ALSO BY ERIC LAX

Radiation: What It Is, What You Need to Know
(with Robert Peter Gale, M.D.)

Faith, Interrupted

Conversations with Woody Allen

The Mold in Dr. Florey's Coat

Bogart
(with A. M. Sperber)

Newman: A Celebration

Woody Allen, A Biography

Life and Death on 10 West

On Being Funny

START TO FINISH

START TO FINISH

Woody Allen and the Art of Moviemaking

ERIC LAX

Alfred A. Knopf · New York · 2017

THIS IS A BORZOI BOOK PUBLISHED BY ALFRED A. KNOPF

www.aaknopf.com

Knopf, Borzoi Books, and the colophon are registered trademarks of Penguin Random House LLC.

Library of Congress Cataloging-in-Publication Data
Names: Lax, Eric, author.
Title: Start to finish : Woody Allen and the art of moviemaking / by Eric Lax.
Description: First edition. | New York : Alfred A. Knopf, 2017. | Includes index.
Identifiers: LCCN 2017002887 | ISBN 9780385352499 (hardcover) |
ISBN 9780385352505 (ebook)
Subjects: LCSH: Allen, Woody, 1935– —Criticism and interpretation.
Classification: LCC PN1998.3.A45 L39 2017 | DDC 791.4302/33092 [B]—dc23
LC record available at https://lccn.loc.gov/2017002887

Jacket photograph by Sabrina Lantos, copyright © 2015 by Gravier Productions, Inc.
Jacket design by Chip Kidd

Manufactured in the United States of America

First Edition

For David Wolf and William Tyrer

"I'm offering up story all the time.
That to me is what the movies are."

—WOODY ALLEN

CONTENTS

START TO FINISH

INTRODUCTION

Woody Allen has so far written and directed forty-seven theatrical films and acted in twenty-seven of them, an average of one a year since 1969, a continuous body of work unmatched in modern cinema. This does not include five films he wrote but did not direct; three he acted in but did not write or direct; one he wrote and acted in but did not direct; and the television movies and shows he has written and directed. Nor does it include *What's Up, Tiger Lily?* (1966), in which his dubbed dialogue turns the Japanese adventure film *International Secret Police: Key of Keys* into the hunt for a top-secret egg salad recipe. Why he works at such a pace is individual to him; how he works and what he has learned from others is, I believe, instructive for anyone who cares about moviemaking.

The idea, the script, the money, the casting, the cinematographer, the locations, the production design, the costumes, the shooting, the editing, the music, the color correction, the mix: the movie. They come in many forms—studio pictures, indies made on shoestring budgets, niche films made for more, action franchises costing hundreds of millions. *Star Wars* or *Stardust Memories, Harry Potter and the Sorcerer's Stone* or *Deconstructing Harry,* no matter the film or its maker, each required vision, determination, and organization to get made. Every filmmaker relies on a vital array of assisting talents. Part of Woody's uniqueness is the outstanding artistic contributors he has attracted and continues to attract to bring his vision to cinematic life. Along with a galaxy of great actors including Cate Blanchett, Michael Caine, Leonardo DiCaprio, Mia Farrow, Gene Hackman, Anthony Hopkins, Scarlett Johansson, Diane Keaton, Geraldine Page, Emma Stone, Charlize Theron, Max von Sydow, Dianne Wiest, and Kate Winslet, to name but a few, he has used the eyes of many of the world's finest cinematographers, notably Gordon Willis, Sven Nykvist, Carlo Di Palma, Vilmos Zsigmond, Darius Khondji, and Vittorio Storaro. Santo Loquasto has provided brilliant production design for half his films, Juliet Taylor has overseen casting for nearly all of them, Helen Robin has kept production rolling for decades, Alisa Lepselter has edited the past nearly twenty films, and the other members of his crews are equally expert in their fields. He could not make his pictures without their valued contributions, but in the end, of course, each film is really his. He has had full control of every aspect of every one, beginning with *Take the Money and Run* (1969)—even though he has writer/director/actor credits on *What's Up, Tiger Lily?*, he considers *Take the Money and Run* his first fully theatrical movie. Unlike with almost every other director, the financing of his movies does not depend on their box-office appeal or the cast he selects. His ideas go from his head to the screen with no impediment between, his scripts unseen by his financiers and distributors. Shooting is over when he is done, regardless if that means exceeding the allotted days in the budget and giving back the cost from his fees. He is present for and decides the editing of every frame, chooses the music, oversees the color correction and the sound mix, and approves the ads that appear in New York (because those are the ones he sees).

Over the years there have been changes in how he makes a movie but few in how he writes one. Both because he has become more proficient and for budget constraints, he reshoots scenes far less often. Filming is faster—usually between thirty and thirty-five days instead of the eighty or more he sometimes needed in the past. He has become comfortable watching a scene unfold on a video monitor rather than observing it from beside the camera. He has taken to editing digitally and, as of 2015, to a digital camera in place of reels of film. His vision and his dedication, however, are unchanged. Now past eighty years of age, there has been no loss of drive or output by this deeply nuanced and singular artist.

By good fortune rather than design, I have been talking with him about his movies and moviemaking since 1971. In the decades since, I have watched him make more than a half-dozen films from the first day to the last and parts of more than twenty others.

His pictures and other projects flow so seamlessly from one to the next that they sometimes overlap. While this book has as its spine the making of *Irrational Man,* in the eighteen months that bookended it he also made *Magic in the Moonlight,* helped transform *Bullets over Broadway* into a Broadway musical, wrote *Café Society,* and created *Crisis in Six Scenes,* a six-part series for Amazon that he later acted in and directed. We were in conversation throughout, talking in his home, in his screening room, on walks along Manhattan's streets. I was with him all through the making of *Irrational Man*. He gave me access without restriction as he scouted locations, decided on costumes, and considered his casting. I sat by him as he worked and we talked between shots about what he was doing, was with him in the editing room for both *Magic in the Moonlight* and *Irrational Man,* and watched as he screened several versions of each. I was present for all I describe here, taking notes as he worked and of what he and others said. More than thirty hours of longer, more formal interviews were recorded. Unless otherwise noted, his quotes as he worked on other films during the past forty-six years are from our conversations at the time.

No two filmmakers work in an identical way; there is not a template that even slavishly adhered to guarantees a compelling movie. Craft is crucial but art is elusive. Copy every move of Bergman, Fellini, Kurosawa, Welles, Godard, Antonioni, Hitchcock, or Scorsese, and you might create a facsimile but not their work of genius. Yet brilliance often sparks innovation, and new art can emerge from observing how a master filmmaker proceeds.

While there is clearly such a thing as a Woody Allen film, his themes vary over a wide range. There is a documentary here, a musical there. A few are in black and white, while most flow over the audience in rich, warm color. Some ask big questions about morality, others are strictly for amusement. Several show his feeling that there will be no judgment or salvation from an absent God, much as he might hope for a spiritual force to provide order and meaning. Others encompass flat-out comedy (*Bananas*); the fragility of marriage (*Husbands and Wives*); faux documentary (*Take the Money and Run, Zelig*); reality smothering fantasy (*The Purple Rose of Cairo*); identity and self-delusion (*Blue Jasmine*); a golden age mundane to those in it (*Midnight in Paris*); the virtue of loyalty (*Broadway Danny Rose*); the fickleness and benefits of fame (*Celebrity*); the vibrant era of his childhood (*Radio Days*); the primal attachment of parenthood (*Mighty Aphrodite*); a life imagined doubly, as a comedy and as a drama (*Melinda and Melinda*); the often stark difference between the man and the artist (*Bullets over Broadway, Deconstructing Harry, Sweet and Lowdown*); *War and Peace* told by Bob Hope, Ingmar Bergman, Charlie Chaplin, and Sergei Eisenstein (*Love and Death*); our futile fight against death (*Shadows and Fog*); a musical with voices purposely not suitable outside the shower (*Everyone Says I Love You*); generational family dynamics (*Interiors, Hannah and Her Sisters, September*); the unpredictability of love (*Annie Hall, Manhattan, Vicky Cristina Barcelona, Whatever Works, Hannah and Her Sisters,* and easily a dozen more); and the personal consequences—or lack thereof—of murder, done as comedy (*Bullets over Broadway, Scoop*), as straight drama (*Match Point, Cassandra's Dream*), or both (*Crimes and Misdemeanors, Manhattan Murder Mystery*), and again as straight drama in *Irrational Man,* which was not titled until months after shooting ended and until then was referred to as *The Boston Story,* as it will be for a while here.

This narrative chronicles every part of the making of *Irrational Man,* from when the idea occurred to when the film was ready for release. The narrative also references all of Woody's other pictures and includes his comments on the directors, cinematographers, writers, and so many others he admires. The best filmmakers absorb the past and yet find their own vision, as you will experience in depth from the way this brilliant artist creates a movie, from start to finish.

Eric Lax, January 2017

CHAPTER 1

The Script

Woody Allen lay fully clothed on the queen-sized bed in his bedroom that doubles as his workroom on the third floor of his Manhattan townhouse, writing a film script in longhand on a legal pad. A bed has been his routine writing spot for decades, even when he is staying in a hotel. What was not routine this day in February 2013 was that he was alternately working on two scripts: one a contemporary drama about a burned-out philosophy professor who unexpectedly finds renewed purpose by deciding to kill a judge he believes is about to ruin the lives of an innocent woman and her children; the other a romantic comedy set in the 1920s about a curmudgeonly magician enlisted to unmask a young woman with apparent powers as a spiritualist. Unsure of which to film that summer to follow *Blue Jasmine,* for which Cate Blanchett won a Best Actress Oscar and his script a Best Original Screenplay nomination, he worked several days on the comedy until his enthusiasm waned and then switched to the drama—until his zest for that one flagged and he returned to the comedy. He might stay with one idea for fifteen minutes or three days before being distracted by the other. Though far from normal, there have been several occasions when he has written simultaneously on two ideas and at least one when he wrote three successive separate scripts in twelve weeks before he had the one he wanted. "I lose confidence," he said while switching between these two, "and I sometimes panic and think, 'Don't try and fix this. Jump ship.'"

But in this instance when he liked both ideas he temporarily fell victim to "obsessional indecision." He picked one and plunged in because he could "see everything falling in place so beautifully—the magician vanishes the elephant and they call him in to help expose the spiritualist and he meets the beautiful girl with the pre-Raphaelite hair." But the idea quickly went "from idealization in my mind to actuality on the printed page and from the Platonic ideal of perfection to all the warts," so he moved back to the murder. He calls this the "automatic anxiety of second-guessing," manifesting his concern that anything he writes will not be the best follow-on to the last film insofar as variety of subject. He says he "could be sitting with *Gone with the Wind* or *A Day at the Races*" and still be anxious that he'd made the wrong choice. While he remains hostage to his uncertainty, his aim is to tell a tale that draws in the audience: "I'm offering up story all the time. That to me is what the movies are."

When Woody finished the handscript of the comedy about the magician in March, he sat at the small table in the corner of his room and used the same Olympia portable typewriter he has had for his entire career to type on yellow foolscap what was on the legal pages, now covered with cross-outs and overwriting in his cramped script.

He then made more changes with a ballpoint pen on what he typed, cut and stapled portions of these further edited pages together, and sent them to Helen Robin, his longtime associate producer, who has typed clean versions of his screenplays for nearly thirty years. He is the sole arbiter of his work. There is no outside authority who can make changes.

"His script is almost prose," she says. A character's "name may be on the left side. As I'm typing it I use a script program that formats on the page but I decide to make a scene cut based on where he's written. My typed version goes back to him with his copy, and after a few days I get back a combination of the original yellow typed pages with cutouts of some of what I've typed stapled and mixed in with handwritten changes. Then I do the next revision and send it to him. That generally goes on until we shoot, usually two to four revisions."

When she returned the first version of the script three days later, he sent her the drama about the professor. Both scripts were soon

The first page of the first draft of The Boston Story, *with the idea of calling it* Crazy Abe *in the upper-left corner.*

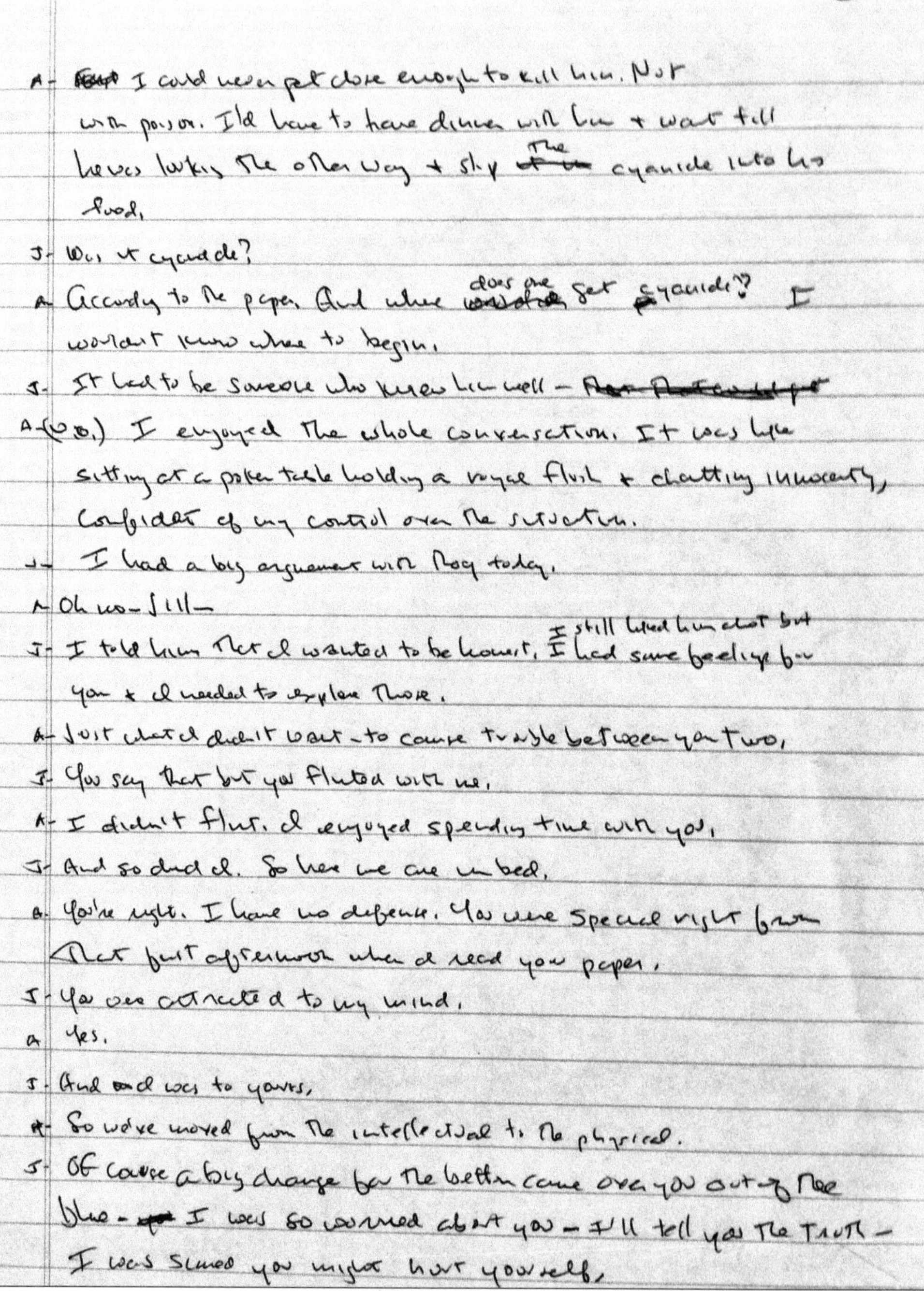

(34)

A- I could never get close enough to kill him. Not with poison. I'd have to have dinner with him + wait till he was looking the other way + slip the cyanide into his food.

J- Was it cyanide?

A- According to the paper. And where does one get cyanide? I wouldn't know where to begin.

J- It had to be someone who knew him well —

A- (V.O.) I enjoyed the whole conversation. It was like sitting at a poker table holding a royal flush + chatting innocently, confident of my control over the situation.

J- I had a big argument with Roy today.

A- Oh no—Jill—

J- I told him that I wanted to be honest. I still liked him alot but I had some feelings for you + I needed to explore those.

A- Just what I didn't want—to cause trouble between you two.

J- You say that but you flirted with me.

A- I didn't flirt. I enjoyed spending time with you.

J- And so did I. So here we are in bed.

A- You're right. I have no defense. You were special right from that first afternoon when I read your paper.

J- You were attracted to my mind.

A- Yes.

J- And I was to yours.

A- So we've moved from the intellectual to the physical.

J- Of course a big change for the better came over you out of the blue — I was so worried about you — I'll tell you the truth — I was scared you might hurt yourself.

After Woody revises, Helen Robin types it into proper script form. As action is delineated only by the initial of the character, she often has to discern a scene's end.

sent to a few trusted readers, including his sister, Letty Aronson, a producer of his films, and Juliet Taylor, who cast them for more than forty years until her retirement in 2016.

No matter the choice, it would be the forty-fourth film written and directed by him in as many years. Such a regular schedule of filming requires nearly metronomic timing, and it allows him to live largely in a world of his own manufacture. Growing up in Brooklyn in the 1940s, he "used to run into the cinema to escape—twelve or fourteen pictures a week sometimes," and cinema is still his refuge: "I get to make the films I want to make, and so for a year while I make a picture I get to live in that unreal world of beautiful women and witty men and dramatic situations and costumes and sets and I can manipulate reality. I've escaped into a life in the cinema on the *other* side of the camera rather than the audience side of it."

Because his alternate life in the movies is so complete, by temperament he cannot begin working on the idea—or ideas—for the next film until the current one is far enough along for him to uncouple emotionally, which usually occurs immediately after he finishes editing and decides on the music.

He does not lack for choices. He told his friend Dick Cavett in the 1960s, "I can't imagine that life could be long enough for me to do the number of projects I have in mind." In a drawer in his workroom is a bag full of scraps of paper with possibilities jotted on them, usually no longer than a sentence or two. Always among them is a constantly updated snippet that reads, "Best three ideas currently." Some notes in the drawer are new additions, others have been there for years—concepts he likes but that have stalled. *The Purple Rose of Cairo* (1985), in which a movie character walks off the screen and into the audience, fermented for years until Woody realized that both the escaped character and the actor who plays him would become involved in the life of a woman who watches the movie every day to escape her dreary Depression-era life.

"The world is strewn with very good ideas that don't go anyplace," he said after completing both new scripts. "It happens all the time, to me and everybody. They get a great idea: A guy walks down the street and finds a wallet and he goes to a house and there's a dead body on the floor. Then what?" He laughed. "It's the *then what?* that kills you."

The comedy about the magician and the spiritualist was another idea he had stored for years, unable to answer what followed after he had established the premise: A world-renowned magician is asked by his lifelong friend, an illusionist of lesser stature, to expose the suspected chicanery of a young woman who seemingly can discern the most private information about people and communicate in séances with their dead relatives. She and her mother, who travels with her, have been embraced by the matron of a wealthy family in gratitude for "connecting her" with her departed husband. The friend explains that the matron is about to give the pair a large donation to establish a foundation for psychic research and that the matron's son has fallen desperately in love with the clairvoyant. There is concern that she will filch the family fortune.

The script had its genesis ten or fifteen years earlier, when Woody and Marshall Brickman—with whom he wrote *Sleeper* (1973), *Annie Hall* (1977), *Manhattan* (1979), and *Manhattan Murder Mystery* (1993)—discussed writing a film about a fake medium and a magician set in the early twentieth century, when spiritualism was at the peak of its popularity. The magician, who is also an escape artist, begins to lose his nerve; he becomes increasingly reluctant to be chained up in a milk can and thrown into the sea and soon ends up in psychoanalysis. Called on to debunk a spiritualist, he accepts the task with brio but soon falls for her. (Woody once read that the great magician and escape artist Harry Houdini was asked to debunk a medium and *she* fell for *him*.) Woody liked that the picture could be easily and inexpensively filmed, mostly in a house, but despite many attempts over the years to advance the story, "it never went anyplace until finally it hit me that the friend who enlists his help is in on the deal." He would make sure in writing the script that viewers would not suspect the friend's duplicity. "Once I had that, I had the whole thing. But for *years* I didn't have that."

In the script, the magician, supremely confident that he will be able to expose the necromancer in no time, instead is confounded by her arcane knowledge about him and his family. His cockiness is replaced first by irritated confusion, then wonder, then hope that after a lifetime of doubt and disbelief in a spiritual world there may actually be one—until finally he realizes that the friend he has trusted and therefore not suspected has given her the detailed personal information.

He enjoyed writing the script so much that he "wasn't sure if it was good enough to do" because such pleasure might have blinded him to problems.

He alternately worked on the tale of the murderous philosophy professor, which, because he thought the place to make it would be at a college in Boston, became *The Boston Story.* It also had rested some years in the drawer after being sparked by a dinner conversation with an acquaintance of his wife, Soon-Yi Previn. The friend was in a protracted court battle with her contractor. She complained that the judge was biased toward the contractor's lawyer: they smiled at each other in the courtroom and the judge consistently ruled in his favor, even though she felt she had clearly shown that the promised work hadn't been finished and what had been completed leaked.

"I was thinking at the table," he said after finishing the script, "if I kill the judge, she'd get a shot at another judge—couldn't be worse than this one, probably would be better—and no one in the world will dream I was involved. I have no connection, no motivation, nothing to do with it. No one will suspect me for a second. It seemed like an interesting idea."

As he always does, he toyed with it comically to see if that would be more effective than a drama, but a drama it became. The professor poisons the judge by surreptitiously switching an identical container of toxic orange juice for the unadulterated one the judge has just bought. Because the men have no known connection, he gets away with it and finds himself transformed from passively suicidal to aggressively life affirming. Then weeks later an innocent man is charged with the crime and the moral dilemma is whether the professor will follow his high philosophical ideals and turn himself in or, feeling alive for the first time in ages, try to kill a friend, the one person who knows what he has done, making that death seem accidental and thus avoiding prosecution for either murder.

Woody considered the mitigating argument that although the judge is corrupt he could well be a decent and loving father and therefore should be spared, but he felt, as a character in the film says, "That's like those Mafia bosses who do horrible things . . . we're supposed to cut them slack because they're wonderful to their wives and children?" To him, it was, "Too bad, it's not enough."

To sidestep that concern, he wrote the judge as a man without a family. As for the professor, he wanted him "to be seen as a psychopath," and to make the point "that murder is not a solution" but rather "leads you down a slippery slope to where you might have to kill somebody else to keep going. If I haven't ruined it in the writing, I think it will be an interesting movie. If you saw this in black and white done by a French or Italian writer and director in the golden age of foreign films"—along the lines, say, of Claude Chabrol's 1958 thriller *Le beau Serge,* which drew on Alfred Hitchcock's 1943 *Shadow of a Doubt,* in which the protagonist tries to commit the perfect murder—"you'd think, 'Hey, this is a great film.' I'm not saying that's so on my end, but it has inherent in it a mature idea. It's a bread-and-butter, meat-and-potatoes adult story."

There are two distinct phases to a Woody Allen script, best summed up by Marshall Brickman: there is the writing, and then there is the writing it down. The writing, during which nothing is actually written, consists of Woody working out in his head every detail of the characters and the plot. Dialogue comes later. What the characters will say is unknowable until it is determined what they will do. Once that is clear, their words will be almost self-evident.

"This is the worst part," Woody says, referring to a period of several weeks during which he alternately lies on his bed, paces the room, and, for "a refreshing change of environment," takes long showers to unlock his thoughts. It is a time of "obsessive thinking" and constant discomfort, during which his hypochondria is in full bloom, his acid reflux is on high burn, and he is in a state of physical exhaustion. The story is constantly at the forefront of his mind, although it has a use-by date. If after a month the way through it remains unseen, the idea is abandoned or thrown in the drawer and replaced with a new one.

"In a chess game," he adds, "I can't see one move ahead. But when I'm writing a script—and it can be a fairly complicated one with lots of characters—I can see far ahead and work out my problems." He likens the process to writing a symphony. "The theme begins here but it's going to resonate three movements later, and if *this* is wrong, *that* is going to be terrible."

He makes no notes or an outline. Early in his career he read *Playwright at Work* by John Van Druten (*I Remember Mama; Bell, Book and Candle; The Voice of the Turtle*) and was persuaded by Van Druten's insistence that a writer should know his story so well that an outline is unnecessary. So he lets it play through his mind in its various possibilities.

"I'm thinking, 'The professor is coming to the college. He's dying to have the job,' and I pursue that for a day. Then I think, 'No, no, it works better if he's jaded and they want him but he wants to quit teaching,' and I pursue *that* for a day. Then I go back to the first possibility, then the second. I think, 'No, it's definitely best if he doesn't want the job and he's emotionally had it. Then he has an affair with another teacher and maybe she's married. No, no, it might be better if he has a relationship with one of his students, the daughter of a teacher. Or she gets a crush on him but he would never have a relationship with her because he's her professor.' I think out these notions, tracking them to their logical conclusions to see which offer the most substantial material."

Something he constantly guards against is clever writing for the sake of being clever. "You can't just have people sitting around making what you hope are wise insights or witty remarks because while they're saying these things the audience is not thinking, 'Hey, that was a great Shavian epigram.' They're hearing it as the dialogue of characters in a certain situation: he's saying this because she's thinking this and he wants to get on her good side. They're watching the *action* of the story. When you lose sight of that, and we all do—I certainly do—you think you're infusing your piece with wisdom, but you're committing suicide. You're just militating against the audience's enjoyment."

Unlike the weeks of thinking through the story, the writing it down seems startlingly easy. He says that once the plot is clear in his mind, "I can lie and write there on that bed all day and it just comes. I'm not writing a play, so it's not like George S. Kaufman, where every sentence has to be perfect. I just *write,* and when I rewrite I might change it completely. It's film, so characters talk like people in real life, they're not speaking poetically like Tennessee Williams writes because in my films that would sound artificial." The day he sees the path through the story is the day the work goes from "very, very unpleasant" to "exhilarating. I have so much energy; I'm almost manic in my conversation. I just bounce along the street and do things like I'm twenty years old." His chronic problem is finding the right ending. It is likely that it will change along the way, and in some instances, such as *Annie Hall,* not be resolved until he finishes editing. (Annie and Alvy meet as friends, and then he speaks directly to the audience.)

Because he is in essence writing a guide for him to direct, his screenplays are widely dissimilar from what a director of a studio film is usually given. He says he admires many movies but few scripts because "through the history of film, screenwriters have gotten the least respect, have the least clout. The studios would get a script and then give it to another screenwriter, and then another. My screenplays don't read like anybody else's because I don't put in any directions. I read a page or two of someone else's screenplay and there's tons of direction in it, every nuance about the character and how he feels a scene should be cut. The movie exists on the page, I guess, because it has to be sold. Mine are just dialogue and a million TBDs [to be determineds]. Theirs, the suits have to read the screenplay, they have to be able to see it in their minds."

He has a different approach to his scripts even from directors who have complete control of their own. Ingmar Bergman, the director he most admires, said he wrote his films "not really understanding what I'd written. Then I shot them, and they meant certain things to me. But what they meant—that I didn't really understand until afterwards. Long afterwards. If my relationships to my own products are so odd, it's because often when I'm writing and shooting a film, I'm inside some sort of protective shell. I hardly analyze what I'm doing or why I'm doing it. I rationalize afterwards."

Woody considers himself more in control than that "on a cerebral level and less in control on a competence level. I start off knowing what I'm doing and what I want to do, and because I'm not competent at it, it turns out to be something different, and I'm surprised." (His assessments of his own work and his abilities raise the deflective art of self-deprecation to a rarefied level.) But he is in complete agreement with Bergman that "the importance of the dreary in art mustn't be underestimated."

"I happen to find dreariness very beautiful," he said some years ago. "I see it in Martha Graham's work. A lot of people watch *Radio Days* and laugh at that early scene when I say, 'I remember my childhood as so beautiful,' and we cut to Rockaway and it is a rainy, wave-tossed day. I meant it completely straight."

While both scripts were out for consideration by his few readers, Woody weighed the ideas himself and said, "*The Boston Story* is a more provocative idea. The magician and the seer is a light, romantic movie—that's what I hate about it. But if I was sitting here with a murder story on my hands, I might be saying the same thing: it's an intellectual-moral-dilemma murder story and that's what I hate about it. Coming after the Cate Blanchett movie [*Blue Jasmine*] it would be nice to do something light and musical and Cole Porter-y. I feel I do *that* well more easily, I feel more at home with it, and I enjoy it more. That's a big consideration. It's more *fun* making that kind of movie; it's more *fun* making *Midnight in Paris* than making a serious movie. I get more of a kick out of staging a scene with a background that I know is the kind of music I like." When he wrote the carriage ride he and Mariel Hemingway take through Central Park in *Manhattan,* he knew he was going to enjoy putting a piece of romantic music behind it even before he chose George and Ira Gershwin's "He Loves and She Loves."

Much has been written about the desire of a comedian to be a tragedian, and there are periods when Woody puts his all into writing a drama, although never one that he would act in. He does not want to play Hamlet; he wants to write *Hamlet*. He knows, however, what he is up against. "If you can do comedy, it's not hard. If you can't do it, it's impossible. The same with drama. Arthur Miller and Tennessee Williams had a wonderful feel for it. For me, it doesn't come as naturally, though I enjoy it more as a spectator. I prefer a Bergman film or *The Bicycle Thief* or *A Streetcar Named Desire* or Chekhov. And so naturally I have an impulse to write something with that seriousness. I haven't been as effective with drama over the years as I have been with comedy, but that doesn't mean I intend to stop trying. I think with *Match Point* (2005) I was reasonably successful, maybe the most successful I've been with dark material, but I'm always struggling with it. I always feel that my natural gift is to be amusing. Look how many people felt that *Blue Jasmine* was a comedy. It was amazing. The Golden Globes didn't know whether to put it in as a comedy or a drama. We said, 'You *can't* put it in as a comedy. It *isn't* a comedy.' [They finally listed it as a drama.] But at the minimum people find parts of it funny, and some find it a black comedy."

In some instances, an idea for one film has its genesis in another. In *Another Woman* (1988), Marion Post is married to Ken, a cardiologist, "who ten years ago examined my heart, liked what he saw, and proposed." A middle-aged woman who shut down her emotions following an abortion when she was in her twenties, Marion is forced to confront her past when she overhears the psychoanalytic sessions of a pregnant younger woman through a heating vent in her office, which is near the analyst's. On the surface Marion seems a woman in total control of herself, but in reality she feels so deeply that her only choice is to deny feelings or be overwhelmed by them.

This was neither the beginning nor the end of an idea for a film based on what someone inadvertently hears. Five years earlier, Woody thought to do a Chaplinesque comedy about a man who overhears a woman patient telling her problems to an analyst in his building. He sees as she walks out after her session that the woman is beautiful and hatches a plot to fulfill her desires and so become her dream man. But he soon questioned the taste of eavesdropping—done even in the most benign way it seemed to him a mean thing to do, and he did not write it.

Then years later he thought of a dramatic version of a woman who hears another woman talking through a wall. The question was, What could she hear that would make such a difference? His first thought "was that the woman's sister and husband are having an affair. She goes home and thinks, 'How terrible.' Then she finds that her own sister and husband *are* having an affair. But that became too Hitchcockian. It was the wrong motif." He used it instead in *Hannah and Her Sisters* (1986).

But the notion of eavesdropping "haunted me for years. Then the idea of someone with a closed life came. I thought it could make an interesting drama. There's more intensity if it evokes the deep feelings in the woman who's eavesdropping." The feelings evoked by overhearing the young woman seep in and trigger buried memories of people in her life.

Woody said with a hint of self-revelation after *Another Woman* was completed, "People have difficulty dealing with their feelings and yet are extremely proficient in their intellectual work and are active in social programs and charities. I'm probably as guilty of that as anyone." He laughed as he added, "Maybe I'll regret that I didn't do it as a comedy." As a few friends took their seats in his screening room to see his edited but not yet mixed cut of the picture, he said, "If I had done this right, I would have made two movies—this one and a comic one. That would be the one that could make money and be successful and this is the one they would cut up for guitar picks."

Eight years later Woody played a character who, tipped off to a woman's intimate details, made all of Julia Roberts's dreams come true in his 1996 musical comedy *Everyone Says I Love You*. For several years, he had talked of wanting to do "an original musical comedy. I'm a sucker for them. I grew up with those great Broadway musicals." Making the film scratched his itch, but even though it had a marvelous cast (in addition to Roberts: Goldie Hawn, Alan Alda, Drew Barrymore, and Edward Norton) and funny musical numbers, it took in only about $10 million in the United States. A main allure of the idea to Woody was that the cast not be trained singers but simply regular people who sound like any of us do at our most unguarded. "What is more ridiculous than a man or a woman singing or dancing?" Woody told the critic John Lahr. "It's the aspiration of your most intense feelings, musicalized. If you took the music away, it would look so silly."

The vote on which script to film was divided. His sister, Letty, was the first to respond, and she preferred *The Boston Story*. Woody felt subsequent readers seemed more inclined toward the magician, and they won the day. He is to a degree mindful of where his projects fit in his body of work and on occasion will discuss with his sister, as he did with Juliet Taylor, whether or not it is a good time for him to develop a given idea. These decisions are not as democratic as they might seem.

"You have to learn to gauge what people say," he explains. "You have to listen between the lines. The same when you're screening the picture, you have to try to intuit not the literal content of what they're telling you they liked or disliked but rather a feel from them about their enthusiasm or how compelled they are by the story. *Midnight in Paris* [2011] was around for ten or fifteen years before I made it and turned out to be a big success. [At first it required more than his usual budget, so it was put aside.] *Match Point* was around for *years* [a story he liked but had not quite worked out to his satisfaction]. Whereas [*Curse of the*] *Jade Scorpion* [2001] also was around for years [other ideas seemed more appropriate at the time] and was not a success at all. It's just not an exact science. You never learn the thing you wish you *could* learn, which is: don't go into this with the judge because the story is doomed from the start. You never learn that."

The sudden idea of having the magician film take place in the South of France in the 1920s reinforced the decision: "I had in my mind the twenties of Matisse and Picasso and the houses that they painted in there, and of Isadora Duncan." He even had a title—*Magic in the Moonlight*—something that often comes along much later, and he immediately asked Helen Robin to clear it. Clearing a title is not always simple. The Motion Picture Association of America (MPAA) Title Registration Bureau catalogues all titles used or registered for future use by the six major studios and many subscribers. There can be trademark issues, in which a proposed title may not be exactly that of a film already made but still evokes one that is registered or, as Woody pointed out, "They'll say, 'Well, Paramount has a movie called *Magic in India,* and they're protesting.' Then you have to go through a process. Usually you win, but it costs money. I want a romantic title for this." At one point in the 1990s, he wanted to call a film *Untitled,* but the Title Registration Bureau said someone else had laid claim to it.

He likes to shoot period films because they offer so much more visually, and he cites Bernardo Bertolucci's *The Conformist* (1970), which takes place in Rome at the height of fascism in the 1930s with flashbacks to earlier times, as an example of a director using design, art direction, and photography to great effect. "I've tried to find good periods that are visually provocative to the photographers and the scenic designers and location managers. *Magic in the Moonlight* and *Midnight in Paris* are very pretty. If the story just doesn't lend itself to a period, I try to do the best job in the confines of the present. *The Boston Story* is a contemporary film on a college campus. But if I'm home and I'm thinking of a story, I know that if I set it in certain periods, I'm ninety percent ahead of the game. If I say, 'This story takes place in Coney Island,' okay, it's fine. But if I say, 'This story takes place in Coney Island in 1935,' I skyrocket the budget and the visuals become enormously powerful right away. [His 2017 film, *Wonder Wheel,* takes place in Coney Island in the 1950s and, a first for him, required many green screen shots—the background was filled in digitally—adding considerably to the budget.] You're dealing not with stark reality but with lighting that's nostalgic and idealized. But I do it knowing that I may not get anything back at the box office because of the extra cost. I've done it a half-dozen times. Early in my career they would say, 'You could do this but you're going to go a million dollars over budget.' I was making a million dollars to write and direct and star in the film, but it was more important that I made a good film so I put in my fees."

He admires Federico Fellini's use of period. "*Amarcord* [1973] is very pretty to look at because it's based on his childhood memories and of course it's exaggerated and stylized and beautiful. *I Vitelloni* [1953] was black and white and of those guys who hang around the town. What can you shoot? In a contemporary picture, people are talking on their cell phones and things happen quickly. It alters the story. If it is shot in a period before people used smartphones, they can't grab theirs and text somebody, they have to grab a yellow cab and go across town. A contemporary setting is great if it's what your story is, but it's not as charming and it doesn't provide the same visual stimulation for the artist."

As Woody wrote the script, he had Colin Firth in mind for Stanley, the magician. They had never met, so his conviction was based solely on what he had seen Firth do on screen, most recently in *The King's Speech* (2010). It was not certain that Firth's schedule would allow him to do the film, but to Woody's relief, it eventually did.

His first choice for Sophie, the American seer, was Emma Stone. Juliet Taylor had told him she could think of no one who could do the part better. Fortunately Stone was in New York making *The Amazing Spider-Man 2* and could easily meet Woody in his editing and screening office. Taylor had warned her that it could be as fast as a thirty-second pop in and out; the get-together was just so that Woody could have a sense of her.

"He's trying to make sure you aren't hideously grotesque in person," Stone recalled later, amused. "It's very dim in that office, so once he saw me in the light he realized I *was* hideous, but Darius [Khondji, the cinematographer] is a real genius. My mom accompanied me to the labyrinth. She looked down at her phone when we came out—we were there four minutes! Actually my friend Jesse Eisenberg had a fifteen-minute interview, which apparently is the longest in history. Jesse and Woody have a lot of similarities." Eisenberg was a lead in *To Rome with Love* (2012) and *Café Society* (2016).

Woody instantly liked her and asked that she return when she could read the screenplay there. After the filming of *Magic* he said of her, "To me she looked exactly like Esther Williams, and there have been moments, you won't see it so easily, she looked to me like Jodie Foster and—you won't see this so easily either—there were times that she looked like Alfalfa [the freckle-faced gawky kid in the Our Gang comedies of the 1930s]. I mean, she's got a protean appearance. She is beyond beautiful." At times he thought that Firth looked like Bob Hope: "The mouth, the eyes, and the nose. I see it very much. I saw it when I shot it with him. I was thinking, 'God, he's funny, who does he remind me of? Yes, Bob Hope.'"

Hope was an enormous influence on Woody, and his performances in many of his films channel Hope's skirt-chasing, cowardly yet full of bravado comedic persona, especially in such pictures as *Monsieur Beaucaire* (1946) and *Casanova's Big Night* (1954). In *Sleeper*, for instance, Woody and Diane Keaton, dressed as doctors, attempt to kidnap what's left of the tyrannical Leader—his nose—from the hospital where he is about to be cloned from the DNA in its cells. As they run through the halls searching for the operating room, Miles (Woody) tells Luna (Keaton) as he takes her hand and pulls it to his mouth, "The trick in these situations is to remain cool."

"Miles," she replies, "you're biting my nails."

"'Cause you're tense," he says.

When they encounter suspicious guards, Miles more or less gathers himself, taps one on the chest, and tells him with perfect Hope bluster, "We're here to see the nose. I heard it was running."

In contrast, the director who has most influenced Woody is Bergman. A wisecracking American and a seemingly dour Swede may be an odd combo, but Bergman has given Woody's films much of their sensibility. In 1953, when he was seventeen, he took his girlfriend to see *Sawdust and Tinsel*. "I was glued to my seat. I thought, 'Who made this film?'" Four years later, the couple went to the Fifth Avenue Cinema in Greenwich Village to watch *The Seventh Seal* and *Wild Strawberries* (both made in 1957). They were transformative for Woody. "From the second *Wild Strawberries* began I was mesmerized. The tension gripped me and never let go. And when I saw *The Seventh Seal,* everything came together—the stark photography, the man on the beach, and then the appearance of the death figure. I was sucked into it. The film resonated with all my obsessions and preoccupations; it's all I thought about and all I was interested in intellectually and emotionally, and it had enormous meaning for me. It was a story told with great imagination, tremendous performances, and fantastic camera work. Bergman was a beautiful magician telling me stories."

He still regards Bergman as "the best filmmaker I've ever seen." In fact, his ambition at the start of his career was to be a dramatist, not a comedian; he saw comedy as a way to get there, even if it was a long road. "I was, as anyone starting out, a product of my influences, but my influences were so incongruous and antithetical. I've always said that I fall between two stools—I am not artist enough and not commercial enough. To the average person, I might look like an intellectual because of my glasses. But to intellectuals, I'm clearly not one."

In the 1980s, Bergman invited Woody to dinner in his New York hotel suite. Woody is always leery of meeting a hero for fear that the person will not be as pleasurable as the work, but he found the evening "a great treat. He was not at all what you might expect: the formidable, dark, brooding genius. He was a regular guy, warm and amusing and insecure about his immense gifts. He commiserated with me about low box-office grosses and women and having to put up with studios."

They developed a friendship that included many long telephone calls between Bergman's Fårö Island retreat in the Baltic Sea and Manhattan. Bergman invited him to visit Fårö but "plane travel bothered me, and I didn't relish flying on a small aircraft to some speck near Russia for what I envisioned as a lunch of yogurt." Woody said after Bergman's death in 2007, "The world saw him as a genius, and he was worrying about the weekend grosses. He was plain and colloquial in speech, not full of profound pronunciamentos about life. [His longtime cameraman] Sven Nykvist told me that when they were doing all those scenes about death and dying, they'd be cracking jokes and gossiping about the actors' sex lives. I liked his attitude that a film is not an event you make a big deal about. He felt filmmaking was just a group of people working. I copied some of that from him. At times he made two and three films in a year. [In all, sixty-seven in sixty-three years, including twenty-five for television. Plus he directed 171 stage and radio productions.] He worked very fast; he'd shoot seven or eight pages of script at a time. They didn't have the money to do anything else. I think his films have eternal relevance, because they deal with the difficulty of personal relationships and lack of communication between people, and religious aspirations and mortality—existential themes that will be relevant a thousand years from now. When many of the pictures that are successful and trendy today will have been long relegated to musty-looking antiques, his will still be fresh."

Another deep but seldom-noted influence on Woody's writing is William Barrett, whose books on existentialism, particularly *Irrational Man* (1958), explicated it by examining its roots in ancient philosophy through Saint Augustine to the nineteenth- and twentieth-century philosophers Søren Kierkegaard, Friedrich Nietzsche, Martin Heidegger, and Jean-Paul Sartre, and through the novels of Dostoyevsky, Tolstoy, Joyce, and Hemingway.

In Barrett's summary: "Existentialism, whether successfully or not, has attempted to gather all the elements of human reality into a total picture of man," which includes our inherent irrationality. For an existentialist, any philosophy that fails to consider our irrational urges cannot be complete.

"Existentialism is no mournful delectation but a humanist philosophy of action, effort, combat, and solidarity," Sartre wrote in *We Have Only This Life to Live*. "Man must create his own essence: it is in throwing himself into the world, suffering there, struggling there, that he gradually defines what this man is before he dies, or what mankind is before it has disappeared." He added, in *Being and Nothingness,* "Life has no meaning a priori. . . . It is up to you to give it a meaning, and value is nothing but the meaning you choose."

This was powerful stuff to a funny twenty-three-year-old who wanted to be a dramatist. Although he flunked out of New York University in his freshman year, he and his first wife, Harlene Rosen, had a tutor from Columbia University take them through its Great Books course. A steady reader and autodidact—he familiarized himself with poetry, literature, art, and music—Woody often puts literary and artistic references in his films. Philosophy, especially existentialism, particularly interested him. The books of the existentialist writers became the "bibles" for Woody and his small circle of like-minded friends. Existentialism flourished in the post–World War II years with the specter of nuclear annihilation now a part of everyday life; we could be dead before we understood what it is to be alive. For Woody and his companions who found no comfort in religion and therefore no sense of a greater power either to turn to or to hold them responsible for deeds however heinous if they went uncaught, a life based on action would give existence meaning. As Sartre put it, "There is no reality except in action." Action might be even more powerful and liberating if it is absurd and beyond societal boundaries, such as Raskolnikov's murder in *Crime and Punishment* or Meursault's behavior in Camus's *The Stranger.*

A traumatic early experience gave Woody context for his outlook. As a child—he was then Allan Konigsberg—he was left in the care of a succession of poorly educated and underskilled women who were paid by the hour and generally lasted only a week or two before quitting or being fired. When he was three the incumbent nanny came to his bed, pulled the covers over him, wrapped him in a bundle so tight that he could not breathe, and said, "See, I could smother you right now and throw you in the garbage, and no one would know the difference." Then she freed him. He has memories of being six or eight and lying in bed in the dark, knowing that one day he would die and how utterly final that would be. His vivid sense that we live under the canopy of death has not left him.

Caught between a comic's insight and a dramatist's wish to deal with the meatiest ideas of life and death, of love and purpose, he incorporated his view of life's inherent meaninglessness into his stand-up routines. "I took a test in existentialism," he would say. "I left all the answers blank and got a hundred."

In another bit he would tell the audience, "I took all the abstract philosophy courses in college, like Truth and Beauty, Advanced Truth and Beauty, and Intermediate Truth, Introduction to God, Death 101. I was thrown out of NYU my freshman year. I cheated on my metaphysics final. I looked within the soul of the boy sitting next to me."

In his *New Yorker* short story "Mr. Big," a detective hired to find God finds instead that God has been murdered by an existentialist.

Absurdity can be restorative. Sometimes an absurd act is the only escape.

The question of why or whether life is worth living is a constant with him. While making *Crimes and Misdemeanors,* he said, "Something I've always been fascinated with and have dealt with in other films of mine is this Tolstoy crisis—he came to the point in his life when he just couldn't figure out why he shouldn't commit suicide. Is it worth living in a godless world? The head says no, but the heart is too scared to take action to end it." There is a comedic yet serious turn on this by his character, Mickey, in *Hannah and Her Sisters.*

At one point in *The Boston Story* the professor, quoting Kierkegaard, tells his class, "Okay—Kierkegaard. When making everyday decisions, we have absolute freedom of choice. We realize we can do nothing or anything and this feeling of freedom creates a sense of dread—a dizzying feeling—'anxiety is the dizziness of freedom.'" (In the long run the professor instead of killing the judge might also have helped himself—though not Woody's story—by recalling Saul Bellow's observation in *Herzog:* "One thought-murder a day keeps the psychiatrist away.")

After choosing to do *Magic in the Moonlight,* Woody said *The Boston Story* would be a contender for his 2014 film, but he dumped it back in the drawer and for a while forgot about it. He really wanted to write a two-handed comedy that he could do with Louis C.K., whom he had come to admire as he performed in *Blue Jasmine,* but he could not think of a satisfying idea.

"I'd rather do a comedy but I just haven't found one that is funny and that has size," he said while still mulling his next project. More than anything, he did not want to do a routine story in a routine way. "I would love to tell a story in a different kind of movie, but there's nothing left in cinema that's different—not the stories but every kind of presentation has been done. Orson Welles was different when he used such stylized shooting in *Citizen Kane,* and then years later Jean-Luc Godard had that rough, very different look [in *Breathless,* 1960, shot with a handheld camera]. I've done the documentary style, first in a crude way with *Take the Money and Run.* Then other people started doing documentaries. I was able to use it another way in *Zelig,* which was a good documentary. People do make unusual things. [Abdellatif Kechiche's] *Blue Is the Warmest Color* [2013] is practically all talking heads, but you don't mind. It's interesting because the heads are interesting. When Bergman wanted to do a movie where he just planted the camera and never moved it at all [*Through a Glass Darkly,* 1961], people went in and out of the frame. But the truth is, you get an idea and the content dictates the form and the content almost always dictates a *reasonably* realistic form. It can be as stylized as Scorsese or Godard shoot, but basically what they're doing has a reasonably fundamental realism to the stories, even if they use a lot of cinematic devices." And so *The Boston Story* came back to mind.

"A different way of filming a story gives you something nice to lean on," he continued. "Some stories you can tell in a documentary style or in black and white or by shuffling the time sequence out of chronological order, but most of them you just tell like a story. *The Boston Story* has a big central idea with some intellectual substance to it and also lends itself to something that is fun to see on a movie screen. It isn't just two people in a room talking. There's something going on.

"It's so hard to think of a great comedy. Shakespeare's to me are just not funny. What's beautiful about them is the language. But they're dopey bumpkin plots, and I never laugh at them no matter who is doing them. Molière, unhhh [*he gives a slight laugh*]. *Pygmalion* is a great comedy; to me it's the only *really* great one. People care about *The Importance of Being Earnest,* but I don't. The Marx Brothers movies are hilarious, as are the W. C. Fields movies, but they're just recordings of their acts; if you remove the guys you have nothing. I love *Born Yesterday,* but that's *Pygmalion* with a different approach to it."

He was troubled by *Magic in the Moonlight,* which was still months from release, feeling, finally, that it was entertaining but slight. Part of the problem was that it came on the heels of *Blue Jasmine.* "You always have problems with the movie that follows a very successful one. *Annie Hall* was very successful. Then I thought I would make *Interiors* [1978], and yes, it was radically different, but following *Annie Hall* was hard. Following *Manhattan* [with *Stardust Memories,* 1980] was hard. Following *Midnight in Paris* [with *To Rome with Love*] was hard. People see *Blue Jasmine,* and it has substance and it's much more serious and it has Cate's bravura performance. The next time they expect the bar is set there, and they want at least that. But then you come out with a little romantic thing in the South of France, and I can see people feeling, 'Well, you know, it's a little throwaway. It's not *Blue Jasmine;* I mean, that was a *picture.*' "

He has, of course, made several groundbreaking films, starting with *Take the Money and Run,* which was the first comedy done in documentary style with newsreel footage and still photos. "I did it influenced by *Kane,*" Woody says of Orson Welles's pseudo-documentary, *Citizen Kane* (1941). "When I got to be a better filmmaker and did *Zelig,* [the late *New York Times* critic] Vincent Canby compared it to *Kane* in certain ways, though I am making no comparisons of quality or stature here." The film had influence beyond the screen: "Zelig" is now the dictionary definition of a ubiquitous, chameleon-like person. "Thank the makers of *Kane,*" Woody says. *Annie Hall* was a novel relationship comedy when it was released: Alvy talked to the audience, stopped and restarted, and he had flashbacks to his childhood that his friends Annie and Rob could also see. *Zelig* masterfully put his character into vintage newsreels. In *The Purple Rose of Cairo,* a film character and the actor playing him duel for the affections of a woman in the audience. But he wishes that once again he could do something new. "I've been working the last ten years so realistically—by realistic I mean so natural—and I wish that I could invent something stylish, just to make a contribution. But you can't just do it, you really have to feel that with the material." When he made *Husbands and Wives* (1995), he "wanted to obey none of the niceties of cinema: people looking in the same direction, cutting whenever I wanted to cut, doing nothing to obey the decorum that you're taught making films."

In *To Rome with Love,* Alec Baldwin's character is often in conversation with Jesse Eisenberg's—in a room, in a car, walking on the street—the only person in the picture who can see or hear him. For all of Woody's desire for a whole film with something different, he says when he has an idea like this he thinks, "Don't ruin it by making the characters talk to the audience because that distances you from the intense reality of it."

He feels only a handful of his pictures succeeded in the way he envisioned them. He has kind words for *Match Point, Husbands and Wives, Vicky Cristina Barcelona, Midnight in Paris, Café Society, Broadway Danny Rose,* and *The Purple Rose of Cairo. Stardust Memories* is a notch below, although when he made it, it was his favorite. *Manhattan Murder Mystery,* he adds, is another of his "personal favorites. It was heavily influenced by the murder mysteries I grew up on." The husband-and-wife banter between Woody and Diane Keaton is reminiscent of William Powell and Myrna Loy in *The Thin Man* (1934) but even more so of a Hope movie. "Especially," he says, "where Keaton and I are in the hotel room checking for where we saw the body and the door opens, and it's the cleaning lady. Look at that scene right after you've watched the opening minutes of *My Favorite Brunette* [1947], until the moment Hope's cleaning lady, Mabel, comes out of the elevator. Notice the shameless burglary. I do a lot of Hope in that movie." But the list does not extend, and invariably he will point out what he failed to do. He admits to being a capable director and wishes his writing were its equal: "For me, the weak spot in every situation is always the writing. I can direct scenes, I can get performances out of the actors, I make nice and pretty shots. That's not so hard—it's not that easy but it's not so hard. A lot of people can do that. I wish I wrote better."

In his *Times* review of *Broadway Danny Rose* (1984), Canby called

Woody "America's most authentic, most serious, most consistent film auteur"—a filmmaker who is the author of movies that are entirely his unique vision and style. Auteur theory, first expressed in the mid-1950s by François Truffaut and other young French critics, championed the work of, among others, Alfred Hitchcock, Jean Renoir, Erich von Stroheim, Howard Hawks, Nicholas Ray, and Stanley Kubrick. Woody is aware that the auteur label is often put on him, but he is not comfortable accepting it without his own qualifications. "I definitely would be considered an auteur, but that doesn't mean for a second that I'm an outstanding director or a good auteur. An auteur to me is simply a person who presents films that he is the author of. It's a category of filmmaking. I'm not putting an auteur filmmaker *above* a great director. I mean [Elia] Kazan might not be an auteur director but he's a truly great director. There are great auteur filmmakers and totally mediocre ones and bad ones.

"I once had this conversation with [Michelangelo] Antonioni over dinner at Elaine's." When? "When he was alive," he says, laughing. (Antonioni died in 2007.) The two knew each other fairly well through Carlo Di Palma, who shot several of Antonioni's pictures, including *Blow-Up* (1966), and twelve of Woody's between 1986 and 1997. "He was looking for a writer for a film and I suggested Joan Didion. I thought there would be a meeting of the minds. If you're a director of such pronounced style and you work with a writer and you contribute to the script, then I guess it counts. But otherwise it's hard for me to imagine that if you don't write the script, if you're doing somebody else's book or screenplay, that you qualify as an auteur filmmaker." There are exceptions. "Hitchcock picked projects that had a Hitchcockian point of view and they all turned out to be unmistakably Hitchcock movies. The same subject matter interested him over and over; he had a clear-cut style and worldview that was his alone.

"There are filmmakers who are brilliant stylists. Scorsese, for example, has a fantastic style. So any material he does becomes a Martin Scorsese movie because he has an individual and creative voice that takes over the material. Oliver Stone has an unmistakable style. It would seem to me that you can be a brilliant stylist and a very great director, but in order to be an auteur it has to be your material that you're presenting to the audience. It isn't just that you're a stylist. Mel Brooks is an auteur filmmaker, but he's not as great a filmmaker as Martin Scorsese."

There are only auteurs, not an auteur style. Their films can overflow with dialogue or be nearly silent. Akira Kurosawa's "*Rashomon* is a masterpiece in every way: the way he chose to tell it, the way he filmed it, the way the actors played it, the way he edited it. In the hands of other directors the scene where the girl is riding a horse through the forest would be viable, but the way he did it—the music, the light coming through the trees, the way he cut it—it's spellbinding. Kurosawa and Bergman use the movies more photographically than verbally, moving photographs to evoke feeling. *Cries and Whispers* is hypnotic. The characters move in a stylized way: clocks tick, people pad around the house, the husband and wife sit down to eat dinner and nobody says anything, but the tension is unbearable. Then she gets up, goes into the other room, and mutilates herself. They use the film to create feeling. But a masterpiece like [Jean Renoir's] *Rules of the Game* [1939] is the opposite. It's very verbal; social mores are explored and characters behave in highly intellectual or cerebral ways.

"So there are no rules. A fantastic film can be as talkative as [John] Huston's *The Dead* [1987] or *The Maltese Falcon* [1941] or as spare as *The Seventh Seal.* It doesn't matter. It's the net effect, like magic tricks. Someone can do an astonishing trick because he has a pianist's digital skill. Someone else will use a stooge to say, 'You're right, I took the seven of spades,' yet he captivates the audience because technique is irrelevant; what's important is the effect on the viewer, and it's the same with movies. The audience watches [Renoir's] *Grand Illusion* [1937] and they're knocked out because it is full of conversational and character conflict. But Bergman makes just as strong an effect with *The Seventh Seal* or *Wild Strawberries*; it's just as good as someone like Fellini, who shoots a film with enormous cinematic technique and bravado. *Citizen Kane* has Welles's bravura directing, but you can also make the case that the bravura style is distancing. In some of Fellini's pictures, you admire the technique, but are you as emotionally sucked into the story as you are by Don Siegel's original *Invasion of the Body Snatchers* [1956]? That's bread-and-butter filmmaking. Simple shots and you're on the edge of your seat the whole way.

"It's what the director sees and hears in his head. In jazz, the instrumentalists play the sound that they hear in their head. So one will sound unbelievably beautiful and another will sound professional but less beautiful. If you take the scenario to *Citizen Kane* and you give it to William Wyler and to Jean-Luc Godard and to Orson Welles, you get different movies. The guys who are good directors will give you interesting movies with a good basic script like that, and the ones that are less talented won't."

After much thought about ideas he could do with Louis C.K. got him nowhere, and another false start, the allure of *The Boston Story* brightened. He went back to the drawer and looked at his ideas and asked himself if there was something he was burning to do. He had thought he would reread *The Boston Story* sometime, just not as soon as January 2014. But after he did he said to his surprise, "Hey, this is not bad. There's a nice story here and these characters *are* interesting. Should I have ever abandoned this?"

So he made it his safety net for the month that he dove back into other ideas, two of which he quite liked. (One, a much-changed, funnier, and livelier reworking of his 2004 play *A Second Hand Memory*, became *Café Society*.) But *The Boston Story* appealed more. He says he found it "stronger. I kept thinking to myself, 'You can't afford to let this get away.' Now, I may regret those words, I may later think, 'God, you *should* have let it get away, it's an embarrassment.' But I thought there is a great part for a guy in this. And as I worked on my side notes and penciled in things, the girl's part seemed to grow. So then I thought, 'There are a *couple* of good parts here.'" After a female professor's part grew as well he found himself with an ensemble piece with much promise but still in need of work: "This is ten times as long as I wanted; there are three scenes in a row indoors at night; there is too much to explain; this is not cogent enough. I corrected all of it. But then I saw my corrections still weren't good enough."

He took the typed script with his handwritten corrections to his bed. As he went over it, he found parts "lacked credibility." He had trouble believing that the professor could act so radically as quickly as written, so he stretched the timeline of his depression and indifference to whether or not he lived by writing additional scenes before the professor decides to kill the judge, which made his sudden switch to being full of life as a result of his choice less jarring. He also realized that his plan for only the professor to narrate the story would not work; to make it more complex, he made the student who the professor befriends a narrator as well. He likes voice-over in his pictures because the audience can hear what the character is thinking.

He also looked to be sure that "I don't saddle myself with the same mistakes that I always saddle myself with"—speeches that are so lengthy that when editing he has to cut them in the middle; scenes that are too long. When he starts a picture, he says, "I think, 'If I can keep the scenes short' "—he snaps his fingers several times—" 'in the first four or five minutes, it really helps me.' If it moves like that—bang bang bang—it gets you into it. But if the scenes are longer in the first five minutes, it's a chore. I've gone through it trying to cut speeches out or down and still retain the ideas, and looking for where to play the scene. I'm looking from my mattress to imagine, 'Gee, are they on a miniature golf course? A carousel? Where can I place it?' Now, I can go up to Boston, or wherever we decide to shoot, and say, 'Look, here's a place where everybody goes up in balloons in the afternoon.' And then I think," he starts to laugh. "Well, I'm not going to do *that* or anything *like* that," he says, still laughing.

He was pleased with the reworked script: "This went someplace." But having written it a year ago and now having rewritten it, he hoped he was not so blinded by what went before that he was unable to see better alternatives. "I'm trying to make the professor someone who's catnip to the ladies—very bright and screwed up. But then you think to yourself, 'What if he wasn't a college professor? What if he was in the advertising business or out of work, or it wasn't a younger girl that's with him, but someone else?' There are other choices that I didn't make that may be better than the ones I made, but it's probably too late for them because things get imprinted on your psyche." Scenes he found too long were shortened; parts of the story too hard to explain were simplified or dropped; where he had three indoor scenes in a row, he moved some of the action outside. And, "I tried to develop the older woman's character [Rita, a chemistry professor who yearns for a more exciting life than she has with her husband] a little more, but I haven't found a satisfactory way to kill the judge. The hard things to get are those big ideas of how to do a murder and then do another so it looks like an accident. I don't want to murder the judge with a gun and certainly not with a knife. You don't want to shoot him because it's not as clever. Plus, he's trying to make it appear that it's not a murder. So he poisons him, but the way to get the poison in his drink still seems a little artificial. I just don't know how else to do it except to somehow put it in the judge's drink behind his back.

"The best idea of all has been done, which is the gradual poisoning in *Notorious* [1946]. That is an *incredible* gimmick. But, of course, you take that in the framework of what Hitchcock would call 'a slice of cake.' In a realistic movie, if you're poisoning someone bit by bit, she'd go to the doctor right away and he'd diagnose what is happening. In the movie, they kept her in a house she couldn't leave, and the doctor was a Nazi in on the plot. It all was unrealistic but completely credible within the framework Hitchcock put you in from the beginning, and you stay in that framework gladly because he's skillful. But in real life," he pauses, "I wish there was a more spectacular way—because it's the movies—to murder." Hitchcock's mastery of suspense allowed him to play us both ways. In *Notorious* we know Ingrid Bergman is slowly being poisoned and our jitters are about if she will be saved, whereas in *Suspicion* (1941) we can only anxiously speculate whether Cary Grant has put poison in the glass of milk he is carrying upstairs to Joan Fontaine. Guilt, actual or presumed, is a hallmark of Hitchcock's films, and the tension is in discovering which.

During the months when Woody mulled how best to write a spectacular second murder, he said he always came back to a struggle by an open elevator shaft. "I think to myself, 'Well, let's take *Shadow of a Doubt* [1943], the great Hitchcock film. Joseph Cotten is struggling with Teresa Wright on the train, and he just falls off. That at least had a train visual going for it.'" He had a couple of notions for how the scene could have an ironic end, assuming he stuck with the elevator idea. "He can't poison another person because this needs to be self-contained. The person could be knifed to death or shot, but that opens up a can of worms. The easiest thing is if it is just an accident. But how many accidents are there? The person could fall out a window. Being hit by a car is a possibility, but that's tricky, because someone might see the license plate or the person doesn't die. I'm just looking for some wonderful way to kill somebody so it looks like a legitimate accident. If someone falls ten floors down an elevator shaft, you can be pretty sure that he is dead. I think the audience would buy a fatal fall. But it's possible there's something like a construction site the person walks past coming home every day, something that I have no concept of so far."

He had the same difficulty when he wrote *Manhattan Murder Mystery*. (The murder story at the heart of the film was originally in the first draft of *Annie Hall*.) He "struggled and contorted and manipulated" until he found the visually exciting ending, in which a killer is shooting at people in a hall of mirrors behind a theater screen on which the hall of mirrors shooting sequence in Orson Welles's *The Lady from Shanghai* (1947) is playing.

The murder in *Cassandra's Dream* takes place in a park at night, and neither the shooting nor the body is seen, nor are the two brutal murders in *Match Point;* only in *Crimes and Misdemeanors* do we see a dead body, her eyes blankly open, a small line of blood on her red sweater, and that is because her eyes fit into a theme of the film—is God all-seeing or blind? Two bloody shootings are seen in *Café Society*. It is not the aftermath of a murder that Woody finds interesting but simply the fact of it. A body is superfluous. "It wasn't about either the killing or the blood, so I didn't feel there was any necessity to just blast people away in front of you," he said after *Match Point*. He is equally discreet when it comes to sex. In that film, for example, the erotic intensity comes from the two stars. He "put them in situations that are sexy to a degree; it's sexier when Jonathan Rhys Meyers rubs Scarlett Johansson's back with oil than to see two people making love, or when he throws her down [in two-foot-high grass] in the rain. There's sexuality without showing any real sex. You get the idea. That's more fun. Real sex, you can see that all you want."

But that does not mean he isn't tempted by more cinematic ideas for doing away with a character. He wrote a Hitchcockian murder in *Cassandra's Dream* to be filmed in the amusement park on Brighton Pier: the victim is upside down on a ride when he is struck by a bullet. He thought that would be "a more theatrical way of doing it. But when I kicked it around, it seemed *too* theatrical for that movie. Everything else in it was realistic." And for *The Boston Story*, however much he might again have wanted the professor to kill the judge in a spectacular Hitchcockian murder, he needed something subtler.

Magic in the Moonlight asks the questions, Is there a spiritual side of life? If not, what do we have to hang on to? *The Boston Story* asks, among other things, Is murder justified if you rid society of a bad person? No matter his subject matter, Woody always finds that his story in some way revolves around an intellectual or moral dilemma that requires argumentation, which he finds annoying. "Philosophy comes into my films all the time," he says while talking about *The Boston Story*. "That this one has philosophical content is," he pauses before saying, "death. That's what will drive the people out. If Hitchcock had this story it would be chock-full of suspense, and if Scorsese had it the emphasis would be somewhere else but it would be exciting. I don't want the movie to be a lot of people in rooms talking to each other. So I have people walking across campus talking to each other, sitting in classrooms, going for coffee after class, and there's a lot of *that*."

His hope is that asking moral questions will differentiate the film from simply a murder story, in the way that *Crime and Punishment* and *Macbeth* are murder stories but also something quite beyond a whodunit. "The tennis movie [*Match Point*] was beyond that," he said. "There wasn't just the killing; it had some character and conflict and ideas. And so I hope that I can do that here. There is no intellectual content in a movie like *Notorious,* but it's as fine a movie as has been made."

CHAPTER 2

The Money

Woody's presentation of on average a movie a year over half a century is perhaps even more impressive in that he has had total control over the script, casting, and editing since his first film, in 1969, something no other director enjoys. He willingly antes up for this. Any overrun of the budget is taken from his salary and fees for writing and directing. His continuous annual production is the result of several interlocking causes. His budgets are small by the standards of Hollywood, where a movie routinely costs scores of millions and, in many cases, $150 million or more, plus additional millions for prints and advertising. *Take the Money and Run* cost $1.7 million; the price now is under $20 million. His first thirty-one films were produced through American studios: United Artists did eight, starting with *Bananas;* Orion Pictures did the next eleven. Then TriStar and DreamWorks did three, Miramax four.

Raising money has always been what Woody calls a "scramble," but even so, he has always had someone who believes in his work and wants to finance it on good terms for him. First it was the late, legendary Arthur Krim, who, with Robert Benjamin, resuscitated United Artists in the 1950s and turned it into a Hollywood powerhouse run by David Picker, who equally admired Woody; Krim liked to say that he entered the movie business with Charlie Chaplin and that he was leaving it with Woody Allen. UA offered artistic autonomy and creative freedom, as well as a percentage of every dollar the film earned, plus payment for writing, directing, and acting, a deal only a small handful of filmmakers enjoy. When Krim and Eric Pleskow left in 1978 to form Orion Pictures Corporation after UA languished following its purchase by the insurance giant Transamerica, Woody joined them as soon as his UA deal was over and stayed until the company closed, in 1999. His films during that time include great critical and financial successes: *Manhattan* (1979), *Broadway Danny Rose* (1984), *Crimes and Misdemeanors* (1989), *Hannah and Her Sisters* (1986), *Radio Days* (1987), and *Bullets over Broadway* (1994). They also include *Shadows and Fog* (1991), which had a budget of more than $15 million and earned less than $3 million domestically. In 1991 Orion was in financial difficulty and the picture opened first in Europe, distributed by Columbia Pictures. Woody says, "I knew when I did that movie that no one was going to want to see it—a black-and-white picture, a simplistic existential story set in Germany in the 1920s and shot in a studio. After Eric Pleskow saw it he commented, 'I've got to say, whenever I come to see one of your films I'm really surprised that they're all so different.' He was groping for something to say as he searched for his cyanide capsule. But it was something I wanted to do and I hoped there would be enough people who saw it that the studio people didn't bother me." Orion executives didn't bother him, although they were not above quietly hoping for a more commercial ending for *The Purple Rose of Cairo.*

That picture is one of Woody's most surreal and most touching. Cecilia (Mia Farrow) is a Depression-era waitress in a small town diner. Married to an abusive and womanizing ne'er-do-well (Danny Aiello), she is a fount of knowledge gleaned from fan magazines about the lives of movie stars and spends her free time living vicariously in the fantasy of films, seeing the week's offering at the local theater over and again. While Cecilia is yet again viewing *The Purple Rose of Cairo,* in which handsome Egyptologist Tom Baxter (Jeff Daniels) is taken to New York by a group of vacationing wealthy Manhattan sophisticates, Tom suddenly interrupts the scene to talk directly to her. ("My god, you must really love this picture. . . . You've been here all day and I've seen you here twice before." "You mean me?" she asks, looking up at the screen. "Yes, you—you—you've—this is the fifth time you're seeing this.") He walks out of the movie, climbs down from the screen into the audience, and soon they fall in love. ("I just met a wonderful new man," Cecilia says. "He's fictional, but you can't have everything.") This raises havoc among the patrons at the theater, who are bewildered by what became of the Tom Baxter character. "I saw the movie just last week and this is not what happened," one woman says. "I want what happened in the movie last week to happen this week. Otherwise, what's life all about anyway?" Baxter causes panic at the studio, as well as for Gil Shepherd (also Daniels), the actor playing him, whose career is threatened because his unpredictable character is on the loose. For self-preservation, Gil comes to town, woos Cecilia separately from Tom, and offers to take her to Hollywood to be with him. Her acceptance forces Tom back onto the screen. But, as soon as Tom is safely back where he belongs, Gil, his livelihood rescued, skips back to California without a word to Cecilia. The film ends with her in the theater once again, lost in the make-believe of Fred Astaire and Ginger Rogers's "Cheek to Cheek" number in *Top Hat* (1935).

Despite the great humor in the film, its ending was the whole purpose for Woody. The inventive storyline aside, its point is that reality inevitably eclipses fantasy. In choosing Gil, Cecilia finally realizes she must pick the real person, which is a step up for her, even if she is left miserable.

"Reality crushes you and disappoints," Woody says. "An upbeat ending would have been trivial. My view of reality is that it has always been a grim place to be—but it's the only place you can get Chinese food. A guy from Orion called after the screening in Boston and asked very nicely, 'Is that definitely the ending?'

"'Oh, yes,' I said.

"'Okay,' he said. But I'm sure the look on his face was a grimace."

As with *Shadows and Fog* and *The Purple Rose of Cairo,* Woody tends to decide on stories that satisfy a particular yen. Occasionally he finds, as he did after *Manhattan,* that the desire is so completely fulfilled that he doesn't want to do another like it again. When he began that film, he was determined to show Manhattan as what he called "a wonderland." He feels he succeeded so well that he no longer has the urge to present New York City in "a pronounced glamorous way. Now whenever I show it, I do show it nicely. But that's strictly en route to the movie itself." The baroque *Stardust Memories* with flashes of Fellini met a similar need for a type of picture.

As Pleskow said, Woody's films so differ that it means his financiers never quite know what they're going to get. He is happy to give them a general sense of what they are in for, but that is all. Some years ago, Woody says, a potential new backer wrote to say "that he understands all my freedoms and would give me X amount of dollars, which was a little on the short side, and all he requires is a five-page synopsis. And we emailed him back that I don't do a five-page synopsis for *me.* I don't do a *one-page* synopsis for me. I've never given anybody who's done one of my films more than three or four lines so that the basic survival fears are mollified—that it's in color, that it's contemporary—because they don't want an Andrei Tarkovsky film, something that takes place in the fourteen hundreds and is in black and white. [One of the late Russian director's most acclaimed films was *Andrei Rublev,* 1966, about the life of the fifteenth-century Russian icon painter.] So I try to give them a vague idea of what I'm doing, but I don't like to pin myself down because sometimes while I'm writing, the very thing I'm writing inspires me to a different idea, and I want to be able to switch over to it. The funny part of it is, for years people have kvetched to me about period films, and every time you see one—whether it's *Titanic* or *Braveheart* or *Gone with the Wind* or *The Godfather*—they all go through the roof."

Still, "the people I have the deal with are all happy," he said of his financiers in the late 1990s. "They pay whatever amount to distribute the film so they have to say they're happy, although every once in a great while they can't hide their disappointment. When I did the musical [*Everyone Says I Love You*], Harvey Weinstein [whose company, Miramax, bought the distribution rights] was mortified. He had paid a lot of money for it, and when he saw it, his heart sank. Usually they can hide their disappointment, but [*laughing*] he was *sobbing.*"

One day in 2012 in San Francisco, when nothing was going right in take after take of a short and seemingly simple outdoor scene in *Blue Jasmine,* Woody said softly, "Guitar picks." Reminded of his feeling the same about *Another Woman,* he smiled wryly and added, "I get that feeling very frequently on my films, that this one can only be salvageable as guitar picks, mandolin picks. I do feel that's probably how Harvey made money on the musical."

As the studio financing system changed in the early 2000s, Woody found a variety of backers elsewhere, and for the next fifteen years he had access to financiers in a small NATO of countries, usually with enticing tax breaks if he filmed there. About two-thirds of his recent films' grosses have come from outside the United States, probably because his pictures have a European sensibility that reflects the influences in his early film viewing. He says that the films he grew up with—those by Bergman, Fellini, Truffaut, De Sica, and Antonioni—"just left an indelible mark on me. The guys I hung out with in Brooklyn were not intellectuals. They liked sports and jazz, played in the schoolyard, hung out, and tried to date all the girls in school. And yet, the movies we cared most about and saw frequently were the European movies. They were more intelligent and more entertaining because they were not submental like so much of what came out of Hollywood. The Europeans worked with more freedom and with much more sophistication. When we were teenagers and saw a European film, there would be real sexual encounters; I don't mean graphic sexual encounters, but instead of seeing married couples in separate beds we would see what was normal and not insulting to human intelligence. The European pictures that came over were sophisticated grown-up pictures."

Despite Woody's European bias, he has long been considered the quintessential New York City filmmaker; thirty-two of his first thirty-four movies were shot entirely or in part there. But between 2004 and 2015 he made only four in the United States (*Whatever Works,* in New York City; *Blue Jasmine,* in San Francisco and New York; *The Boston Story,* in Rhode Island; and *Café Society,* in New York and Los Angeles) while making eight in Europe: *Match Point, Scoop, Cas-*

sandra's Dream, and *You Will Meet a Tall Dark Stranger,* in London; *Midnight in Paris* and *Magic in the Moonlight,* in France; *Vicky Cristina Barcelona,* in Spain; and *To Rome with Love,* in Italy.

A few disparate things collectively made the decade of shooting in England and Europe a more attractive alternative to New York or another U.S. city. Over so many years, films set in the same locale can give an air of sameness regardless of the scenario. Because he has used nearly every photographically interesting part of Manhattan as a location, finding fresh spots that suit his stories gets tougher by the picture. And a change of venue is often invigorating. But the chief reason is that getting money under the terms he demands was increasingly difficult. For decades, the largely independent studios were happy to finance his projects. Over the years, though, they have become almost entirely owned by huge corporations that demand more and more oversight on their investment. When in 1968 his managers Jack Rollins and Charles Joffe negotiated his first writer/director/actor contract for *Take the Money and Run,* Palomar Pictures asked what it would take to come to an agreement. "Put two million dollars in a paper bag, give it to us, go away, and we'll bring you a picture," Joffe told them. Which they did and Woody has done ever since.

His move away from the studios began in 1993. Jean Doumanian, then his closest friend for more than thirty years—they met when he performed in Chicago early in his stand-up years, had dinner often, traveled together, even shared a phone answering service—and her partner Jacqui Safra, a Swiss investor and member of the Safra banking family, became his producer and financier through their privately held company, Sweetland Films. TriStar had financed his two previous films, *Manhattan Murder Mystery* and *Husbands and Wives*. A contract for three projects (*Bullets over Broadway, Mighty Aphrodite,* and *Everyone Says I Love You*) at a cost of $18 to $20 million each was signed, and as the years passed there were verbal agreements for six more (*Deconstructing Harry,* 1997; *Celebrity,* 1998; *Sweet and Lowdown,* 1999; *Small Time Crooks,* 2000; the TV version of *Don't Drink the Water,* 1994; and the Barbara Kopple documentary *Wild Man Blues,* 1997). Woody traded participation from the first dollar earned for a smaller fee but a larger percentage of the profits. It seemed the perfect union not only of close friends but also of an artist with supporters who appreciated and understood the way he works. But a fast partnership demands fastidious accounting. Despite years of urging from his then business manager, Stephen Tenenbaum, and his producer of twenty-one films, Robert Greenhut—who had left after finding it difficult to work with Sweetland—to get detailed financial summaries of the pictures, Woody assumed his money was safe with people he trusted. In 2000, though, he sued Sweetland for a reported $12 million in unpaid royalties to him for the eight films he wrote and directed, and the friendship with Doumanian ruptured. The case went to court but toward the end of the trial was settled for an undisclosed amount awarded to Woody. Before the case, Sweetland was set to finance and produce *The Curse of the Jade Scorpion,* but after the abrupt end of the partnership a deal was quickly made with DreamWorks SKG to finance and distribute the movie. DreamWorks also did the next two, *Hollywood Ending* (2002) and *Anything Else* (2003). Fox Searchlight Pictures then picked up *Melinda and Melinda* (2004).

None of these was a great financial success. By the time Woody was ready to make *Match Point,* which originally was set in the United States, the studios were no longer content with putting millions of dollars in a paper bag and going away. They wanted to be treated less as a bank and more as a partner. They wanted to see a script and to know whom he was casting. They were still willing to give Woody final cut, although once on this soapy slide of diminished control, who knows how long it would have been before they tried to renegotiate *that*? He acknowledged that this request was reasonable, but it was not how he was accustomed to working and he didn't intend to change his habits. He has said throughout his career that if he could not have total control over his films he would stop making them and instead write books or for the theatre because he feels, "the guys in the suits don't have the faintest idea about what is good acting or what's good storytelling." He adds that he has "no talent or connection with investing," so for the same reason he doesn't tell the backers what to do with their money, he does not want them telling him how to fulfill his vision for a film. When first English, and then Spanish and French companies said they were content to be just bankers and offered financing with no strings of approval or consultation attached, he was happy to accept their offers and work mostly abroad for a decade, beginning with *Match Point* in London.

In the years following, financiers in at least a half-dozen other countries across Europe and in South America (he is particularly popular in Brazil and Argentina) vied for Woody to make films, but then an attractive American offer came along. Edward Walson, whose father, John Walson Sr., started the first U.S. TV cable company, met Woody at a party in 2006, and they discovered a shared interest in jazz. Walson became a producer of *Relatively Speaking*, the 2011 trio of Broadway plays by Woody, Elaine May, and Ethan Coen, and he has several other Broadway credits including *Cinderella* and *An American in Paris.* He financed *Blue Jasmine* and has also produced several pictures other than Woody's.

In 2013, Chicago investor Ronald L. Chez made a cold call to Tenenbaum, saying he would like to bankroll Woody's films. Tenenbaum at first did not take the call seriously—how often do strangers phone to say they want to offer millions of dollars?—but Chez, a fan of Woody's films, was serious. He and Walson financed *Magic in the Moonlight* with Chez as executive producer. Adam Stern, the son-in-law of Woody's sister, Letty Aronson, assembled a group of investors, and in 2014 an agreement was made among them, Walson, and Chez to finance Woody's next four films at the equivalent of 18 million 2014 dollars, with Walson and Chez providing the largest shares. Woody pays any overage from his fees. In keeping with Woody's practice, they do not see the script and have no say on casting, editing, music, or any creative aspect of the picture. They settled on an $18 million budget because experience has shown that amount allows a good chance for profit on an Allen picture. Usually the domestic and many foreign distribution deals earn back close to the budget even before the picture is released. Part of the agreement was that Woody could make one film with another financing group, which he did with Amazon Studios for his larger-budget 2017 film, *Wonder Wheel.*

He is aware of the latitude he has. "It's a very good thing for someone who's been around as long as I have and my age to make a four-picture deal with complete freedom," Woody, who was seventy-eight at the time, said after the agreement was signed.

His financiers have not suffered. *Midnight in Paris, To Rome with Love,* and *Blue Jasmine* took in about $325 million in worldwide box-office receipts, about half of which was returned to the distributors. This would not impress American studios. After *Midnight in Paris,* which pulled in $150 million—$57 million of it in the United States—"no one called and said, 'We'd like to back your next picture,'" he says. "Not a single studio offered us a nickel after that picture." Only Sony Pictures Classics wanted to distribute it, "because they're a very artistic-minded outfit and they're tuned in on me. They're a very small-budget place, they don't pay a lot of money for the films [a reported $1 million and $4 million for prints and advertising] and I understand that. But nobody else wanted it." (One company did offer to pay for prints and advertising but with no money up front.) A reason Sony Classics is so attuned to Woody is that co-president Michael Barker worked with Krim and has much of his sensibility. They were the U.S. distributors for Woody's seven films between 2009 and 2015, which had a total U.S. gross of about $130 million, ranging from $3.2 million for *You Will Meet a Tall Dark Stranger* (plus $31 million foreign) and $5.3 million for *Whatever Works* (and $30 million foreign) to the $57 million for *Midnight in Paris* (with another $95 million foreign) and $34 million for *Blue Jasmine* ($65 million foreign). Distributors in various countries buy the rights for those territories.

With the acquisition of the largely independent film studios by conglomerates, corporate Hollywood, which prefers gambling $100 to $200 million on a picture in the hope of it garnering $1 billion or more in ticket sales, is not interested in financing let alone giving total control of a project to a filmmaker with even a comparatively tiny budget, even if it was very profitable. The stakes are too small.

What amounts to a blockbuster for Woody is just a good weekend's take to them. After *Love and Death* (1975) earned superlative reviews across the country and a total of $20 million in domestic box office ($91 million in 2016 dollars), Charles Joffe told Woody, "If you have to get reviews like that to make this kind of money, I don't know how we're going to last in the film business, because you're not going to get reviews like that every single picture."

"When I look in the *Times* at that little box of top tens in the financial section," Woody said years ago, "I'll see pictures that were just *crucified* critically. They will have been out for two weeks and they'll have made sixteen to eighteen million dollars and they're considered catastrophes. But if I could have made that in the United States over the years with my films, I would be in *clover*."

Even so, he has not done badly, if only because of sheer volume. The day after he finished editing *Magic in the Moonlight* in September 2013—there would be additional technical work some weeks later—he talked about his streak of annual production. (No films were released in 1974 or 1977, but two were in both 1987 and 1989.) "It says nothing about my filmmaking skill," he offered. "It's testimony to me being like a business hustler." He acknowledges that it is a special achievement but claims it is more a function of his stringent work habits and good fortune in backers than design. "I don't think of it as a streak," he said. "I just don't know what else to do. You saw yesterday, I finished the film to that point and for a couple of weeks I'm off until we start the mix. So when I woke up this morning, I did the treadmill, took a shower, and then I'm sitting at home. What am I going to do? So I went to my drawer and got stuff out to look at it. What would I do if I wasn't working?"

His rhetorical question is evidence of his tungsten self-discipline and work ethic. He once described himself as a "digger ant," and it is an apt assessment. In the same way that he practices the clarinet every day and exercises on a treadmill each morning, he works at writing, or thinking about what he will write, every day. He and his friends speak about his ability to compartmentalize his life so that no matter what may beset him, he can still work. If he has a three-story elevator ride, he will assign himself a question to ponder during it, not only because he is pathologically claustrophobic—during a trip to Norway in 1990, he had the driver go two hours around the coastal mountains rather than take the direct several-mile-long tunnel through them—but more so because he does not want to waste time.

As for making a film a year, "people think it's a feat. It's not a feat. I've got the funding for it already. So the day I finish my script I just send it over to Helen [Robin] and she budgets it. Somebody else finishes a script, they've got to have six million meetings with movie stars to see whom they can get to play the part and raise the money and get a director and get a studio. I don't have those problems. I write it and when I'm finished with it, I do it.

"There's nobody standing over me saying, 'I want to see the dailies' or 'You can't reshoot unless I give you permission.' I remember when I did *The Front* [1976] with Marty Ritt and he had to ask permission to reshoot something. The guys flew in, or they flew the dailies out to Columbia in L.A., and the studio guys looked at them and said, 'Yes' or 'No, you can't.' And even forty years ago that was unheard of to me. If I wanted to reshoot something, I reshot it. It's working on a small budget, giving up a lot of money but having complete control. There are guys who write a screenplay and make more money than I'll make writing and directing and starring combined and working a year on the thing. And then if it doesn't make money—and if it goes over budget I have to kick in from my salary—I get very little. But paying that price, I've made whatever I want, when I want." The regularity has the bonus of him being able to keep a core crew who know to keep the time free—among them associate producer Helen Robin, production designer Santo Loquasto, and editor Alisa Lepselter.

There are critics and filmgoers who question why he makes a movie a year. Their argument is that if he spent longer on a script it would perhaps result in a better or more polished picture. This misses the point that almost all his scripts have marinated and been rethought and reworked over many years. "More time couldn't help," he says. "My films are the best they can be. Nothing is sacrificed for speed."

The simplest answers to why he makes a film a year are because he can, and because, "like Ingmar, I want to work." He has the script, he has the money, he has the roster of big-name actors clamoring to be in his movies, and he always has the drive to be productive. His pictures usually draw well, usually at least break even, and often are very profitable. His ten films made between 2005 and 2014 (*Match Point, Scoop, Cassandra's Dream, Vicky Cristina Barcelona, Whatever Works, You Will Meet a Tall Dark Stranger, Midnight in Paris, To Rome with Love, Blue Jasmine,* and *Magic in the Moonlight*) cost a combined $180 million to make and earned more than $680 million worldwide at the box office alone, on top of which there was income from DVDs, television, and other residual sales. The total box-office gross for all the films he has directed is in excess of $1.23 billion, a little more than half from foreign sales. Of the 12 films made between 2002 and 2014, three had cast members nominated for an Academy Award; two (Penelope Cruz and Cate Blanchett) won. Three of his scripts were finalists in the Best Original Screenplay category (*Match Point* won). *Midnight in Paris* received a Best Picture nomination. If one adds up all the Oscar, BAFTA, Golden Globe, Screen Actors Guild, and Writers Guild awards and nominations, as well as major awards in foreign countries, over the years his films have been nominated 199 times and won 131 times. For someone who never accepts an award because he says it is impossible to say one work of art is better than another, these achievements have no meaning. But even if he is indifferent to them, they are a decent gauge of sentiment about his work by critics, audiences, and his peers. Because of his philosophy about awards, he is not a member of the Academy of Motion Picture Arts and Sciences nor has he shown up to accept any of the three Best Original Screenplay, one Best Picture, and one Best Director awards he has won. This has not stopped the Academy from nominating him sixteen times for his screenplays, seven times for his directing (he is tied for third most all-time), and once as an actor. The only time he has attended an Oscar ceremony was as a surprise to the audience in 2002, in the wake of the terrorist attacks on Manhattan's World Trade

Center the previous September 11, to urge producers to continue making films in New York.

He does not undertake the project he thinks will make the most money but rather the one he most wants to do, knowing that some are destined not to be smashes but that in the long run his backers will come out ahead. He works at his own pace. Why should he artificially regulate his work when it is his artistic process and not the public's acclaim that gives his life meaning? Picasso painted prodigiously. Some canvases are better than others. Woody writes prodigiously. Some films are better than others. Their work speaks for itself.

He likens his pleasure in making a film to a songwriter or painter who wants to create something pleasurable and then has the fun of doing it, "like a kid in art class." He certainly has a style—his regular use of old New Orleans jazz and standards from the American Songbook of the 1930s and 1940s is a simple giveaway—but he lets the content dictate the form of the film. The vertiginous handheld camera movement of *Husbands and Wives* reflects the agitation of that story. The brilliant faux documentary *Zelig* combines old film stock and the technical effect of putting Leonard Zelig into newsreel footage of the 1930s to make a completely different sort of movie. A casual viewer would not know these are the work of the same person, whereas it would not take much of a leap to see that *Notorious* and, say, *Dial M for Murder* are by one artist. He said for many years that if he worked out a tale that requires special effects, he would do it (and did with *Wonder Wheel*), just as he did when he had one best told by alternating the past and the present (*Midnight in Paris*) and another in which jump cuts add to the effect of the story (*Deconstructing Harry*).

"There are a million decisions you have to make yourself," he says. "Sometimes creative people have either an assistant or a partner that they collaborate with or who give them feedback. I do at the early stage when I finish my script. But finally you're in charge and entrusted with millions of dollars. I knew from my first film that if you didn't make the decision you just sat in the room. At some point if you don't make a decision you won't have a project. I marvel at how big a scale directors such as Francis Coppola and Steven Spielberg work. They not only control the material, they do it in an artistic way."

The Boston Story is a return to one of Woody's favorite subjects. His meditations on murder have three different outcomes. In *Bullets over Broadway, Manhattan Murder Mystery,* and *Scoop,* the killer is identified and caught or killed. In *Cassandra's Dream,* two brothers pull off the perfect crime, but while one sees the murder as the path to a fresh life, the other is undone by conscience, and after a fight, neither lives. *Crimes and Misdemeanors, Match Point,* and to a large degree *The Boston Story* are bookends to *Cassandra's Dream.* A murderer has no regrets, his conscience does not bother him, and he goes unpunished by society because in a godless universe there is no justice if you go uncaught.

Woody's sister, Letty, considers *Cassandra's Dream* (2007) one of his best films, but it did not resonate with audiences and was a rare financial loss. Made for $18 million, it grossed under $1 million in the United States and $22 million worldwide, about half of which went to theater owners. He had hopes for the movie with its Dostoyevskian undertone of crime and punishment, but they were short-lived. "I knew I was dead with that film in Cannes when the overseas press was questioning me. They love me and are always very nice, but then one lady stood up and asked, 'What did you expect us to feel with this picture?' And I thought [*groans*] . . . I said, 'Well, I hoped you would get involved with the characters and enjoy the story,' but I knew then I was sunk."

Crimes and Misdemeanors is highly regarded by critics and filmgoers (it made $19 million domestically in 1989 dollars, about the same as its budget, and much more foreign), but less so by Woody, who thinks it "mechanical" because he worked too hard to pull together the intertwined dramatic and comedic stories. However, he feels he avoided that in *Match Point*. To him, that film "flowed organically. I just happened to have the right characters in the right place at the right time."

Time in the sense of when his pictures are made is not a concern because as they are not tied to historical events or current issues, they're not of a time. He doesn't write about common problems on the minds of people in the particular period he makes the movie. Certainly he never uses the music of the time. "*I'm* not of a time," he said some years ago. "The problems I have always reflected could by chance have been on the minds of people or not, but they never are social issues. They're always psychological issues or romantic issues or existential issues. They'll always be what they were. If it's a bad picture, it will always seem a bad picture. And if it's a good picture, it won't seem dated whenever you watch it."

His divergent influences and his personal style have, he adds, put his pictures "in a strange limbo. They've been—I don't know what to say—not commercial and not art, and yet some are profitable."

CHAPTER 3

The Cast, the Cinematographer

1

"I could never get a job as an actor if I had to read."

When Juliet Taylor first worked with Woody to cast his films in the early 1970s, he simply gave her a finished script and she suggested actors. In the four decades since, he has come to solicit her advice routinely, not only, as with *The Boston Story*, on scripts, but often to ask if she even likes an idea before he sets to writing it, or what she thinks of an idea if he can get a specific actor for it. (Taylor's last film for him was *Café Society*, although he still asks for her advice about the top of the cast, and he still shows her scripts and early versions of the edited films.) Apart from casting more than forty Allen films, she did the same for *Taxi Driver* (1976) and put Meryl Streep in her first film, Fred Zinnemann's *Julia* (1977). She has such broad and deep knowledge of theater and film actors that she can pluck the match for a part from the thousands held in her memory.

Most movies are dependent on the studios or financiers agreeing to the actors in them, and the films often are postponed until the desired—which means bankable—actor is free. In Woody's films, "nothing ever hangs on an actor," Taylor says. "He won't change his schedule for anybody." However, he has changed projects. On at least one occasion after reading a script, she told him that she did not like it and he did not make it. She watches the first cut of his films and feels she "can say anything to him" about both casting and her opinion of the picture, including the title. "We all can," she said while still working full-time. "He will listen to everything and be humorous about it. He just takes things in. You can give him the worst news and he'll say, 'Okay.' He's so nice about it, always."

They began working together on Woody's second film, *Bananas* (1971), when Taylor was an assistant to the highly regarded casting director Marion Dougherty; beginning with *Love and Death* (1975), she cast every film until *Café Society.* In recent years, Woody was the only director with whom she worked, for the last twenty with her associate, Patricia Kerrigan DiCerto, who collaborates with other directors as well. Taylor first reads a script to absorb the characters, and her initial conversation with Woody is solely about the story, because his first interest is whether she thinks the screenplay will work. Once that is settled, they talk about who might play in it. Then, Taylor says, when she looks at her lists of actors, "it's sort of an instinctive thing, it just hits you," as to who might be right. "If you're lucky you'll feel this way about a number of people who could be very different from each other. It gets scary when you see only one person who you think can do it" because the actors Woody picks to star in his movies are in high demand, and it is better to have a selection. Even so, he often gets his first choice.

"It seems like it's almost on every actor's bucket list to be in a Woody Allen film," she adds. "Agents call all the time to ask that their clients be considered. There also are certain people he knows want to be in his films and it makes him feel good when he has something for them." Cate Blanchett is one. He knew of her interest and felt she would be ideal for *Blue Jasmine*. The actors' enthusiasm is not financially based. All players in an Allen film, no matter their star wattage, are paid only a bit above the Screen Actors Guild minimum of $3,239 a week, plus a per diem allowance. None receive any portion of the film's receipts, although some initially don't believe this. Over the years actors have turned down roles because of the pay, but Taylor says, "The only people who have turned us down over money are men." One reason may be that Woody's parts for women often draw great acclaim. "He always makes women look better, act better, than they ever have before. He always dresses them beautifully. He has great taste in clothes and style. It may be as simple as that. He loves women; he really appreciates their minds. He identifies with situations they find themselves in." Male stars in their forties and fifties are the hardest group to cast because they are so in demand, are paid tremendous amounts, and often produce their own pictures. Some years ago Taylor asked Jack Nicholson if he was interested in a part. "Flattered you thought of me," she, in a good imitation of Nicholson's voice, recalls him saying, "but I need to make some money." Dustin Hoffman has said he regretted as a young actor turning down offers from Woody, as well as from Fellini, Bergman, and Spielberg.

Actors with a reputation for being difficult on a set need not apply. Woody has no interest in having to prove who is in charge, and for some years earlier in his career, Taylor would tell actors' agents, "I just want to make sure that they know if there is a problem, it will be over in one day." George C. Scott gave her an immediate reply: "Okay, fuck you!"

There have been times when a script Woody wants to do is economically unfeasible. Initially, *Midnight in Paris* was one. When he first wanted to make it, some of his production team were concerned that the many 1920s literary and artistic figures in the picture made it too esoteric to be even remotely commercial, and that the actor he was interested in using was not well enough known to help with the draw; at the time it was particularly expensive to shoot in Paris, and making the film would have far exceeded his usual budget. So he made *Match Point* instead. Then in 2009 the French government offered substantial financial breaks for movies made in the country, which allowed Woody to have a more comfortable budget. But there remained the problem of whom to cast in the lead.

"If you don't get who you want for the way it's written," Taylor says, "then you have to think about what else to do. You don't want to get the same thing but down a notch. It's better to find an exciting way to do it written differently, with someone who can bring real life to it and who's fun to watch." The main character was originally written as a young eastern intellectual. To better suit Owen Wilson's style and persona, Woody rewrote him as a laid-back blond Californian.

It can take a couple of months to decide on the leads and usually six months before the last of the supporting parts are filled. Woody's penchant for secrecy runs deep, so players know only as much as is necessary. Actors in secondary roles are given just the pages of scenes they are in. No matter a star's magnitude, prospective lead actors go through the same process. A representative of Woody's comes to wherever the person is, hands over the script, and waits outside until it has been read. Then it is collected and taken away. As Woody's longtime production designer Santo Loquasto puts it, they are given "pages written with milk that have to be held up to a candle to read before all trace disappears." In Emma Stone's case, she read the script for *Magic in the Moonlight* at Woody's editing and screening suite and left it behind when she departed a couple of hours later. She accepted the role immediately.

Actors are willing to do this, and be paid as little as they are, because they know an Allen film most likely will give them a great part to shine in. (Eighteen actors in his films have received an Academy Award nomination; seven have won. William Wyler's actors garnered thirty-six and won fourteen; Woody is third on the win list.) The roles he writes for women are particularly strong, perhaps because his only sibling is a younger sister and he has seven maternal aunts, all of whose children were daughters, so his childhood experiences were largely with them. But just because he writes great parts does not mean that every actor enjoys the process. Most by nature have a certain level of insecurity that makes it hard for them to accept that they have done good work. Woody knows this well and is sympathetic, even if he is unable to do much about it.

"Marion Cotillard [*Midnight in Paris*] was ambivalent," he said one day in the library of his home before going to France to film *Magic*. The room is lined floor to ceiling with filled bookcases, save for a TV inserted in front of a sofa. "I think there are certain actresses—maybe actors too but often actresses—that don't know how good or attractive they are. They find it hard to believe. When I did that Greek movie with Mira Sorvino [*Mighty Aphrodite,* 1995, which won her the Best Supporting Actress Oscar], she was always insecure, not appreciating how pretty she was, and how smart she was, and how gifted she was. She was always critical—her most severe critic. When Cate Blanchett saw *Blue Jasmine,* she said, 'Oh, I love the movie. I don't want to say anything about *myself.*' Marion was like that, too. It happens so often that people who are wonderful have a tough time accepting how wonderful they are. So she suffered a lot when we made the French picture, unnecessarily. I don't think Cate enjoyed herself when she made the movie."

Woody seldom socializes with his actors and rarely spends time with them between setups for scenes. His expectation of the people he casts is simple: he believes they can bring their character to life or he would not have hired them; he cast them for their inherent skills and he expects to see those on screen. If he does not like a reading, he shoots another take, or ten takes, often without saying what he wants done differently. Implicitly he is knocking them out of their comfort zone, to move them from being less an actor and more the person experiencing the words they're saying. This can be disconcerting, but for him, making movies is about performance. By Blanchett's account on *60 Minutes,* Woody said of the first day's shooting, "It's awful. *You're* awful." But to a fine actor such criticism, however blunt, can be stimulating. "I like to be terrified," she went on to say. "I think it's the only way to work for me. I'm much better with truth. Even if it hurts. When you're stretching yourself, as a role like *Blue Jasmine* did for me, you risk falling flat on your face." And end up standing with an Oscar.

For Cotillard, who in 2014 was named the Most Bankable French Actress of the Twenty-First Century and who won the Best Actress Oscar in 2007 for her portrayal of Edith Piaf in *La vie en rose, Midnight in Paris* "was a tough experience . . . because it took me a long time to actually believe that I was on a set with Woody Allen," she said in an interview at the New York Film Festival. "I met Woody Allen five days before we started shooting, and we didn't really exchange things. We discussed a little bit about the vision of this character, but I had very little information. Then being on set with him . . . I was always scared that he wouldn't get what he wanted because we had talked so little. . . . I'm very happy that I worked with him. . . . I could have done better." Woody disagrees with the last part: "She is a great actress and was wonderful."

For his first twenty-five or so films, Woody tended to cast people he knew and was comfortable with, most notably Mia Farrow, who starred in thirteen, as well as Diane Keaton, Dianne Wiest, and Tony Roberts. (He had an example for this predisposition in Bergman, who used Max von Sydow in eleven pictures, Liv Ullmann in ten, and Bibi Andersson in nine.) Woody sees only a small fraction of the films, plays, and TV shows Taylor watches. Over the years, she has convinced him to look farther afield, "but there are a lot of people he does not know. He'll say, 'Gosh, if I don't know them and they're already thirty-five years old, they can't be all that great.' And I'll say, 'No, that's not true.' He is still a little reluctant with new people, although much, much better than the earlier days. But he has good casting instincts, which I almost always agree with."

Over the many weeks of looking for a cast, in the past Taylor would show Woody clips of actors whose work he did not know but who she felt might be right for a part. The system continues today with DiCerto. If he likes what he sees, there is a quick face-to-face interview, "quick" meaning about one minute. He was so shy about talking to people when he made *Bananas* and the several films following it that he would sit silently in the back of the room, doing his best to be invisible, and listen to Taylor and first assistant director Fred Gallo interview prospective players. He has improved considerably since then but still keeps the interviews very short. Taylor warned those who came that the brevity of the encounter was no reflection of Woody's enthusiasm. Now, as before, they are not told what part they are being considered for or anything about the film. Each interview is an almost verbatim repetition of the last. The supplicant is brought into the screening room. Woody can quickly discern if an actor is right for a part, evidenced by the high caliber of the performances in his films. He is standing toward the middle, comes over, shakes hands, and says a version of, "Hi, I'm shooting a film starting in July. We thought you might be right for one of the parts, and today I just want to see how you look." Usually the actor stammers out something reasonably appropriate. Then Woody thanks the actor and he or she leaves. Once, after he said to an actress, "I wanted to see your face," she replied, "Well, here it is."

"Thanks for bringing it," he told her.

He knows an actor's work from performances or clips he has been shown but will occasionally ask the person to read for a part. He gives no instructions beforehand. His main concern is naturalness of voice. "It's awful, having to read," he says. "I could never get a job as an actor if I had to read. The problem with actors is, when they come in and just stand around talking, they're fine," but when they slip into the character on the page, they "immediately lapse into two hundred years of acting lessons. They don't sound like a real person." He listens and looks intently while DiCerto alternates lines with the actor. Sometimes he will slip into a chair a foot away and lean in to see an actor's face from the side as closely as possible, imagining it on the screen. He sometimes asks the person to do the reading again. When the audition ends, there are slightly awkward thank-yous and goodbyes after what is by its nature an awkward encounter.

Woody was able to get the leads he wanted for *The Boston Story.* While he rewrote the script following the completion of *Magic in the Moonlight,* he thought the part of Jill, the college student who befriends Abe, the professor, might be suitable for Emma Stone, who had impressed him with her work as Sophie in *Magic.* But, prudence overcoming enthusiasm, he waited to be sure he did proper diligence before offering her the role. He and Taylor discussed several others who might play Jill, but nothing dissuaded them from their initial feeling that Stone was the best choice. Woody knew from conversations with her during the making of *Magic* that she hoped to tackle more dramatic roles, and he was sure she could play them successfully. A script was sent to her in Los Angeles. The courier waited two hours while she read it and then took it away. She had immediately accepted the more comedic part of Sophie but took a day to think about this dramatic role in order "to understand Jill," she said later. The part offered her two bonuses. "It was a huge honor" to be asked to do another Allen film. "He knew I was desperate to play [*laughing*] Blanche DuBois in *Streetcar* and Nina and Irina in *The Seagull.* I was very touched to be asked because he knew that this subject matter and these characters were very interesting to me."

Woody says, "Watching her do comedy, you can see she'd be a great dramatic actress."

For Abe, Joaquin Phoenix came to mind to both Woody and Taylor. Woody had never met him but thought he would bring an extra dimension to the part. "He's really amazing," Woody said during casting, "like Cate Blanchett but a guy."

The part of the chemistry professor, Rita, was cast by serendipity. Taylor and Parker Posey were judges at the 2013 Krakow Film Festival, and as Taylor read the script of *The Boston Story,* Posey, fresh in her mind, immediately seemed right. It was an offer Posey had long hoped for but was beginning to think would never come. A favorite of independent directors such as Christopher Guest and Noah Baumbach, she could easily imagine herself in roles in many Allen pictures. It got to the point where, she half jokes, she "couldn't even see Woody's latest films because I was so upset that I wasn't in them."

Posey had her first interview with Woody in 1993, when he was casting *Bullets over Broadway,* so she knew how short the meeting would be. "At the interview he was so nice. I walked into the screening room and he's there. I was startled. He said, 'It's nice to see you.' And I started gushing about him. He said, 'I just wanted to meet you to make sure you weren't crazy.'" Soon after getting the part, she broke her wrist. Woody offered to write her into the script wearing a cast but she declined; by the time shooting began, she was able to take off the soft cast for her scenes.

Woody and Taylor considered several New York actors for the part of Roy, Jill's college boyfriend, but even though bringing in an actor from abroad requires a waiver from the Screen Actors Guild, Woody felt the most appealing was Jamie Blackley, a rising English actor with a flawless mid-Atlantic American accent.

In all, there were thirty-nine speaking or credited parts and another sixty-two small, uncredited ones. The decision of which roles were cast from New York and which were cast from closer to the shooting location was in large part financial but also artistic. Taylor found a Boston casting director of good reputation who put actors on tape reading many of the featured roles. Woody, Taylor, and DiCerto decided intuitively if they were right. If Woody particularly liked an actor he interviewed in New York, he said they should find something for that person, subject to his and Taylor's considering whether it was essential for the role to bring the actor from New York or if they would do just as well to cast it locally. The budget is always an issue, and local hires mean less additional expense.

2

"I know what I want and I can describe it. I have no idea how to get it."

Actors bring the characters to life. Directors of photography shape the life and look and mood of the film through the camera. Woody has used many of the world's finest cinematographers: Sven Nykvist (Ingmar Bergman's cameraman for most of his pictures and for *Another Woman, Oedipus Wrecks, Crimes and Misdemeanors,* and *Celebrity*), Carlo Di Palma (the dozen films from *Hannah and Her Sisters* to *Deconstructing Harry*), Ghislaine Cloquet (*Love and Death*), Zhao Fei (*Sweet and Lowdown, Small Time Crooks, Curse of the Jade Scorpion*), Vilmos Zsigmond (*You Will Meet a Tall Dark Stranger, Cassandra's Dream, Melinda and Melinda*), Remi Adefarasin (*Match Point, Scoop*), Javier Aguirresarobe (*Blue Jasmine, Vicky Cristina Barcelona*), Vittorio Storaro (*Café Society* and *Wonder Wheel*), and, most productively, Gordon Willis, who died in 2014. Willis shot eight films between 1976 and 1985 including *Annie Hall, Manhattan, Zelig,* and *The Purple Rose of Cairo*. Among his twenty-nine other films are *Klute* and *All the President's Men,* plus all three parts of *The Godfather*. Woody says Willis set the standard for how he shoots. Willis once said, "Woody and I hate the same things and like the same things. Our minds are cross-indexed very well."

One difference between them is that Willis wanted to be deeply prepared for every shot before the first day of shooting, and Woody is happy to come to the set without a plan and instead do what comes to mind after he sees it, a trait that he says "plays into my laziness. I don't like to do homework and I don't like to think about it, so I get there and do it. Gordon, as great a cameraman as I've seen, liked to go over the scene and ask, 'How are you going to shoot this so I can see what you need?' I would always accommodate to his way of working. Before every picture he would come over to the house and we would go over each shot, and when we would get to the set he would ask, 'Show me how you're staging this.' It's not the way I usually do it, but I wanted to accommodate his genius. Carlo di Palma was the perfect bad brother for me because he was [*laughing*] completely laissez-faire. The two of us would get there in the morning with no idea of how it was going to be shot. And Carlo would say [*slipping into a slacker Italian accent*], 'Come and see where the sun is, it's cloudy. . . .' I was the same way: 'What's the minimum I can get away with this morning?' "

Woody talked of a meeting with Willis before *Annie Hall*. "He said, 'You're on the analyst's couch and she's on the analyst's couch. What are you thinking of doing there?' And I said, 'Well, we shoot it and then we split the screen.' And he said, 'What about if we build the set so we pan from one to the other?' Then we went on to the next shot, a basketball game at Madison Square Garden. 'How are you going to shoot it?' he asked. And I said, 'Well, maybe through the players with a long lens.' He'd say, 'Yes, that's one way you could do it,' and then we'd talk it down." But Woody was not entirely without plans, as in how he wanted to accent his favorite and least favorite places. "When we went out to California I said, 'Let's make it sunny in an annoying way and in New York always have end-of-the-day sunlight or grey.'

"On *Stardust Memories,* I usually would design the shot and then Gordie would look at it and say, 'Great,' or 'We have to tweak it,' and he would make a decent idea into a very good one. There were occasions he said, 'Pretentious,' and we wouldn't do that shot. I never argued with him or said, 'Look, I'm the director and I want that shot.' I always deferred to wiser, more gifted guidance. I'm good at working with people because I have great respect for them and defer to them." Once he did not. At the end of the first week of shooting *Hollywood Ending,* Woody fired the acclaimed Haskell Wexler, whom he considers "one of the all-time great cinematographers. All one has to do is look at the Kazan picture *America America* [1963]. But he always wanted to shoot a million angles, and I kept saying, 'I don't have the patience, we don't have the money, we need to move on.' And the next scene we'd be back at the same thing." He will occasionally overrule his cinematographer if he feels there is something critical in the script that the shot will interfere with, especially if, he said, "I'll never get a laugh if we do it that way. In one picture with Gordie [*Annie Hall*] there was a Nazi in a fantasy, and without telling me he shot it so the swastika armband on the Nazi reflected in the lenses of my glasses. I thought that was a terrible idea and told him we couldn't do that. But ninety-nine percent of the time with all of them, when they say to me, 'I think we'd be better off here,' or 'Light that half and leave this other half off,' I defer to them. I once said to Gordon, 'You can't see her, she's in the dark,' and he said, 'Well, you can *hear* her.' So I learned by doing it that he was right. Not everybody has to be lit up and the camera doesn't have to be on the person talking—or on anybody."

Many directors, Woody obviously included, prefer to use the same cinematographer again and again. Bergman made twenty-one films with Nykvist; Walter Hill ten with Lloyd Ahern II; Scorsese seven each with Michael Ballhaus and Robert Richardson; Clint Eastwood thirteen to date with Tom Stern. Jean Renoir was his own cinematographer, to great effect.

In 2003 Woody brought in Darius Khondji to shoot *Anything*

Else. Khondji had just finished *Panic Room* (2002), and among his forty films to that time were *Se7en* and *Evita.* He returned for *Midnight in Paris* and *To Rome with Love,* then *Magic in the Moonlight.* Woody hoped to use Khondji for *The Boston Story,* but he had committed to shoot James Gray's *The Lost City of* Z at the same time. Because of that film's projected high budget and difficult locations, however, its production date was not firm. There was the possibility he would be free, and Woody wanted to give him every chance. By early March there still was no resolution on Khondji's film. Woody was firm in wanting to shoot during July and August, but he told Khondji he would not hire a cameraman until the last minute. Boston, he said, was still the front-runner location "because I want something that's a little fresher than New York for me." In May, Gray's film was postponed to 2015 and Khondji was free to return for what would be his fifth film with Woody.

One day Woody talked about the similarities and differences among his various cinematographers.

"Gordon was slow and meticulous and had a million different complex angles—he was always painting with light," he said. "Darius is the same; he, too, is very poetic in his photography. Sven was also poetic and worked fast. He was a Swedish cornpone, a guy who liked to chop wood, and absolutely sweet. He got his effects with very few lights, and very quickly. He was a great black-and-white photographer. I was the one who convinced him to shoot warm because that was not his tendency, and then he started to like that. He would come in and bang-bang-bang, two or three things and you're ready to shoot and the final effect would be very beautiful. It's what your own body rhythm is. Some cameramen want a lot of equipment and they work with tons of lights. Others don't; it's just what poetry is in them for the photography." For a night shot on the Montebello Quay for *Everyone Says I Love You,* in which the Goldie Hawn character seemingly dances in midair, "Carlo had days to light that thing. We had rented every light in France. Notre Dame was lit and the other side of the Seine was lit—we must have had five hundred lights." Also, European filmmakers such as Bergman worked with smaller budgets than their

American counterparts and thus had less time both to make their films and set up their shots—one reason European directors and cameramen often employ the zoom lens to such great effect.

Willis and Nykvist were in many ways opposites whose strengths Woody put to good use. Willis saw the whole frame and was not concerned specifically with the actors. Nykvist, through his long association with Bergman, was preoccupied with actors, the prerequisite for Bergman: every scene they did is framed and lit to illuminate the actors' faces, a style Nykvist referred to as "two faces and a teacup." Woody is of course interested in the actors but has a bigger interest in the total frame. Early in the filming of *Another Woman* in 1987, their predilections inadvertently played out in a scene with Gene Hackman and Gena Rowlands, shot at the end of a hallway. Only after Woody looked at dailies did he realize that Nykvist had lit it far brighter than he wanted. "Gosh," Woody said, "it's so light, so bright. I thought it was going to be dark up in that hallway, just light coming in through that end window. I picked that hall for the look."

Nykvist, puzzled, said, "If that was the lighting we never would have seen the faces of the actors. It would have been a very pretty picture but we wouldn't have seen the actors' faces." This is the one point on which they had to learn to work together; otherwise, they were in great harmony. The shot was much darker in the finished film. The scene is a good example of the differences in style between Nykvist and Willis, and where Woody's preference lies, which is somewhere in the middle between the two. "I want to see the actors' faces to a degree but I'm much more willing not to see them than Sven would imagine or Bergman would be. I'd be perfectly willing to do that scene where at first you didn't see the actors' faces, just saw light coming through the window, and as the camera moved in you saw their faces a little better. I don't want it ruinous, but I go much further than Sven is used to going. Everything else we did felt natural; I like to shoot long masters with no coverage and so does he."

The styles of Willis, Di Palma, and Nykvist, each beautiful, differ in other ways as well. Woody once said of Willis, "Gordon's is a very American style. He would have been sensational working with John

Ford. His shots are superbly lit, like Rembrandt." Di Palma, on the other hand, liked the camera constantly in motion—an extreme case is the jerky handheld camera that mirrors the emotional atmosphere of *Husbands and Wives.* He set moods beautifully and used color brilliantly. His mother was a florist, and he once told me that growing up surrounded by the bright hues of flowers was a major influence on his work. Nykvist liked to move the camera but not as much as Di Palma.

Woody knows the difference between what he sees in his mind as he writes and what he can shoot. "I can never recreate on the screen what I envision when I'm writing a script. I remember when Bergman was writing *Winter Light,* he and Sven went and sat in many churches watching the light change until he said, '*That's* the light I want.'" During the filming of *Another Woman,* Nykvist told me, "*Winter Light* is Ingmar's favorite. I changed my style of shooting with that film: there were no shadows except for the end, where it means something. I started using boards [similar to black poster material, used to redirect or block light] to get the right light. Then I realized that it worked for color, too."

Woody also wants a certain light, "but I don't do anything to get it," he says. "I think to myself, 'I'd like the soft sepia light that you get just as dusk is beginning to fall on a summer's day.' But I don't go to Central Park days before and wait and say, 'This is the right time to get that light.' If I have the light that night, great, and if not, I rewrite the scene or find another solution. I *always* prefer a warm picture. Blue is fatal. It's very tricky. I never used it with Gordon. It's too cold. This picture [*Another Woman*] is kind of monochromatic. Yellow would crush. Maroon turns to mud. White was dangerous to Gordon. Sven said on *Cries and Whispers* it was a pleasure because a red picture is inherently warm. When the film was color corrected and they took the red out of the faces, the walls kept the red yet left good skin tone.

"Gordon is sort of like the Platonic ideal of a cameraman. Everything was perfect, every composition, every lighting, he knew everything about cameras and photography and film and emulsion and he never made a bad shot in his life. He just couldn't and wouldn't. Darius makes everything very beautiful, and he's obsessional in the best sense of the word. When we did *Midnight in Paris* he researched what the streetlights of the twenties were like so he could reproduce their look, as if anyone's going to say, 'Well, the filament in the streetlight is different than it should be.'" Khondji also studied the images of the Hungarian-French photographer and filmmaker Brassaï and other photographers of 1920s Paris for guidance. Woody sought out Arthur Penn for advice before doing *Take the Money and Run.* He had recently seen *Bonnie and Clyde,* which he considers "one of the best American movies ever. I asked him to tell me what I should be looking out for, and he told me how he had looked at many vintage photographs of small Texas towns and banks and framed his shots based on them."

Surrounded by such technical talent, Woody professes to have none. Shooting a scene requires a number of decisions in advance: selection of the lens, what f-stop, the color density, and so on. But "none of that is on my mind. I wouldn't know one f-stop from another. I know what I want and I can describe it. I have no idea how to get it. I have to tell the cameraman and he has to get it for me. Now, I do make up the compositions of my shots. There are directors who don't look through the camera; they rely on their cameraman. I could never do that."

With so much prior collaboration, Woody and Khondji quickly agreed on the look for *The Boston Story.* Woody talked about Carol Reed's *The Third Man* (1949), with Orson Welles, as a way into the story because, like Hitchcock, Khondji tells himself a story within a story when he films. He wants his work to reflect the director and says that Woody arrives on set with "a blanker page and far less baggage" than he, and that he has "great poetic imagination." In early discussions they talked about the warmth of the photography—Woody generally prefers a "rich, saturated look"—and when the subject of screen ratio naturally arose, Khondji suggested that as they had in *Magic,* they use anamorphic, a format they both appreciate because a wide screen has room for a lot of information. For that film Woody liked that it would allow a broad view of the French countryside, a chance to see the terrain in all its beauty.

Often called CinemaScope or Panavision, anamorphic allows for a large rectangular image on the screen with a ratio of 2.39 units wide by 1 tall, rather than the more common, squarer image of 1.85:1. When shown on television, an anamorphic film has to be squeezed to fill the screen, and much of what is on the far sides of the original is lost. (When shown in proper proportion, there is a black border top and bottom that forms what is called a letterbox—so named because the rectangular shape mimics that of a mail slot.) In this instance, Woody was drawn to anamorphic because he has had "good luck with it on intimate pictures," notably in *Manhattan*. Among others of his films in CinemaScope are *Anything Else, Blue Jasmine,* and, of course, *Magic in the Moonlight*. For him, "the more intimate the picture the more a wide screen helps, the opposite of what you think. When I first talked about this with Gordon, they had only done widescreen with war and cowboy pictures. We thought we would do it with *Manhattan* because the tension between the intimacy and the panoramic screen would make the film visually more interesting."

After deciding to use anamorphic again with *The Boston Story,* Woody, his genial pessimism in full bloom, said ruefully, "You know, always going in hoping for the best, and inevitably disillusioned."

CHAPTER 4

The Locations, the Production Design, the Costumes

Locations—houses, rooms, streets, cafés, countryside, anywhere the action takes place—need to have a look that evokes the sense of the script and gives it visual and emotional reality. Woody prefers actual places that can be redecorated with minor adjustments rather than sets built on a soundstage; *Shadows and Fog* and *September*, the exceptions that prove the rule, were completely shot on manufactured sets. On the occasions in other films that a set is required (the fun house mirrors in this film, for example), Santo Loquasto designs and oversees its construction, just as he oversees all sets and locations. He is responsible for the look the camera sees.

Loquasto first worked with Woody in 1980 as costume designer on *Stardust Memories*, then *A Midsummer Night's Sex Comedy* and *Zelig*, after which he switched to production designer for the past going-on-thirty Allen movies made in the United States. Apart from his extensive film work, he is a renowned costume and production designer for the theater; he has been the scenic and/or costume designer for more than seventy shows, Woody's included, and is in the Theater Hall of Fame. He has received nineteen Tony nominations (including for his set design of *Bullets over Broadway* in 2014) and four awards, plus several Oscar nominations. He has also designed sets and costumes for productions by the American Ballet Theatre, the Metropolitan Opera, and Woody's 2008 direction of Puccini's

Gianni Schicchi for the Los Angeles Opera. He is a bespectacled, neatly bearded man with an ironic outlook, a quick wit, and a sober visage that breaks easily into laughter.

Adventure comes with his job. For *Whatever Works* (2009), he constructed a bedroom and corridor for the Upper East Side apartment of Boris (Larry David) at the Astoria Studios, in Queens. As Woody walked with Loquasto around the set, he turned to him and said, "Oh, where's the kitchen?"

"Your heart stops," Loquasto recalled. "I said, 'What are you talking about?' He said, 'Well, he goes down the hall and gets a glass of milk.' I said, 'Woody, that's not scripted, you know?'" In looking for an appropriate space for the art gallery in the film, Loquasto found one with a residence above it. One look and he said to Woody, "This is where he lives," and he immediately agreed. "It was this sprawling place. He could do whatever he wanted," Loquasto says. "There was a kitchen he could go into, we covered up some things and built others, and it worked perfectly—sadly after another set had been built, but these things happen. You realize you can change something enormously to accommodate and take advantage of a better location."

After nearly thirty years of working together, Woody's complete trust in Loquasto has earned him a special status with the production crew, who call him "the Woody Whisperer" for his ability to infer what he needs and to deliver unhappy news. Woody often greets him by asking, "What's the bad word?"

"I'd like to think I help but only as a privilege," Loquasto says. "I certainly have his ear to tell him all the bad news. I'm always sent in to say, 'We lost the location and we have no money.'" Loquasto is one of two crew members—the other is Helen Robin—who are comfortable making wisecracks at Woody's expense, to both their amusement. As they stood in an apartment in San Francisco before shooting a scene of *Blue Jasmine,* which many critics would liken in part to Tennessee Williams's *A Streetcar Named Desire,* Loquasto said, "I'm still very anxious about the parallels of this to *Streetcar.*"

Woody looked placidly at him and answered, "Oh, no. Don't worry."

"I suppose you're right," Loquasto replied. "What you have going for you is none of the poetry and none of the sex."

"He has spoiled me, that's the truth," Loquasto says. "The way he works, his control. You don't have creative producers and all those other people with their opinions to deal with the way most films do. You go to Woody. He defers to the cinematographer, and I do too; I work for Woody and the cinematographer. We have similar taste, and I want to think I understand the way he views things. I kind of know when I think it should be different, and I try to vary things accordingly. He allows me just to go after it. Even though I want his approval, I don't have to wait to show him fifty-three samples."

Christie Mullen first worked with Woody as a location assistant on *Sweet and Lowdown* (1999). She breaks out the necessary locations from the script, then meets with Loquasto and the location designer to decide on what to scout.

Mullen, whose North Carolina roots are in her voice, says that as Woody considers locations, he is as much the writer as he is the director, thinking of changes in the script he can make to match the scene. "He is seeing the fictional story in the reality of the world, and that's a really good thing to work with. He is very decisive when it comes to locations. He knows what he wants and doesn't want, but he can change his mind. If something's not available or too hard, he'll say, 'Okay, let me work on that.' A lot of directors don't have that confidence or experience; you're just going around in circles: 'Can we see ten more Italian restaurants?' 'No, there aren't ten more. Use your imagination, please.' He'll take off his glasses and look closely at a photo and ask, 'What can I do here, and over here?' He asks me a lot about the reality of where we're going and who the people are. When we were scouting cookie factories for *Small Time Crooks,* he said, 'Why would they want to do this?' "

What seemed a simple task for *The Boston Story*—find a classic verdant campus in a city full of colleges where they could film for ten to fifteen days—turned out to be an impossible one. For a month, Mullen called colleges and universities, to no avail. Many had summer sessions or other activities and so would be too crowded. Others did not have the small-college look Woody wanted. Still others had a policy against having film crews on campus. A few were willing to have one for a day or two but not two or three weeks. And administrators at places that might otherwise have been a possibility wanted to read the script so they could see how their institution was being portrayed, something Woody never allows. He will give a very vague synopsis, but in this case he had to add that an unspecified crime is committed. This was not a selling point.

Mullen began looking at prep schools outside Boston, knowing "you can make anything into anything else. It could have been a nursing school, if it had the look." But nothing did, and so *The Boston Story* would have to be filmed elsewhere. The Episcopal Church's General Theological Seminary on Manhattan's West Side had the right look, but the quad was a bit small. It could have been used in conjunction with other, similar locations, but Woody still wanted something fresh and new outside New York where he could take his family for the summer.

Loquasto suggested Brown University in Providence, Rhode Island, but like the schools in Boston, it was not willing to have a film crew on campus for more than a day or two, especially with only a vague synopsis that included an undetermined crime. The Rhode Island Film and TV Office, however, was eager to help. They suggested the University of Rhode Island, but Woody found it too sprawling. He constantly thinks about the logic of his scripts and wanted a small area so people in the story could realistically keep running into one another. Mullen suggested they drive around Providence and Newport to see if either town looked right. A local scout hired by Mullen suggested they swing by Salve Regina University in Newport, even though it does not have the classic campus look Woody envisioned. Instead, many nineteenth-century mansions on a bluff overlooking the Atlantic constitute the school, but it is beautifully landscaped, with areas of flowers and lawn and massive old trees. As soon as the car stopped, Woody was out and looking intently. Mullen immediately called the college to get the okay for him to wander around.

"My biggest fear," she says, "is showing him something he likes and not getting permission to use it."

Woody liked everything he saw, knowing that the untraditional layout would require tying buildings together in an unconventional way. Fortunately, other film crews had worked there and administrators were not spooked by the prospect of one hundred people milling about for several days, but they did want a better sense of the crime. Woody was now set on using Providence and Newport and time was running short if he wanted to make the film on schedule. As a safety measure, Mullen and Robin were looking into colleges a couple of hours north of Manhattan and told Woody that if he wanted Salve Regina he would have to tell officials more. He wrote a description of the story in which a murder is committed without revealing by whom, and that was accepted.

At the end of May, Loquasto and Mullen meet with Woody and Helen Robin at the Manhattan Film Center to go over photos of possible locations in Newport and Providence. Over the past weeks they and several locals they hired looked for restaurants, houses, stores, parks, and other sites that might work in the film, and the possibilities are stored in Mullen's laptop computer. She sets it atop the record cabinet in the screening room, next to a black banjo case belonging to Eddy Davis; Davis and others in Woody's band often practice with him in the room. In the predigital era, Mullen would arrive with cartons of files with photos of possible locations. Sometimes Woody would look at them and say, "What is this, another box of compromises?"

The four stand to watch the slide show. They expect most of the action to take place in Newport, with a few days of shooting in and around Providence, forty-five minutes away. A critical location is the park where Abe will slip the poison to the judge. Several possibilities follow one another on the screen. The first is too picture-perfect and clearly is in Providence because the statehouse is in the background. Others seem ho-hum. Then one divided by a broad walkway appears.

There is an area with playground equipment, but the park is large enough to offer isolation for the exchange of cups to go unnoticed by others, and Woody starts to imagine the scene there. Plus there is a coffee stand with tables outside it across from one side of the park where the judge could get his drink after he finishes his Saturday run, making the two scenes less time-consuming to shoot. The question still to be answered is, Just how will Abe pull off the poisoning? At this point the idea is for him to accidentally knock over the judge's coffee cup and offer him the poisoned replacement. (It will later be changed to orange juice.)

Thinking aloud, Woody says, "If he gets his coffee, why doesn't he sit here at the stand and read his paper? He has to be sitting somewhere else so he can take the offered drink. If there is a bench nearby in the park, he would go to somewhere more comfortable." Still thinking, he adds, "I assume just after he runs he buys coffee and the paper and goes to read it for an hour. Our guy can just be walking along and knock over his cup."

"Is the judge sitting or standing?" Loquasto asks.

"We'll have to work that out," Woody answers, then stops to consider another, larger coffee shop where the judge could go, but then he shakes his head. "It might be too big a deal. Maybe it is better for students." In the film it is where the Emma Stone character, Jill, and her boyfriend, Roy, make up.

Some photos garner a lot of conversation. Others are quickly dismissed.

Loquasto says that a room with a high ceiling "looks like a place where Jill might have piano lessons."

"It could be but it's not what I had in mind," Woody says. Next picture.

It is of a wooden barn, a possibility for a horseback riding scene, and Loquasto offers, "I'm thinking back to *Bullets.* We had one of those confrontation scenes in a stable. Maybe here as well?" An earlier photo looked too much like a farm. The next photo is of a hundred-year-old stone barn in Portsmouth that seems promising. Loquasto is looking for interior stalls. "This is not good with the fluorescent lights on," he says, "but I hung lights in the other stable—is that a viable idea?"

"Possible," Woody muses. (They do use this location.)

Small details are important. Loquasto likes the crosshatched windowpanes in a room. Other details are larger, such as what sort of house does the judge live in? An otherwise suitable one seems too big for someone who lives alone. Where will the reception to welcome Abe to the college be? Woody doesn't like the notion of a sedate club and prefers a large home, perhaps the college dean's. What about the place where Jill and Abe overhear the mother weepily telling her friends about the judge's treatment of her? A restaurant is a likely spot, but the choices are a problem.

"How many casual restaurants do we have? Because I hate most of them," Loquasto says.

Woody says, "It has to be a place that has booths or something where you could hear—not tables side by side."

The script calls for a party at the home of a student named Danny, whose parents have just purchased a Willem de Kooning painting. Jill, in an attempt to coax Abe from his doldrums, invites him to come with her and Roy. What the house looks like is still undetermined. Loquasto has several to show and offers, "It might be a modern house."

"What is the exterior?" Woody asks. "It should be nice. There are perhaps a dozen people there."

A pleasant-looking modern house comes on the screen. "I worry this is small to work in," Loquasto says.

"It *could* work," Woody says, more musing than pushing for it.

"There is a bigger one," Loquasto tells him.

"It would be nice if it could be sort of isolated on a few acres," Woody says.

"Darius will want to shoot night for night [using actual outside darkness]," Robin reminds them.

Woody retires to one of the forest-green chairs by the screen at one end of the room to think. After a few seconds he asks, "What's the boy's name?" Danny, he is told. "This kid Danny, his father's not a teacher, he just lives in the area."

"Emma's father is a music professor," Robin reminds him.

Still thinking aloud and filling in one of the many TBDs in the script, Woody says, "Danny's dad is a hedge fund guy or a lawyer or a doctor."

This exchange is emblematic of how fluid his scripts are at this stage and how easy it is for him to adjust scenes to fit locations. In a week or two the party scene will be altered even more after Sophie von Haselberg reads for the part of April, a student friend of Jill's. In the original script she has only a couple of brief appearances, but Woody so likes her naturalness that he enlarges her role; it will be her parents who have bought the painting and she who is hosting the party. Danny will stay in the film but simply as one of those in the room.

The script calls for a second party but does not specify where it will be. Woody thinks that it likely would be in a house, but it could be a birthday celebration in a bought-out bar. He envisions dancing: "In the 1960s there wasn't a movie that didn't have a disco in it."

Loquasto, looking at a photo of a big, open room where there could be line dancing, says, "We'd have to make it smaller so it doesn't look like a roller rink—and *not* a disco."

A picture of a lovely beach comes up. Woody immediately says, "What about one of those on the beach for the barbecue?"

"Clambake," Robin says.

"Right, a clambake."

"Walks by the water would be quite beautiful, with crashing surf," Loquasto says.

A lighthouse on the rocks comes on the screen. Woody perks up. "What about that lighthouse? I like that. We could have a clambake outside the lighthouse. I'm tempted to make it more in the afternoon."

"Or magic hour," Loquasto suggests [the time before sunset when the sun is low and everything is saturated in golden red light]. Robin groans because shooting into the long summer evenings would make it more expensive.

Woody, still looking at the picture, says with some energy, "I am more and more drawn to this. It is a very exciting location and we can change the party to a clambake. I can just rewrite that scene so it will fit." (He does, but in the end there will be only one party, in a house; the lighthouse will be where Abe tells Jill they must only be friends.)

The financial circumstances of Jill's parents are another TBD. Both teach at the college. How they live is part of a broader question of how all the faculty live. In Woody's mind, faculty housing is next to the campus and should not be inconsequential. (While scouting locations in Rhode Island ten days later, he several times points to dilapidated or very inexpensive residences and smiles as he says, "Faculty housing.") There is a photogenic block of adjoining red brick Federal-style homes in Providence, known as Athenaeum Row, that Woody has thought might serve as faculty homes. "It would be nice to split it up," he says, "some brownstone, that row of red brick houses."

"Maybe that's where the parents are," Loquasto suggests. But Woody has a different idea.

"I saw their place as more homey. They're a nice, sweet family. I could see putting Abe in an expensive red brick house because he's a celebrity and have someone say something to explain that this is for the resident superstar, whereas the girl and her parents have a sweet house." In the end, the judge will live in one of the Athenaeum Row houses but no faculty members. Jill's parents will live in a cozy-looking Cape Cod on a corner by a park that was not scouted but that Woody saw while looking at another house nearby. The Cape Cod is smaller inside than the proposed house, which made it harder to move the camera, but to Woody, who tends to like small, the look was just what he wanted. (When a set is built on a soundstage, the rooms are always much larger than normal to accommodate the equipment and crew.)

He looks through the photos for interesting storefronts but finds few. Always wanting something unique, he says, "A dolls' hospital would be nice."

There is the question of where to set a romantic meal between Abe and Jill, when he gives her a birthday present. A number of restaurants are considered, but Woody feels they look too corporate, too much like a place where the judge would eat. "They could have take-out in a car and be just as romantic," he says.

"I think our friend is going to be the car," Loquasto says. The script calls for car shots of Abe; of Jill, Roy, and Abe going to a party; another of Rita and her husband; and now this.

"Once you have them face-to-face it doesn't matter where he gives the gift," Woody says, still mulling. "You know what else makes it romantic is if it's raining."

Loquasto says he will work on the rain idea and fills Woody in on his search for an arcade or fair for a scene with Abe and Jill, where they kiss for the first time. "In Newport there's this little arcade. They don't have the chicken," he says, referring to a trained fowl at a place in New York's Chinatown that was unbeatable at tic-tac-toe, "but they have a photo booth."

Woody is unimpressed by a photo of a store with stuffed animals and cheap plastic toys. "Tacky. A fair should be a fair."

Robin arches her eyebrows. "If you want to shoot in the middle of the country, I am sure we can find you a *great* amusement park."

They also are on the lookout for a dark bar where Abe and Jill go after the amusement park and he tells her not to get involved with him.

"It could be a conversation in the car," Woody offers.

"The problem with a closed top is that you don't have much latitude," Loquasto reminds him.

Woody shakes his head. "I never think of those details."

Selecting locations from photos means less time for Woody driving around Providence and Newport looking for them. A scouting trip with Loquasto, Mullen, Robin, and the local staff is planned for the next week. Scouting is among his least favorite activities—too much time going from place to place. Loquasto mentions that if they can't see all the locations in a day, he will bring Khondji up the following one and they can continue. Having found the main locations, Woody reacts with alarm. "A *one*-day trip. I can do it from pictures. For me to go and stand there and say, 'This is great' is silly."

Loquasto shrugs. "Like Alfred Hitchcock from the car—he just rolled down the window."

(It was a one-day trip. The best find for Woody was an empty 1920s twenty-six-story bank building [the tallest in Rhode Island] with a basement elevator room three floors below the ground floor, where the professor can disguise malice as an accident. By fiddling with the controls, he will keep the elevator in the basement when the doors on a high floor open. His plan is to then shove his victim into the empty shaft, making the death seem the result of equipment malfunction. Many tangled wires lie at the bottom of a closet that houses the controls. Woody looks at them for a moment and says, "Harpo [Marx] would pull out the spaghetti wire," and mimes doing so. Elevators—all small, enclosed places—make Woody so claustrophobic that rather than ride in one, he trudged down and back up the 108 stairs from the lobby.)

More details. They talk about the scene where a faculty member and her husband break up. Perhaps it is raining. "We could see the house wide with the porch, then go in," Woody says.

Loquasto nods. "Rain gets you a lot of places." In the film, the scene plays out entirely in the car during a heavy rain.

Photo by photo, one of the central assumptions of where the story will be filmed changes as they show that Newport does not have as many appropriate locations as imagined.

"Providence has a more consistent look," Woody acknowledges. "It would be better if the college is just on the outskirts of the city and the basic playing field for the story." Newport, which was to be used in about 80 percent of the filming, will instead be in about 20.

The session is nearly finished. Woody is quiet for a moment and then says, "I couldn't dare shoot the movie in black and white, could I?" The films of his youth in Brooklyn were largely in black and white, and they shaped his view of the world and especially Manhattan, that magical place across the East River. He considered making *Another Woman* in black and white; *Stardust Memories, Manhattan, Zelig, Broadway Danny Rose, Celebrity,* and *Shadows and Fog* are in it, each for a reason. "Manhattan has a black-and-white feel to it," hence the choice for *Manhattan*; he shot the horse-drawn carriage ride he takes with Mariel Hemingway in the same spot that James Stewart and Eleanor Powell took their walk in *Born to Dance* (1936) because that's what gave him the idea. He felt *Shadows and Fog*, a film modeled on

German expressionism, needed to be in black and white, even though he knew its chances for success were diminished by the choice. By 2000, he recognized that black and white is just a headache: "It is a pain in the neck these days, though every once in a while I like to shoot in it. The labs are so unsuited to black and white and there are so many technical problems: static on the film; when you make edits they come out and you have to have the whole film coated because the temperature of the lamp melts the black-and-white stock going through the projector." But he still fancies the look.

"You're asking the wrong person. I love it," Loquasto quickly responds. Despite their enthusiasm, both know this is a fantasy.

"The problem is strictly financial because TV won't buy black and white and countries like Japan won't play it," Woody says matter-of-factly.

As soon as the locations discussion ends, Suzy Benzinger, the costume designer, comes in to talk over how the main characters will be dressed. Costumes give a subtle but immediate sense of a character's personality. Her first film with Woody was the TV version of *Don't Drink the Water* (1994). Starting with *Deconstructing Harry* (1997), she has done costumes for most of his U.S.-filmed pictures; those done abroad use someone local. Both stand by the cabinet where the computer with the location slides is still open.

Without preliminary chitchat, Woody says, "I want Joaquin to look handsome and charming. No facial hair but a five o'clock shadow is okay."

Benzinger nods. "Keep him in this world: oxford cloth shirts, one pair of colored pants, one jacket. It would be nice to have stuff he can pull out of a pocket." She shows Woody a picture of a relaxed-cut deep tan jacket that she has in mind: "Something we can age up."

"These are all the colors I think of all the time. I don't want him to look like one of those male models."

"Layer him with jeans that fit like pants and plaids."

"My feeling is that he would not give two seconds' thought to clothes but that he would have the sense not to get Miami Beach," Woody says.

"Oxford shoes, lace up, brown, beat-up nice leather. He can pull a tie from his pocket and can tuck in the shirt when he needs to."

"Would we be better off with two jackets instead of one?" Woody asks. "Just so people don't look up and say, 'Oh, the same jacket'?"

She laughs. "I can stretch the budget for two jackets." Actually, the budget is extraordinarily low, about $25,000.

"Over the years he's been a ladies' man, only recently he's come to the end of his rope."

"A modest wardrobe—jackets, a suit, sweater." But her larger concern is seasonal. "This film date was originally spring but now it will run into late August? If that's the case, I suggest you either lighten up the colors or get heavier. You're going to the end of the semester?"

"We can adjust," Woody says. "I don't want to take the leaves off the trees."

"It's better if the story covers a short period of time. It is New England, so there's a change." (The action will take place during a summer session.)

"Joaquin's thirty-nine, right?" Woody asks, thinking of Abe. Abe needs to have a bit of age on him to have reached this point in his life. "If he was forty-two in the movie, forty-three . . . I've never laid eyes on him. I've seen him on screen, of course. We've spoken briefly on the phone. He was very nice. He had two questions for me. Then I said, 'I'll see you at the wardrobe test.' Scarlett [Johansson] told me he is very nice to work with."

All this takes less than ten minutes. Benzinger suggests they move on to Emma Stone's hair. Woody says, "First I said to her, 'You should be playing this as a blonde.' She said, 'Please, no, I have no pigment and it will wash me out, I'll be a ghost.' I said, 'Do whatever you want. The actor I've just hired for your boyfriend is twenty-two. Just don't look like his aunt.'"

"She doesn't wear wigs, although all leading ladies now do," Benzinger tells him. "She wants to keep her bangs. I asked her how she looks in braids. She said, 'Cute.'"

"Did you ask her what color she wants?"

"Red trending to auburn."

"As long as she's comfortable."

"I have the lightest tones for Emma's clothes: pale-ish beige and green. They're pretty and sweet—soft."

Woody nods in approval. "Simple and adorable."

He moves on to Parker Posey. "Make Parker soft and pretty. I didn't want to cast Angelina Jolie—she's a biology teacher and Angelina's too amazing looking, but don't give her gloves." (In the film, she teaches chemistry to make a plot line work better.)

"I have her in petrol blue—pale and teals, not the blue you hate." (For years Woody disliked darker blue because it tended to cool the screen. Recent advances in technology have fixed that, but by now it has become traditional for him not to use it.)

"Okay," he tells her, and they're done.

As in most of Woody's films, the rest of the cast will be dressed in varying tones of khaki and muted autumnal hues so their costumes do not bring attention—"fifty shades of beige" is how Helen Robin describes the palette. Extras are told what clothes and colors to wear. Anyone who shows up wearing an identifying label—a T-shirt with a logo, for instance—is put in something at hand because there is not the time or money to get legal clearances to photograph trademarked clothes. In a film like this with many extras, Benzinger goes "to the Salvation Army every day to stock up."

"Woody has a certain aesthetic and it's very classic," she says. "Not much pattern, though a character piece here and there. You can't use a lot of red because the eye goes to it automatically. Woody misses *nothing*. If I put something in he doesn't like, the camera won't go there." An instance where he wanted the audience's eye attracted is in *Interiors* when Pearl (Maureen Stapleton), the new paramour of Arthur (E. G. Marshall), makes her first appearance. Through the film until then, the rooms, décor, and costumes are muted, mostly greys and whites. Suddenly the bright red of Pearl's dress shocks the eye. She is a mood-changing gust, a slightly vulgar but effervescent, life-grasping character amidst a controlled, inhibited patrician family.

When Woody is in a film, he wears clothes made by Ralph Lauren, as do many characters, because, as Benzinger points out, "he makes stuff that shows beautifully and is cut beautifully. And they are so incredibly generous to us."

Generosity is welcome, and needed. The costume budget for *Blue Jasmine,* extras included, was $35,000, but because of Cate Blanchett's stature, designers were happy to loan or give clothes, including an $8,000-plus white Chanel jacket. Benzinger's atelier is in her Greenwich Village loft, where she also washes, dyes, irons, and ages costumes as needed, hanging them in the apartment or on the small rooftop terrace. To give the Chanel jacket the distressed look to match Jasmine's character, who has not accepted her reduced circumstances and so still wears her now-tatty trappings of wealth, Benzinger sent it to the dry cleaner, dunked it in water, and hung it on her rooftop clothesline. She eventually got the desired look but says admiringly of the tailoring, "It's hard to wreck it."

When Woody watches any film, he is aware of what makes a scene interesting and draws him in, and he instinctually separates the photography from the scenic design. "People will say after seeing [Kubrick's] *Barry Lyndon* [1975], 'Oh, this is fantastic photography.' When I see it, I'm thinking it's beautiful photography, but the locations are what's great." It is the same with costumes. "In a contemporary film, you don't want them to be affecting. There are some costume designers and directors who, when there's a stagehand, will dress him in overalls and a sweater or a vest. The flaw, whether it's acting or costume design or photography, is always excess: overacting; doing more than necessary. You're aware that there's too much—the character would never wear a beret. You want a car, they get a Ferrari. You usually have to say, 'No, plain Chevy.' You almost never have to say, 'Do more.'"

A Woody Allen film is carried on Helen Robin's back. Normally a movie has a line producer and also a production manager, but Robin fills both roles. "Where there is a lot of dealing with studios there is more to do," she explains. "I'm sort of like the be-all stopper, so why not just do it?" She is a no-nonsense New Yorker with a high capacity for organization and a sense for detecting when someone is trying to sneak anything past her. When something goes awry, as things in film production are wont to do every ten minutes, she has likely anticipated it and is already at work to right it. She describes herself as "one of those people who's a pessimist because I believe somewhere in my childhood I must have done something optimistic that didn't turn out and I thought to myself, 'You know, you feel better if you plan for the worst.'" She is as tough or as pleasant as a situation demands, and wickedly funny.

Her first job after Woody has settled on a script is to work out a shooting schedule. After that she worries about the budget. "Every year there is x amount of money, regardless of what he writes, regardless of where it is," she said after budgeting *The Boston Story,* "so I kind of know how many days we can afford to shoot regardless of where we are, which is generally thirty-five days. So I break down the script. There is a program called Movie Magic Scheduling. You go into a script with a pencil and a ruler and every page is considered eight-eighths of a page. I highlight the cast, any key extras, an animal, a vehicle—anything off the beaten path—and then type in 'Interior school day, two-eighths of a page.' You end up with strips of a hundred odd scenes and then you do the jigsaw puzzle of putting them together. The thing that's easy for me, easier than for people in my position on other pictures, is there is the pretty much constant factor of having to get it done in thirty-five days. I know how he shoots. I have to take into account the DP [director of photography] we are using for time, as some are faster than others. We have a starring cast and I know I have to get everything around their schedule. Once we know the bulk of the cast and how they fit in, the schedule is made round the cast.

"You don't think about the daily cost when you're doing the budget; you have to look at the larger picture. You take each department separately: here's how much my designer is going to make, the people they need. Period is more expensive because more needs to be done. Ninety-nine-point-nine percent of the time the budget does not come out to be the number you have. There are things that are not malleable, like Woody's lifestyle and everybody else's. So you sit there and say, 'Should we be making a movie in another city or another country where so many people have to be moved and put up?' This film was the perfect example. It could have been shot anywhere in the USA. I think Boston became fixed in his mind because it is the quintessential college town, but as soon as we knew we weren't going to get Boston we could have done it anywhere. We could have done it cheaper in New York City. The only one that loses is him. But it's his vision."

Over the following six weeks, she oversaw the complex logistics of setting up a production office in Warwick, between Providence and Newport; hiring a crew of more than 120 and caterers to feed them during the day; negotiating with unions on work rules and local governments for various permits; setting the shooting schedule that started at thirty-three days but was soon rebudgeted to twenty-eight, turning a headache into a migraine; and finding a hotel to billet the crew, as well as houses for the senior production people. Not least, she and Letty Aronson had to find a house with a good kitchen for Woody and his family with space for all, including their au pair. His location home requires three essentials: powerful and reliable air-conditioning; a treadmill, or a place where a rented one can be placed; and, most important, he says, aware of his quirkiness and with some amusement, "a good clean shower that has some intensity and sufficient hot water so that none of us is ever in a position where the water is not hot or just dribbles out." Plus, as he likes to shave in the shower, it must have good light and a place to stick his suction mirror. "The shower is a major, *major* consideration. I couldn't do it otherwise. It would ruin the entire filmmaking thing for me. I would check into a hotel."

This would not be a first. When he performed in St. Louis at the Crystal Palace in the 1960s, on the bill with the late, highly talented jazz singer Irene Kral, his pay included room and board. But his quarters, though otherwise perfectly pleasant, did not have a good shower, so several times a week he would walk down the street to the Howard Johnson's motel, rent a room, have a long and vigorous wash, then check out. "It took my whole salary," he says.

In preparation for the start of production on July 7, there were days of technical scouting, during which the heads of the various departments looked over the locations to work out what they would need. Khondji considered what the camera crew would require, and he and Woody decided the location of the camera for exterior shots. The lead actors gathered for a day of test shots for their costumes, filmed in a warehouse by the production office.

The day after—five days before shooting was to start—Woody, Soon-Yi, and their teenage daughters, Bechet and Manzie, are settled in a huge stone house with suitable showers on many gated acres, with an undisturbed view of Newport's Second Beach a mile away and on to the horizon. At nine p.m. the family will fly to Barcelona with producer Edward Walson on his plane for three days of pleasure before shooting starts Monday. This will give his family at least a short vacation trip together before his daughters embark on their separate summer adventures. Even so, it is hard to imagine any other director zipping off in the last days before shooting begins. It is nearly five p.m. and Woody is seated between Suzy Benzinger and Helen Robin at the counter in the large stone-floored kitchen with an imposing La Cornue stove, looking at an iPad with the film of the wardrobe tests, making the decisions on how the three central characters will look. Soon-Yi is busy with preparations of her own in another part of the room. The talk turns to other films and other performers and the personal quirks of many. Benzinger mentions that as actors grow older, their usually imagined physical complaints are more often expressed.

"Really?" Woody, an ever-ready hypochondriac—although he prefers to say he is "an alarmist"—asks in disbelief. Soon-Yi looks up and without missing a beat says, "Look at you, Woody." Everyone laughs, no one more than he.

There are a couple of dozen rooms in the three-story house, including a floor below the kitchen that has two large bedrooms and a billiards room with an almost walk-in fireplace. "The lord of the manor," Woody says derisively of his situation after the wardrobe decisions have been made. "But I feel good about the script, I feel great about Emma and Joaquin and Parker Posey and the people I've cast. Once I start shooting I just wish I could shoot straight through twenty-four hours; that would be a help. It's when we knock off Friday night, I've got the weekend and that's tough for me. I can't get through the weekends." When he films in London or Paris or Barcelona, it is a different story, there is plenty to do, but not so much in Newport for someone who dislikes the sun and being on the ocean. He is already thinking of options. "Maybe if I went back to New York or hopped over to Boston or something for a sightsee. In two weeks I have to go to the opening of *Magic* in New York and then Chicago so that will" [*he pauses and laughs again*] "create enough anxiety to get me through the weekend." A sure way for him to lessen that anxiety is to work; he still is "compulsively" fiddling with the script. "I keep seeing things, though I'm not sure they're better. Maybe they're just lateral moves that seem better because they're new."

The crew, and especially those involved with costumes and locations, have been working flat out for weeks. Woody has paced himself to be at top strength when the filming begins, often to the frustration of those who want only to do their best work on his behalf but cannot always get his attention to make a choice on what he wants. He is more comfortable making decisions at the time he is ready to shoot than he is with settling everything in advance, because that takes away the spontaneity he thrives on. He acknowledges the inevitable difficulty with this for people whose job it is to be sure everything is as prepared as possible, but this is how he works and others learn to adapt.

He uses the analogy of a baseball pitcher about to face a tough team, trying to hold himself in check until shooting starts Monday. "Then you bear down on every single scene so when you get in the cutting room, you have it all. There's a tendency when you're in your sixth week of shooting and tiring and things are not going so well to say, 'Look, it's freezing out,' or 'It's hot out,' or 'It's late, make that take and let's get out of here,' but later in the cutting room you regret it. So the pitcher must bear down on the bottom three hitters in the order. You can't let up on them just because they're not the good ones;

every little thing, every car pass by matters. Then later the picture still may not be good for a billion other reasons, but you won't feel as I did *years* ago. The first five years after I started, I didn't bear down on every shot. I'd slough some off and not do the best I could and I regretted it. I kept asking myself, 'Don't you learn? Remember in the cutting room you wished you had a close-up of the inkwell so you could shorten the scene?' The time comes when the AD [assistant director] asks, 'Anything else here?' And instead of saying, 'I better make a close-up of the inkwell,' I'd say, 'No, let's move on.'"

The quick trip to Barcelona is a pleasant diversion to pass the time until shooting starts, but he is ready to get on with the work. "This place is what I wanted, this script is what I conceived, and here I am counting the minutes until I start, notching the headboard of the bed with my knife and drawing the line through the five days."

CHAPTER 5

The Shoot

Films are virtually always shot not in order of scenes but in the order that best limits expenses. Usually all scenes in a particular location are done at once, and when possible, supporting actors do all their work over a portion of the shoot so they need not be paid and housed for the whole production.

This chapter follows what happened on the set from the first day to last, over seven weeks, rather than the script from beginning to end.

1

"I cut the persiflage."

Woody's call for the first day of filming is eight a.m. in the Fastnet Pub in Newport, which has the authentic look of an ersatz Irish pub. A picture of the lighthouse that appears to pin Fastnet Rock to the ocean off southern Ireland hangs prominently on a wall. At one end of the large room is an accommodating bar with taps for draft beer and dozens of liquor bottles in front of a wall-length mirror behind it. Several neon signs advertise brands of beer. A pool table stands in a smaller area off the main room.

By the time he arrives, more than a dozen gaffers, riggers, and grips, whose call, along with the rest of the crew, was 6:05 a.m., have hung lights from rafters and clamped framed black cloths called flags onto three-legged century stands to modify the light, and set up twelve-by-twenty-foot sheets of Ultrabounce, a white reflective fabric, tied within rectangular aluminum pipe frames, to deflect and diffuse the light and make it seem natural. The camera crew—operator, two assistants, and the loader—have set up just inside the door so the camera can pan down from the pool table in a raised area at the back of the room and pick up Jill (Emma Stone) as she walks toward the bar at the far end with a friend and there discovers Rita (Parker Posey) sitting on a stool; an accidental meeting in scene 101. The pan is a last-minute change by Woody, who wants the visual cue of the pool table to tell the audience this is the same bar they will see from a different angle in scene 126.

The sound mixer is in another corner, and producers Edward Walson and Stephen Tenenbaum are jammed into a small area behind the camera, seated on a narrow, thin-cushioned bench. Near the camera are two video monitors on which Woody and Khondji will watch the takes while listening to the dialogue through headphones. For less cramped locations the sound mixer is with them in what is called the video village. Woody's long-legged director's chair is in front of the display; he has myopia in his right eye, and during takes his face is only a few inches from the screen, which shows the shot as it will appear in theaters. Because anamorphic spreads out the picture, it runs across the middle third, letterboxed with black atop and below. Beside him is Virginia McCarthy, the script supervisor, who logs every shot and makes notes of its particulars—the continuity—on her iPad with an app for the work. She times each take with a stopwatch, and her continuity is every detail of the movie: the type of shot—wide, long, full, medium full, medium close-up, close-up, dolly; where the actors are; any changes in dialogue; whether a take was better for the soundman or the cameraman; and so on. Those Woody wants printed are highlighted in green, those not, in red.

Danielle Rigby, the first assistant director, who runs the set with a quietly firm manner and has worked with Woody on four previous films, places the forty-five extras in their twenties meant to be patrons of the bar. As she does, Woody reads the nearly four full pages to be shot (every morning he and all relevant crew receive the day's portion of the script on 4.5-by-5.5-inch sheets of paper called sides) and says with some surprise, "This is a long scene." He pauses and remarks with emphasis, as if reading the words for the first time, "This is *long.*" Loquasto laughs and tells him, "You say this every morning." He has been here since 4:30 a.m. to be sure everything is set up exactly right. He grew up over a beauty salon and then a bar in Easton, Pennsylvania, but says he can't mix a drink. "Four years of college and three years of graduate school—Yale drama, pre-Meryl, as everyone asks—and *this* is what I do?" he says in mock horror.

Woody is dressed in cream-colored trousers, a beige long-sleeved cotton shirt with a frayed collar, scuffed brown Varda shoes, and a well-worn waxed canvas brimless hat made by Borsalino, one of a variety given him by the manufacturer when he was in France to film *Magic.*

He rolls up the hat and stuffs it in a rear pocket of his trousers, then steps onto the camera dolly and looks through the eyepiece, adjusting it: "I need to get my prescription," he says. The observation is delivered in a way that makes the crew who hear him laugh. He walks over to Jill and Rita and tells them to drop the general greetings at the start of their scene, about a quarter of a page. "I cut the persiflage," he says when he comes back. "It's a long scene and we need to get to the meat." (Later he adds, "I made the cuts because it's like when you go out in your nightclub act: you practice it and practice it and then you get out onstage and you realize, 'I can't say that, I'm going to *die* if I say this! I need to cut from joke one to joke nine and leave all that other stuff out.' The same thing here. I get to the set and I think, 'Oh, god, that looked great when I read the script ahead but now that people are saying it, it takes forever.' So I quickly made cuts, which I do all the time. To me it's what I call Reality Setting In. Everything that has gone before is speculation. Now there's no more posturing, you're on the set, you hear how awful the dialogue is, that's it. Reality sets in and you're on a downward spiral.") He goes back over to Jill and tells her to sit or stand, as she likes—"whatever's comfortable"—when she starts to talk with Rita, who is already seated at the bar and needs to show she has had a couple of scotches.

Just after nine thirty everything is in place for the first shot. Khondji makes one last check of his light meter and adjusts a spotlight. Letty Aronson arrives and squeezes in beside Walson. "Finished already?" she asks brightly. Rigby calls out to the extras, "Lots of energy in the background—you're having a great time at the bar." It is easy to tell from her voice that she is Australian. (Her father was the great editorial cartoonist Paul Rigby.) "Rolling," one of the camera crew calls out. A chorus of production assistants in and outside the bar echo it loudly; a very noisy way to demand quiet. Anyone in earshot must stand still and say nothing so no unscripted noise ruins the take. "Background!" Rigby yells out, and the extras start to play pool. "And . . . action!" The camera starts on the pool players. It begins its pan. The film magazine jams.

"Of course," Woody says.

"This happened on the first shot of *Magic,*" Khondji reminds him.

"I hope this is a first day of filming I don't have to reshoot," Woody says softly, no doubt recalling the several times, including on *Magic,* he has had to redo scenes because the look was not what he wanted or there were lines he wanted to change or the actors had yet to find a rhythm.

There are five separate setups for the scene: this establishing shot of the bar in which Jill runs into Rita and they say their first lines; a single of Rita over Jill's right shoulder; one of Jill over Rita's left shoulder; and a close-up on each. Snippets of these will be pieced together to produce the maximum dramatic effect. "We're going to do more coverage than I usually do because this script is more intimate and psychological," Woody says. In most of his pictures, he relies whenever he can on master shots that capture the scene in one go.

A scene shot on a soundstage often lacks the verisimilitude of one done in an actual building but benefits from being a controlled environment with no extraneous noise. A scene such as this, filmed in a bar in a busy neighborhood, benefits from its reality, but a take is subject to ruin by a car horn or other interruption that disturbs the intimacy of the dialogue. There are some adjustments that can be made, but in general the sound mixer is hostage to the SNR—the signal-to-noise ratio. The louder the actors speak, the more he can turn down the background sound; the softer they speak the greater the random noise picked up. This is a scene that requires the actors to speak relatively softly, and so David Schwartz, the mixer, has to do the best he can. He says that there is a discernable noise outside but to go ahead. "Speak up over the hum," Woody calls out in frustrated bonhomie. Almost every director overcomes such problems with additional dialogue recording (ADR), also known as looping, where actors come to a sound studio and resay the lines to match the movement of their lips on screen. But Woody feels that it is impossible to improve on the dialogue of the moment and prefers to have the noise and the better delivery rather than no noise and inferior delivery. Also, what is a problem for a professional sound person is often not one for Woody or a regular audience member.

They do a new take. This time the magazine does not jam. "That good for you?" Woody asks Khondji. It is. "Let's do one or two more," Woody says. The next is no good almost from the start; he gives the thumbs-down sign to McCarthy but lets the actors finish the scene so as not to disturb their concentration. The third take is okay, the fourth no good. Part of the problem for him is that for the past six months he has heard the dialogue only in his head. Listening to actors speak it is always sobering, especially on the first day, because reality inevitably overcomes imagination. After the take he pulls his earphones down to his neck and says with a rueful laugh, "When you hear them say the words, you realize how bad the writing is."

This is a constant with him. With two exceptions, the film in his head becomes something different the moment he hears the initial words of dialogue because the voice in his mind is not that of the actor in the film. The first time the voice in his head matched that of the actor was when Martin Landau spoke his initial lines in *Crimes and Misdemeanors*, because Landau grew up a block away from Woody's childhood home in Brooklyn and spoke precisely in the cadence and tone of the neighborhood. The second was with *Match Point:* when he heard Jonathan Rhys Meyers deliver the voiceover, he says he thought, "'My god, did I write that?' The narration being read with a British accent sounded sensational to me." But usually it is a case of, "When I don't have to meet the test of reality, when I'm at home writing, I can imagine an argument going on at the edge of a pier between George C. Scott and Paul Newman. Then I do the film and I get good people, but the voices don't sound like what I thought they would sound like and the pier doesn't look the way I envisioned—he can't jump off it because he'd break his neck. So now he has to run to the end of the pier and do something else. Everything keeps evolving and evolving, or more frequently, devolving, and that's the problem. Ninety percent of the stuff is worse than you conceived it."

They move on to the medium close-up of Jill as Rita details her theory about Abe being the judge's murderer. Woody wonders if the conversation in the first take isn't too lighthearted and asks for a more serious version so he will have a choice in the editing room.

The scene begins with a couple of exchanges between the two women and then:

JILL

I ran into Ellie Tanner who said you had a theory about Abe.

RITA

Oh my god—don't get me started . . . you want some single malt scotch?

JILL

She said your theory is very funny.

RITA

Yes, it's what's called a crackpot theory but it's not totally off the wall.

After the shots of Jill, the camera is moved to the other side for Rita's two shots. Rita is meant to sound as if although she has a theory, it is probably a crazy one. The conversation lasts more than three minutes, and there are many takes. Woody says to print the first and fifth, although Posey, an accomplished actor, for some reason has trouble making the crackpot theory line sound as conversational as he wants. He goes to her and lightly says a version of the dialogue: "It's funny, you're going to think I'm nuts and it *is* a little crazy but you might believe it . . ." Posey thanks him and tries again without success and of course gets more nervous and flustered with each take. The situation is an actor's worst nightmare. Everyone in the room feels the tension as he or she roots for her to get it to his liking. (She, however, took the trouble like a pro. "I was fine with it," she said afterward. "I wasn't crying in my trailer.") After a few more unsuccessful tries Woody goes back to her and suggests in perfect conversational tone: " 'This is crackpot and you probably won't believe it,' or 'I know this sounds nuts.' " After a couple more unsatisfactory takes he says to her, "Repeat after me" and "Use my words," but the easy delivery is hard to get until in the ninth take it falls into place. "That was very good," he says, and they do a few more. In one of the latter takes, melting ice in Rita's glass makes a loud, gurgling sound over her dialogue at the end of the scene. After the scene is cut together in the editing room, there is no trace of difficulty; Posey does her usual superb job.

Because as the leads Stone and Phoenix are in nearly every scene, by necessity they have complete scripts and therefore know the full story. All other actors in the film—in every Allen film—don't. He believes actors don't need to know the plot or what happens in scenes they are not in; it can only complicate their performance and make it more studied than natural. By human nature they will create their own sense of what the story should be rather than just say the lines naturally and spontaneously in the moment of filming. So, unlike many directors who meticulously rehearse their actors—Mike Leigh, for instance, spends weeks at it—Woody virtually never rehearses his (except to work out the blocking of the shot), and on the few occasions when he has had to rehearse a scene on set, he later wished he had filmed the rehearsal because the dialogue sounded the most natural. He sees no reason to change.

Woody, during the first shot of the first day of shooting, explaining to Parker Posey how he wants her character Rita to sound. He often has to reshoot scenes from the first day, but after several takes, this came out as he wanted.

"Over the years I've worked my way, and I've gotten wonderful performances from the actors—I don't get them *out* of the actors. The actors don't rehearse, many have only their sides, they come to the set [*snaps fingers*] and go just like that, and they're wonderful. And when they see the picture, they couldn't be more delighted with their performance. So no one has ever complained to me about it before, during, or after. No one has ever said, 'If only we could have rehearsed this more.' Nor has anyone ever complained to me about not getting a full script. [But then most actors are diffident and would never challenge a director, especially one of Woody's stature.] So much of the business is garbage, starting with the many meetings and the endless time in getting the project on, and the money wasted, and the pretensions. It's just common sense getting together and doing it. It's proven all the time by people who don't have any money and don't have any time and get together and do perfectly fine work."

When she sat down at the bar for her first scene, Posey was

unclear whether she was in a comedy or a drama but did not ask, which was fine with Woody on both counts. They had exchanged brief pleasantries during costume tests a few days earlier, but that is all virtually every actor gets: no deep information about the character; no rehearsal; no visit to the trailer on the first day to say hello and welcome aboard. Just: Here we are; let's get to work. Woody is confident the actors can deliver the performance or he wouldn't have hired them. His approach is so widely known that it is not a surprise. Still, there is knowing it, and there is experiencing it. Thrust under the gaze of a deeply admired writer-actor-director who suddenly is asking you to do something differently can make the mind freeze. For some, as Loquasto puts it, "I'm sure they go deaf. I'm sure there is the panic: 'I can see his lips moving but I can't hear what he's saying.'" But it also can be enormously liberating to be allowed the freedom to become the character without any overlay yet know that Woody will respond and offer an alternative if needed.

After Posey completed her work in the film, she sent me a note to explain the combination of challenge and thrill in doing the part.

> I came home and found the letter he wrote to me offering the part. It wasn't an offer though, just simply "Dear Parker, Rita is . . . Best, Woody." It was just a paragraph describing her succinctly and briefly, and along with that I got about twenty pages of sides. The letter said nothing about Rita's being "a lonely woman" . . . that was one of the things he'd say intently to me that first day, the twenty-takes day. Along with "she's in an unhappy marriage," the letter described her as a flirt and "loose" and that she has feelings for Abe and a "fantasy" that he will take her away. I knew she was a fantasist, but this "she is a lonely woman" wasn't expressed to me in writing. I thought even though she was in an unhappy marriage, she has the passion to follow her desires and is at a point in her life where those desires can be manifested positively. "She is trapped" was another emphasis he made about Rita in that first scene with Emma. (I mention this feeling to Abe on the cliff later in the story.) I knew she had this longing

> but since I hadn't read the whole script I had no idea if this was a bleak Woody Allen picture or a lighter one. That first day, in the first scene shot, I started to intuit it was on the heavier and darker side. And that I was intentionally being kept in the dark. I sat facing out, away from the bar, and observing the students—as well as waiting or looking for Abe, and Woody said, "What are you doing? It looks like you're sitting there waiting for the camera to land on you." I wasn't going to say "No, I'm not, I'm just zoning out in a daydream" or "Darius indicated to me to face out because that's where the lights were set up," which was true. I wasn't going to enter into that kind of dialogue but rather acquiesce. I remember thinking, "He's right, I am waiting for the camera to land on me" and then got hit with the downward spiral of "I don't know how to act anymore, I have actually forgotten how to." He is directing me, and I'm going to land in that projection and that's what I'm here to do, that is my job, being the subject. It was exhilarating and terrifying working that first day, but I know he is a master at what he does and that it got so convoluted. I can best describe it as being in a wave pool turned on very high and in all sorts of directions and say, too, that he was there with me in the water. I remember laughing and telling him I felt like he was chiropracting me. As a side note, I was in fact IN one of those wave pools as a kid and gulped a big wave that had me terrified. I survived it, obviously.

The next day Woody talked about the scene. "The first shot went very well. We did Emma first because Darius wanted to start in that direction. And I figured, 'Good, Parker will be doing it over and over again off camera.'

"I was trying to say nice things to her: 'You're going off on the wrong road, and once you're off on that road you play it brilliantly, but that's not the idea. I want you to go on the *right* road and play it brilliantly.' I'm trying to think of nice things to say but also tell her she's not doing it right. I loved her final work." And he cast her in his next film.

He is more willing now than in the past to be quite specific with actors about how to deliver their lines, although it still is something he prefers not to do. "I remember the three young girls [Natalie Portman, Gaby Hoffmann, and Natasha Lyonne] in the musical I did [*Everyone Says I Love You,* 1996], when they were in Zabar's and the handsome guy walks in," he once told me. "I had to *kill* myself to say, 'No, you guys have to do it like *this.*' [*mimics near hysteria*] Sometimes the acting is tentative because the actor is insecure or he can't believe I mean him to be that broad. My instinct in broadness is very strong. So I'll put my hand on my face [*makes very broad gestures*], and I want them to go all the way, I mean really all the way. So I expected the kids to act that way and they didn't. They were much milder, much more inhibited. I finally got them to do it and it looks funny on the screen."

Funny on the screen is something he knows how to achieve and other comic actors trust him to let them show. On a very rare occasion a comedian in a role will ask if he can change a few words to accommodate his particular way of speaking and thus make his jokes land better—Andrew Dice Clay did it on *Blue Jasmine* and Woody immediately agreed—but virtually all adhere to the script. Larry David has a several-minute monologue in *Whatever Works* that he rehearsed for days to get every word correct. Woody is so highly regarded as a comedian and director by comics that even the most successful can seem in awe. While making *Deconstructing Harry,* Billy Crystal and Robin Williams were overheard saying to each other, "Can you believe we're on a Woody Allen set?"

What comes as a surprise to some of even the most accomplished actors is Woody's proclivity for master shots and the necessity to have several pages of dialogue memorized. An actor will sometimes show up and ask Suzy Benzinger, "Is it really true that we're going to do this in one?" It is a lesson quickly learned and not forgotten. "Actors with a lot of theater experience do it best," she says.

Posey's difficulties do not extend to her second scene of the day, nor for the remainder of the film. In scene 126 that afternoon, in the same bar where she met Jill, Rita and Abe talk over a drink about running off together, leaving the college and her husband.

ABE (V.O.)

(seated at a table in the bar)

That night I made passionate love with Rita and even entertained the thought of taking her with me to Europe.

RITA

I would leave him in a minute—are you serious about Europe?

ABE

What if I was?

RITA

It's too good to think about—to start over in Spain or Rome or even London.

The tension of the morning disappears with her first words, delivered in a seamless combination of excitement, hope, and not quite daring to believe this could be true. Still, extra takes are required. One is excellent but spoiled by a camera malfunction; another, the best of the lot, is sullied by a sudden car noise outside. Woody is exasperated by the delays but later says, "What they consider a sound and camera problem may be nothing. I learned that years ago."

Posey continued in her note:

> And then the second scene which was that little scene in the bar with Joaquin towards the end of the movie where she tells him she'd leave Paul in a second and her fantasy of leaving this academia life starts to come true. When we came in to shoot (this was Joaquin's first shot), Woody said to me again, "She is a lonely woman" and went back to his chair and we did it just 3 or 4 times—the temperature was right the first two times but the third time I was out of the water of it and he said "Make sure your voice doesn't get too soft, you don't want to sound actressy" and I scream-laughed and stood up and pretended I had gotten stabbed in the gut and he retorted,

> "That was deliberate" and I said, "Do it again!" and pretended to get stabbed in my other side. It was funny, he laughed. I was relieved. But it's all that stuff you learn from good acting teachers, to act is not act but to be and to live the part in the moment. Why should he indulge my fantasy of what the part is and my thoughts on the character? What a waste of time for him! My work was to listen to him and make adjustments as best I could to be who he saw her as.

Woody finds every first day awkward while actors get their footing. "I've had first day problems with some of the best actors in the world," he recalls. During *A Midsummer Night's Sex Comedy* (1982), José Ferrer became upset when Woody asked him for fifteen takes to get a line the way he wanted it. The incidents this morning and with Ferrer illustrate what Woody expects from his actors as well as the difference between his ease in being on his own set and the nervousness of actors working on their first scene with a director they greatly admire. Throughout the film Woody had "a wonderful time" with Ferrer. "I thought he was a total delight in every way. But finally he said to me [*in a good Ferrer imitation*], 'Now I *can't,* you've turned me into a *mass* of terrors.' And I thought to myself, 'My god, you're *José Ferrer*. How can I turn you into a mass of terrors? You're this wonderful actor and all I'm doing is saying, "No, that's not really the way I wanted, do it again."' So I guess I'm insensitive, because I just assume that they should take my requests for granted."

Those who have worked with Woody for a long time think there is some insensitivity to personal feelings but more impatience to get it right, although the effect on an actor can be the same. Loquasto once said to him after he unconvincingly tried to reassure a player that all was going well, "You do have the touch of a very clumsy proctologist at times." But the proof of his method is in the decades-long list of superb performances actors have given him. Hitchcock said, "All actors should be treated like cattle," but Woody feels the opposite. "I rely on actors, let them change all the lines they care to, and never direct them unless I think they're doing it wrong."

After finishing the scenes at the bar, the crew move a couple of blocks for scene 40: Abe and Jill walking and talking after leaving a movie theater. After she provocatively suggests that she might help unblock him, he tells her he doesn't want her closer. The theater's marquee advertises a Northern Lights Film Festival, showing what sort of film the pair has seen without having it in dialogue. In the glass case in front of the theater is a poster that the audience cannot fully make out because the shot starts as an extra wide, then switches to a medium full on Abe and Jill as they walk. But because Loquasto believes in making everything completely believable, and because no one, including Woody, knows what shots he will want until they get to the location, the poster details the festival in fictional titles and directors (and fanciful dates) thought up by Loquasto and his staff that give a tip of the hat to Woody's sixty-five-year-long admiration of Bergman's films.

NORTHERN LIGHTS FILM FESTIVAL

Films of the Northern countries of Europe are often noted for their moody symphysis of the principles of mortality and existence.

The Northern Lights film series is a celebration of this deep and pensive school of cinema.

SWEDEN

Friday 9/27—*Sisters of the Sun* Jernberg, 1959

DENMARK

Saturday 9/28—*Duo* Angstrom, 1980

NORWAY

Sunday 9/29—*Rhapsody* Johansson, 1967

ICELAND

Monday 9/30—*The Unfortunate* Bergen, 1955

FINLAND

Tuesday 10/1—*Dag and Kristina* Jernberg, 1975

ESTONIA

Wednesday 10/2—*Autumn Wishes* (*Svårmod*) Olsson, 1977

Thursday 10/3—*The Thirteenth Turn* Lundquist, 1963

Friday 10/4—*Principle* Jernberg, 1970

Saturday 10/5—*Words, Silence* Magnuson, 1964

Before many directors begin a film, they make elaborately drawn storyboards of every scene, the shots they want to make already decided. Hitchcock was one of the first major directors to do this. A storyboard is particularly useful for an action film; Victor Fleming's drawings for *Gone with the Wind* were done in color, the burning of Atlanta meticulously scripted. Contemporaries of Woody who make a storyboard include Steven Spielberg, Joel and Ethan Coen, and Martin Scorsese.

Woody, like Clint Eastwood and Christopher Nolan (except for big action scenes and special effects), does not. He prefers to come to the set and see what looks best at the moment, and so he and Khondji consider various angles of tracking Jill and Abe as they exit, cross the street, and walk beside the park in the square opposite the theater. They start with the camera looking down at the couple through the leaves and branches of a tall tree, then lower it to eye level. The first take "misses the point," Woody says, "because there is no need to see them walk out first." In the next take too many background people walk out ahead of them. For the third the camera starts in the tree and Jill and Abe follow after several couples, so it looks more natural and midstream. This is the first scene Stone and Phoenix do together. It begins with Abe's voice over the action. (My comments are in parentheses.) The lines from this and subsequent scenes are taken verbatim from the shooting script and do not include changes made during filming.

ABE (V.O.)

I spent a lot of time with Jill—walks, talks, coffee, museums. One time the Campus Cinema Society was showing *The Seventh Seal,* the old Bergman film, and I took her.

(Abe and Jill exiting)

JILL

Thanks for that movie. It was such a treat to see it with you. I would not have gotten all the philosophical references and I love the way the central character is searching for some act to give meaning to his life and finds it in protecting this simple family going through the forest.

[They have crossed the street and are walking on the sidewalk along the park.]

ABE

Sometimes if you find that one act—

JILL

You teach, Abe, it counts.

ABE

Not satisfying.

JILL

You write.

ABE

I've given up. It's all bullshit. My bullshit book on Martin Heidegger will not make a scintilla of difference to the world.

JILL

How do you know?

ABE

I set out to be an active world-changer and ended up a passive intellectual who can't fuck.

[Jill has fallen a step behind Abe. She hesitates, eyes cast down, then raises them and speaks tentatively.]

JILL

Maybe Rita Richards couldn't get your creative juices going but you ever think maybe I could?

ABE

Uh-uh, Jill—don't go there.

JILL

(closer now to Abe)

I know you like the time we spend together and you must know I care about you. Christ, it's obvious to everyone.

ABE

Including your boyfriend?

JILL

Am I ready to make an exclusive commitment? He is but I have a lot of questions.

ABE

Maybe we're seeing too much of each other. Maybe I shouldn't monopolize your time.

JILL *(unscripted)*

(Pauses, her face hardens. She speaks flatly.)

Okay.

[She turns and walks on.]

"It's hard to make dialogue work in that blocking where people walk and talk," Woody says after the shot. "I do it so every part of the picture is different. It would have been effective if I had had them sit on a park bench and say the same things, but I want to make it—and Darius wants to make it—so the picture has scope and size. It's not easy to walk and talk those emotional things." I remark on how Jill falls just a bit behind Abe as he says his juices have dried up and then comes back to him. "Yeah, Emma played that great. I didn't have to tell her a thing. Those were all her choices. I told her nothing. She never asked me, never told me she was going to do that, she just played it that way and it was a treat for me to watch her. Her instinct was great—*his* instinct was great. The guy's so tortured, everything he says" [*he laughs*] "is dredged out of him. But this should be good for the character."

The next morning's first shot is part of scene 89, Jill and Abe riding bikes together down a country road. Despite Abe's determination not to become intimate with Jill, they have just become lovers, and the ride is meant to show them happy and relaxed together. A polo field runs along either side of the narrow asphalt road lined with grand old chestnut trees at peak greenery. While the crew readies the shot, Woody stands in the road talking with his fourteen-year-old daughter, Manzie, who will come to the set almost every day for the first month of shooting before going to summer camp.

A normal shooting day often lasts twelve hours and sometimes more. It is also the norm that about 85 percent of that time is spent moving equipment and readying the lights and camera for a shot; perhaps thirty minutes of film will be printed for dailies. Actors spend most of the hours they are on call in their barely comfortable eighteen-foot-long campers with a fold-out table, a couple of chairs, a small upholstered built-in bench, and a toilet, parked with the wardrobe trailer and one for the production assistants at the base camp. Woody does not have a trailer to repair to between when the details of a shot are settled and the setup is done. Depending on how much time there is—and sometimes there can be two hours—he plays chess on his phone or takes care of whatever business is at hand with his assistant, Ginevra Tamberi, or sits in the back of the black Chevy sedan in which he is driven to and from the set, its windows up, doing his daily long tones, tonguing, and articulation exercises on his clarinet, or deals with production questions from Helen Robin. Sometimes he stands around and chats.

"I went to a polo match once and was completely bored," he says, looking over the playing fields, "and I'm someone who loves all sports, even timber sports and tugging trucks." For a man whose shoes it seems are soled with sidewalk, this is alien territory. He looks around and stamps one foot. "You know where I wish this was? Madison Avenue." However, he is better off than a year earlier. After several days of shooting in the dirt and grass surrounding a country home in *Magic,* he stamped the same foot on the ground—a thunderhead of dust rose up—and said, "If I don't get on pavement soon, I'll go crazy."

At last it is time for the first take: Abe, wearing jeans and a polo shirt, and Jill, in a short skirt and flimsy top that shows a bit of bare midriff, ride down the lane, the camera in the back of a truck in front of them. The shot is pretty but it also is static and boring—just the two of them coming straight for the camera. Woody suggests a change in the action but first wants a change of Jill's costume. After seeing the shot and surroundings, he feels jeans and plaid shirt are more appropriate and that the skirt and top can be better in an evening scene.

In keeping with his intent to bolster the intimacy of the picture and its psychological aspect with more coverage (shots from different angles and lenses to vary the look for the scene) than usual, several takes track the bicycles weaving along the road, the cheerful and carefree riders coming close to each other and then separating before coming back together. The shot is intentionally long to strengthen the

Jill (Emma Stone) and Abe (Joaquin Phoenix) the day after their romance begins. The shot is intentionally long to strengthen the sense of excitement in a new love affair. Rather than have them ride straight ahead, Woody wanted the bikes to come together and separate often.

sense of excitement in a new love affair and the complete pleasure the couple take in each other.

"Originally Darius had a straight-on shot and that was fine for a little piece," Woody explains while the actors and the camera truck go back to the starting point for another take, "but it goes on forever. And I know how these work from my experience with *Vicky Cristina* when I did a bicycle shot—of course the terrain was more interesting in Spain, they were going through towns and around walls. So I'll have all the pieces. It won't go on forever, but in a romance it has a real exhilarating feeling, going back and forth."

The company moves a half mile for scene 99, a prelude to scene 101, Jill and Rita in the bar, shot yesterday. In this one, Jill and her friend Ellie talk on horseback as they return to the barn. It is a turning point for Jill, who in the scene before says of the murder, "When it wasn't on the front page or the six o'clock news staring me in the face I gave it no thought until one day when I ran into Ellie Tanner when we went horseback riding."

The film cuts to the two of them talking as their horses walk along a grassy path. (Roy is Jill's college boyfriend, whom she has emotionally shunted aside for Abe.) What Ellie has to say plants the first seed of suspicion in Jill that Abe may not be what he seems.

JILL

And Roy felt I wasn't being fair to him and he was right. But I didn't know what to do. Abe—he's so damn interesting.

ELLIE

You know Rita Richards?

JILL

Yes, I know—if you're going to tell me Abe has had an affair with her. I mean who on the faculty hasn't been to bed with Rita Richards.

ELLIE

She has a theory about Abe Lucas.

JILL

Yes?

ELLIE

She thinks he's a good suspect in that case of the murdered judge who's all over the papers.

JILL

Of course she's kidding.

ELLIE

Yes. Half kidding.

JILL

How did she come to this bizarre conclusion?

ELLIE

I don't know. We were having a good time at her husband's barbecue. I think she said Professor Lucas had argued that the judge deserved to die and a lot of talk about the aesthetics of committing a perfect crime. I forget the details. It was a barbecue and I was concentrating on the ribs.

Jill is taken aback a bit.

The picturesque stone barn has an archway, toward which the dirt and stone path incline. Horses stand in an attached paddock; others are enclosed across the wide grass path parallel to the barn that the women will ride down. Several hours of planning and labor have gone into designing and then setting up the shot, nearly two hours alone for the grips (strong and agile women and men who assemble and move a vast array of equipment wherever needed—on the ground, on rooftops, outside second-story windows) to lay down and level the track on the uneven ground for the camera to follow the horses coming toward it, through the turn and into the barn. For added richness, the shot is to be filmed during magic hour.

Neither Stone nor Kate McGonigle, who plays Ellie, can ride, but

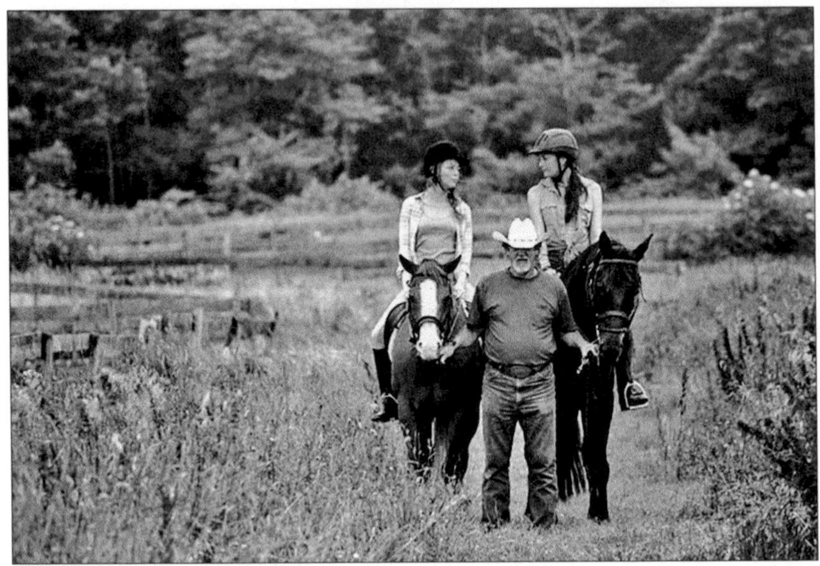

The wrangler and the uncooperative horses.

the production company has hired movie horses—animals that walk when prompted and don't require guidance by the rider. At least that is what they are supposed to do. The wrangler helps Jill and Ellie into their saddles. The sun is in perfect magic hour splendor. The camera rolls. The wrangler leads the horses forward a few feet to establish their pace and then dives behind a large clump of thick, tall weeds at the side of the trail so he will not be seen. The women begin their conversation—and the horses stop. Woody is mildly amused.

In the second take, the horses start then almost immediately stop again. Jill and Ellie kick their heels and shake the reins but the horses know they are rubes and don't move. Woody laughs a bit. Take 3 is the same. Ellie and Jill flail their legs like flippers but again the horses stand still. Woody is laughing so hard his face is in his hands. This clearly is not going to work; he will have to come up with another location so they can do this without animals. When the next day he watches the takes in dailies, he laughs deeply again and says, "Hitchcock knew what he was doing when he used all that rear projection, even though you could tell what it was."

Stone laughed uproariously after the fiasco. "He put a *horse* in the picture? I sat down with him right before they put us up on the horses and said, 'Woody, you can't do this to me. Listen, I can't go up on the horse.'

"'Why?' he said. 'What did it do to you?'"

She shook her head in mock disgust. "I was bucked off a horse when I was ten years old and haven't gotten on one since. I asked him, 'Why did you write a horse scene?' 'I thought it was *nice,*' he said. 'Let's just *try.*' I was already having a meltdown. Having a meltdown is the easiest way to make Woody laugh. I was in full meltdown mode. The *horse* melted down. There are moments I think I'll remember forever, and him cracking up at me not being able to ride a horse is one."

The next morning is more serious. Scene 45, a critical part of the story, takes place in a coffee shop (the exterior shot is of a diner several blocks away because it is a more interesting-looking building): Jill and Abe are in a booth, talking across the table; then Jill whispers to Abe to come to her side and listen to what is being said in the booth behind them. What he hears is the catalyst to justify the murder he will commit, and what he thinks to himself after listening to the conversation is what happens when a casual dinner conversation is turned by a dramatic sensibility into a screenplay.

CAROL

I don't know what to do—I'm at my wit's end.

HAL

Who's the judge?

CAROL

Spangler—Thomas Spangler.

BIFF

How this guy ever wound up on family court . . .

HAL

They're political appointees. Some are okay but a lot of them are just bums who are getting paid off.

CAROL

But it's not right. He awards the kids to Frank. Frank doesn't even look after them. Frank doesn't even want them. He just wants to hurt me.

BIFF

It's true—this guy doesn't care about his own kids.

CAROL

(near tears)

I deliver the kids, they don't want to go, they're crying. What does Frank do? He sticks them in a corner at the garage he works at and they sit underground all day. They should be playing—in the fresh air—with the other kids. And now he's thinking of switching custody to Frank.

EVE

On what grounds?

CAROL

No grounds—because he has some kind of relationship with Frank's lawyer.

EVE

Switching custody would be a disaster.

HAL

It doesn't make sense.

CAROL

I brought in the kids' teachers, the kids' doctors—they're all on my side—it doesn't matter because the judge is friendly in some way with Frank's lawyer.

BIFF

And you can't get him recused?

CAROL

(cries at the end)

My lawyer tried and failed. Now of course the judge hates me with a vengeance. I can't keep paying all these legal bills and the judge knows it—so every time I want something, he says, make a motion, and I do, and he turns me down but it costs me everything I've got and in the end I'm going to lose the kids.

HAL

And you're sure he's cozy with Frank's lawyer.

CAROL

They look at each other, they smile. I just got a bad break drawing this judge.

EVE

It's so unfair.

CAROL

I'm due in court in six weeks if he doesn't postpone it as usual—he knows the delays help Frank. I haven't had a decent night's sleep, I wish I could take the kids and move to Europe. I actually thought of taking them out of the country.

HAL

And hide for the rest of your life? You'll be a fugitive.

EVE

I feel for you, Carol. And you're such a good mother.

CAROL

(choking back tears, frustrated)

I hope the judge gets cancer.

ABE (V.O.)

He won't get cancer because wishing doesn't work and the way the world goes the meanest bastards rarely get what they deserve—if you want him dead you have to make it happen but you'd never be able to pull it off and even if you did you'd be a prime suspect. On the other hand, I could kill him for you, lady, and no one in the world would dream I did it. I could rid you of this roach and end all your suffering. It was at this moment that my life came together. I could perform this blessing for that poor woman and no one would ever connect me to it. I don't know any of the parties involved, I have no motive, and when I walk out of here I'll never lay eyes on any of these people again. All I need to know is the name: Judge Thomas Spangler.

The sidewalk and street outside the windows by the booths are filled with lighting apparatus. Were the actors in their adjoining booths next to the windows that run along the side of the café filmed in natural light, the result would be uneven, alternately too bright or too shadowy, and change steadily as the sun moved across the sky. The grips set up an array of equipment outside the windows that includes large spotlights and aluminum-rod frames of Ultrabounce as large as twelve feet by twenty feet to emulate unchanging daylight in the café.

"Grips shape the light," key grip Billy Weberg says after he and his crew have set five 15,000-kilowatt spots and an equal number of frames of Ultrabounce to diffuse the light into the café and keep it steady throughout the day. Weberg, in his early fifties, is compact and well muscled and owns a forty-foot trailer with every possible piece of equipment that reflects or diffuses light and the myriad tools for holding them in place, each with an arcane name: Cardellinis, gobos, grid clamps, baby plates, C-clamps, Big Bens, junior plates, century stands, apples, pigeon plates, and pancakes (a pigeon is often clamped to a pancake). There is Bead Board (beaded white polystyrene in sizes

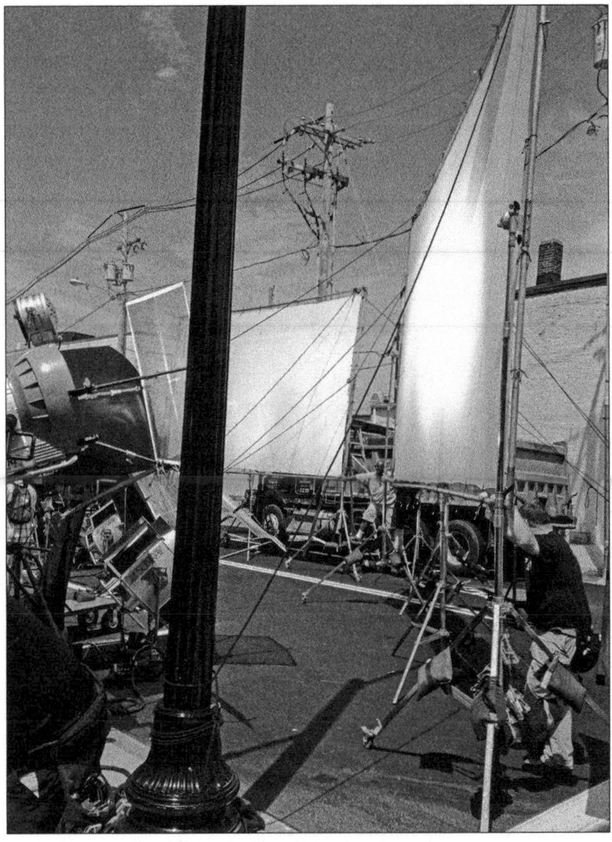

Sheets of a reflective material called Ultrabounce keep the light the same from shot to shot. Natural light would change as the sun moves or is darkened by passing clouds.

from two feet by two feet to four by eight) that reflects light, and there are Bead Board holders (thin, flat plates that grip the board), variously called onky-bonks, flappers, Billygrips (after British cinematographer Billy Williams, who used polystyrene regularly for his lighting arsenal), platypus, and clamps. "We bring the director and cameraman's vision to life by use of intelligent muscle," he adds, walking through his trailer with several hundred thousand dollars' worth of paraphernalia, all neatly stacked, boxed, or hung in the appointed place. "The process hasn't changed much in the past hundred years. We've just improved the quality of the equipment."

The scene takes all day to shoot and requires a dozen variations of lenses and setups to cover the individuals and groups as the story spills out over three minutes. After one take Phoenix asks Woody if he is locked into a certain position in the booth as he hears Carol's tale of woe. "You're completely free to move wherever you like," Woody tells him, "so long as you don't wave your arms above your head."

The single shot of Abe when he hears Carol say, "I hope he gets cancer," has to hold for forty-nine seconds to cover the time it will take Abe to speak his voiceover. McCarthy clicks on her stopwatch, nods to Woody when the time is up, and holds it so he can see.

"Perfect," he says. "My eggs are ready."

As they always do, crew members not working during a shot check their phones and email as the camera rolls.

• • •

The idea of a judge denying custody of children to a parent is personal to Woody, and although it was not the impetus for his writing *The Boston Story*, it is often on his mind.

In June 1993, following a bitter and sensational fight that played out in the media worldwide, Mia Farrow was awarded custody of their three children. They had been an unmarried couple for twelve years and were the adoptive parents of a boy, Moses, fourteen, and a girl, Dylan, seven, and the biological parents of a boy, Satchel (now Ronan), five. (Farrow said in a 2013 *Vanity Fair* article that the boy's father is "possibly" Frank Sinatra, with whom she began a romance at nineteen, married at twenty-one, and divorced four years later but remained close to in the following decades.) Farrow and her second husband, the composer André Previn, had three biological sons and adopted three girls, one of whom was Soon-Yi Previn, born in 1970 in Korea. For the length of the Allen-Farrow relationship, the couple lived and slept in separate apartments on opposite sides of Central Park, she on the West Side, he on the East. Woody says the romance cooled after Satchel was born in 1987.

In 1991, Woody and Soon-Yi Previn began a relationship. Not

surprisingly, this caused emotional havoc. Farrow lashed out. Woody says she called him many times late at night to scream at him, saying, among other things, "You took my daughter, and I'm going to take yours," meaning Dylan. Woody's sister, Letty, says she was told the same in a separate conversation. During one call to Woody, Farrow warned, "I've got something planned for you." When he jokingly asked, "What are you going to do, shoot me?" she answered, "No, this is worse."

In early August 1992, Farrow accused Woody of sexually abusing Dylan at her country home in Connecticut. (Dylan had recently turned seven.) Precisely where he allegedly did this changed over time: first in the TV room, where several children and at least one babysitter were with Woody; then on a staircase; finally in an attic storeroom.

Woody has steadfastly denied the allegation, and all investigative evidence bears him out. And subsequent to the abuse allegations, child welfare officials would not have allowed Woody and Soon-Yi to adopt two daughters following their marriage in 1997 if there had been the slightest evidence of guilt.

After the molestation allegation, Woody voluntarily took a lie detector test administered by Paul Minor, the chief polygraph examiner for the FBI from 1978 to 1987. Minor wrote in his report: "Following careful analysis of the polygraph tracings, it is concluded that deception was not indicated and that he was, therefore, truthful."

Farrow had Dylan examined by a doctor for any signs of abuse. None were found, but by law the examination had to be reported and investigated. In September 1992, the Connecticut State Police commissioned the Child Sexual Abuse Clinic at Yale–New Haven Hospital to conduct interviews, perform tests, and make a judgment as to whether the allegation had merit.

The report, issued in March 1993, concluded that after what it listed as nine interviews with Dylan alone between September 18 and November 13, 1992, and others with each parent separately, two babysitters, and two psychotherapists who had evaluated Dylan and Satchel—interviews that extended into the first week of January 1993: "It is our expert opinion that Dylan was not sexually abused by Mr. Allen." It went on to say, "There were important inconsistencies in Dylan's statements," "She appeared to struggle with how to tell about the touching," "She told the story in a manner that was overly thoughtful and controlling," and "There was no spontaneity in her statements, and a rehearsed quality was suggested in how she spoke. Her descriptions of the details surrounding the alleged events were unusual and inconsistent."

The Clinic drew its conclusions from "three hypotheses: First, that Dylan's statements were true and that Mr. Allen had sexually abused her; second, that Dylan's statements were not true but were made up by an emotionally vulnerable child who was caught in a disturbed family and who was responding to the stress in the family; and three, that Dylan was coached or influenced by her mother, Ms. Farrow . . . We believe that it is more likely that a combination of these [latter] two formulations best explains Dylan's allegations of sexual abuse."

Acting Justice of the New York Supreme Court Elliot Wilk, who presided over the custody fight that followed, decided not to accept the Yale–New Haven conclusion, which was based on numerous and extensive interviews of all relevant persons, and on which the prosecutor declined to proceed. The forensic experts destroyed their interview notes after writing their opinion and were unwilling to be examined in court. The judge, who to some observers seemed sympathetic to Farrow during the proceedings, felt this "compromised [the court's] ability to scrutinize their findings and resulted in a report which was sanitized and, therefore, less credible." In May 1993, Wilk awarded custody of the children to Farrow and despite the experts' opinion that Dylan would benefit from visits by Woody, ruled that he could not see her for at least six months. In fact, he has not been able to see her in the twenty-five years since the day the allegation was made. He spent years and millions of dollars trying to make contact, even just by phone, for her to know "that she was not abandoned," he said in 2000.

Wilk wrote that Farrow was "not faultless as a parent" but that her "principal shortcoming with respect to responsible parenting appears to have been her continued relationship with Mr. Allen." He added, seemingly based largely on her testimony, that Woody was not "an adequate custodian for Moses, Dylan, or Satchel" and that "Allen's behavior toward Dylan was grossly inappropriate and that measures must be taken to protect her." Yet later in 1993, the New York State Department of Social Services announced that their child welfare investigators had closed their own fourteen-month-long inquiry. In a letter to Woody dated October 7 and later reported in *The New York Times,* they wrote, "No credible evidence was found that the child named in this report has been abused or maltreated. This report has, therefore, been considered unfounded."

Apart from Wilk, the court of public opinion has not been favorable to Woody. Some people simply feel that despite the absence of any investigative findings against him, if he could start the relationship with Soon-Yi, he could do something worse. As for his relationship with Soon-Yi, Woody said afterward, "We were in love, and those older children never for a second thought of me in a paternal way. Their father was André Previn. They knew it." Recently he added, "I've taken a lot of flack about my falling in love with Soon-Yi, but it's so worth it and I wouldn't trade a second of our time together."

While *The Boston Story* was being made, I was given new information about the case from a member of the Farrow family who lived in the house at the time and who tells a different version of what to date has been largely a one-sided story. I include it here not to rehash the unpleasant past but because it might reshape the prism through which so many view Woody's work.

Moses Farrow was born in Korea in 1978, afflicted with cerebral palsy. He was abandoned in a telephone booth, taken to an orphanage, and adopted by Farrow when he was two. In 1985 she adopted Dylan; in 1991 Woody became Moses's adoptive parent as well.

Now a thirty-nine-year-old family therapist, Moses speaks of the atmosphere his mother created in the home as one in which "I felt the constant need to gain her trust and approval."

In his earliest memories, "I was awoken in the middle of the night by Mia. I was in kindergarten. I slept in the girls' room with [my adopted sisters] Lark and Daisy, on the lower bed of the bunk. Mia pulled me out of it. I was still half asleep as she repeatedly asked in a harsh tone if I had taken her pills. It wasn't out of concern that I had swallowed any, but rather to accuse me of having stolen them from her. She took me to her bathroom. I was crying as she stood over me, scowling. I told her a dozen or so more times that I hadn't taken them, but finally I said what she wanted to hear. I was forced to lie. Simply telling her I took them didn't suffice, however, and more questions ensued. I had to elaborate on the lie and tell her I had taken four or five pills because I thought they were Tic Tacs. She pulled me over to the sink and directed me to put her bar of soap in my mouth and then instructed me to wash out my mouth, telling me that lying is a bad thing to do. Once I dried my mouth, she put me back to bed. The next day I searched for the missing pills and found them under the cabinet between the toilet and the bathtub, but I never mentioned this to her out of fear of getting into more trouble. This was the first time I felt truly fearful of her, and it was the start of her instilling fear in me. It began the very long and impossible task of gaining her approval. I can recall numerous times when she let me know the burden was on me to gain her trust.

"The summer between first and second grades, she was having new wallpaper installed in the bedroom I slept in, across the hall from hers on the second floor of the house in Connecticut. She was getting me ready to go to sleep, and when she came over to my bed she found a tape measure. I didn't even know what it was. She had a piercing look on her face that stopped me in my tracks. It was really scary. She asked if I had taken it. She used that familiar voice I had become attuned to as she explained she had been looking for it all day. I stood in front of her, frozen. She asked why it was on my bed. I told her I didn't know, that perhaps the workman left it there. After a couple more demands for the answer she wanted, she slapped my face, knocking off my glasses. She told me I was lying. She directed me to tell my brothers and sisters that I had taken the tape measure. Through my crying and tears I listened to her as she explained that we would rehearse what should have happened. She told me that she would walk into the room and I would tell her I was sorry for taking the tape measure, that I had taken it to play with and that I would never do it again. We practiced at least a half dozen times. It became late, I was afraid and had cried myself out. Once she was satisfied, she took me to the rocking chair and rocked me. After a short while she brought me downstairs and made hot chocolate for me before putting me to bed. That was the start of her coaching, drilling, scripting, and rehearsing.

"Over the next few years, I continued to become more anxious and fearful. At that point, I had learned to fight, flee, or freeze. I often chose the latter two. For instance, as a young child, I was given a new pair of jeans. I thought they would look cool if I cut off a couple of the belt loops. When my mother found I had done this, she spanked me repeatedly—as was her way—and had me remove all my clothes, saying, 'You're not deserving of any clothes.' Then she had me stand naked in the corner of her room."

Monica Thompson was a nanny in the Farrow household from 1986 to 1993. In a January 1993 affidavit to Woody's lawyers reported by the *Los Angeles Times,* she said that around 1990 she saw Farrow slap Moses across the face because he could not find a dog's leash. "The other children were horrified and told their mother that it could not have been Moses who lost the leash. Farrow told the children that it was not their place to comment on the incident. The children were scared of their mother and did not like to confide in her because they were afraid of what her reactions might be." (Thompson acknowledged that in 1992 she had told Connecticut police that Farrow was a good mother and did not hit her children but that she had said so because she was pressured to support the charges against Woody and feared losing her job. She resigned in January 1993 after being subpoenaed to testify in the custody battle.)

On at least one occasion, Moses fought back. "One summer day in the Connecticut house Mia accused me of leaving the curtains closed in the TV room; they had been drawn the day before when Dylan and Satchel were watching a movie. She insisted that I had closed them and left them that way. Her friend had come over to visit and while they were in the kitchen, my mother insisted I had shut the curtains. At that point, I couldn't take it anymore and I lost it. I yelled at her, 'You're lying!' She shot me a look and took me into the bathroom next to the TV room. She hit me uncontrollably all over my body. She slapped me, pushed me back, and hit me on my chest. She said, 'How dare you say I'm a liar in front of my friend. *You're* the pathological liar.' I was defeated, deflated, and beaten down. Mia had stripped me of my voice and my sense of self. It was clear that if I stepped even slightly outside her carefully crafted reality, she would not tolerate it. Yet I grew up fiercely loyal and obedient to her, even though I lived in extreme fear of her. Based on my own experience, I believe it's possible that Mia rehearsed with Dylan what she ended up saying on video. As Mia had done with me, it's conceivable she set the stage, the mood, and scripted what was to take place."

Around the time of the custody trial in 1993, a person who went often to the Farrow home found Dylan crying one day. The story has been confirmed with someone else who often visited. "Dylan asked me, 'Is it okay to lie?' She felt she didn't want to lie and wondered, What would God think? She wanted an Attic Kids doll, but Mia forbade it. This was shortly before Dylan was to speak with someone connected with the trial. She said, 'Mom wants me to say something I don't want to say.' Then the next week she had the Attic Kids doll with a yellow dress. I asked, 'What happened?' She said, 'I did what my mom asked.'"

The story does not surprise Moses, who adds, "This I can speak to with confidence. Mia's ability and intent to mold her children to do her bidding was matched by her living in constant fear that her secrets of abusive parenting would be divulged and the reputation she built as the loving mother of a large brood of adopted kids would be destroyed. My biggest fear was that we would be rejected, *excommunicated* rather, from her and the family. I lived in constant threat of this happening. When you are an adopted child, there is no bigger fear than to lose your family."

Soon-Yi Previn says, "She just liked to pick on people. She chose the easy, vulnerable targets. She had a fierce temper. On one occasion she kicked me and hit me again and again with the phone. She was always physical and violent with us. I learned to stay away from her and keep in survival mode, but Moses got the brunt by being too innocent, too sweet, to grasp the situation. She was regularly mentally and physically abusive to him."

After Woody and Soon-Yi began their relationship, Moses spent "many days and nights with Mia offering support." One day Moses went by himself to the end of the driveway of the Connecticut house to denounce Woody to the assembled media throng.

"Being thirteen, I felt that this was the right mind-set," he says. "I was showing loyalty to my mother. Mia already established with us that 'You have to be with me or you're against me. We're in a battle. This is a custody fight. We have to stick together as a family.' "

As the custody battle continued, however, Moses found that despite his reflexive loyalty to Farrow, he was emotionally torn between his parents. In a meeting with Judge Renee Roth, who had overseen his adoption, Moses recalls being told that Woody had proposed that Moses come to live with him. The powerful feeling to undo an injustice echoes the distraught mother in *The Boston Story*—a mother about to lose custody of her children. "I believe that Woody knew what kind of mother Mia was at that point," says Moses. "He was trying to protect *his* kids and was trying to offer a better life with kindness and love and affection. That's who he is." Because he found "the loyalty Mia demanded was overpowering," Moses chose to stay with her and soon became a boarding student at Kent School in Connecticut.

He had a psychological evaluation done in the wake of the high emotions of the custody case. "I shared my truth and told the psychologist that I felt like I was a pawn. I was torn between both Mia and Woody. After the report was submitted, I received a very upsetting call from Mia at school. She said, 'You've destroyed my case! I can't believe you said that you are torn. You have to recant your statement. You have to call your lawyer and make this right.' " Moses did as he was told.

He recalls his boyhood relationship with Woody as the opposite of the relationship he had with his mother. "Woody would come over to our apartment every morning at 6:30. I used to love to wake up before the others, and he and I would be at the kitchen table together. He would always bring two newspapers and half a dozen or so massive muffins—blueberry, corn, wheat. He'd open up *The New York Times* and sit there turning pages, and I'd take *The New York Post* and go straight to the comics and word puzzles. We would read together before waking Dylan. It was peaceful and memorable. He'd make a couple of slices of toast with cinnamon and honey and be there as she ate her breakfast. He really seemed to enjoy taking care of her. He was a caring father to me. He helped me feel good about myself, and I felt he did everything he could to include us in his life." (Woody's production company for many years was called Moses Productions. He had another called Dylan and Satchel Productions.)

Moses believes that in no way did Woody sexually abuse Dylan. The molestation accusation against Woody was "calculated. Mia had a judge who seemed sympathetic to her case; she found a lawyer who helped craft her arguments, she used her influence as a mother over her own children and used it to gain favor in the media."

He adds, "The instance of Mia telling Woody that she had something planned for him is the way she operated. On the one extreme, she went on uncontrollable rages, but she also made careful plans. She instilled fear. She demanded obedience. It wasn't just a few slaps on the cheek but extremely disproportionate actions. Now that I no longer live in fear of her rejection, I am free to share how she cultivated and brainwashed me as she has done with Ronan and Dylan. In 2002, I told Mia I wanted to reach out to Woody. Her initial response was understanding and motherly: 'I can see you miss having a father, and I'll support you.' Not twenty-four hours later, however, she told me, 'I forbid you to contact Woody.'" Nevertheless, he did and they reunited. Farrow has broken off with Moses.

On February 1, 2014, while Woody was in the midst of the preproduction and casting of *The Boston Story, The New York Times* printed in its Opinion Pages an open letter from Dylan in which she detailed the alleged 1992 sexual assault by Woody: "[My father] told me to lay on my stomach and play with my brother's electric train set. Then he sexually assaulted me . . . I remember staring at that toy train, focusing on it as it traveled in its circle around the attic. To this day, I find it difficult to look at toy trains."

It is a heartrending letter, all the more so because undoubtedly she believes every word of it. But the attic was not the first place the alleged abuse happened, and apart from the letter's details not being consistent with what she told the Yale–New Haven investigators, Moses says there is a central problem with the recollection: "I assure you, there was no electric train set in that attic. There was nothing practical about that space as a place for kids to play, even if we wanted to. It was an unfinished attic with exposed fiberglass insulation. It smelled of mothballs, and there were mouse traps and poison pellets left all around. My mother used it for storage where she kept several trunks full of hand-me-down clothes, that sort of thing. The idea that the space could possibly accommodate a functioning electric train set, circling around the attic, makes no sense at all. One of my brothers did have an elaborate model train set, but it was set up in the boys' room, a converted garage on the first floor. Maybe that was the train set my sister thinks she remembers." Farrow described the attic area in a deposition made in 1992 as "a crawl space . . . where the eave kind of drops."

Moses told *People* magazine in 2014, "Of course Woody did not molest my sister. She loved him and looked forward to seeing him when he would visit. She never hid from him until our mother succeeded in creating the atmosphere of fear and hate toward him." He added that on the day of the alleged abuse, along with Woody, there were six or seven children and nannies in the common rooms and that none of them went where they were unseen by the others. He emphasized how important it was to the children to avoid getting on their mother's "wrong side."

Farrow declined to respond to *People* regarding Moses's accusations but tweeted, "I love my daughter. I will always protect her." She added that she expected "a lot of ugliness" directed toward herself. Dylan said in the same *People* article that because Moses's comments betrayed her and her family, "My brother is dead to me." She also said that she and her siblings were never beaten but were sometimes sent to their rooms.

Monica Thompson was not in the house the day of the alleged incident but, according to the *Los Angeles Times* article, said in her affidavit that when she came to work the next day, "Moses came over to me and said that he believes that Ms. Farrow made up the accusation that was being said by Dylan." It has been argued that because Woody paid her salary she is somehow less reliable, but he paid her only indirectly; he says her wages came out of $1 million he gave Farrow for the general welfare of their children.

On the 1970 album *On My Way to Where* by Dory Previn (she married André Previn in 1959 and divorced him in 1970 after he impregnated Mia Farrow) is a song about incest, "With My Daddy in the Attic." The lyrics include: "And he'll play / His clarinet / When I despair / With my / Daddy in the attic." Woody says that Dory—who died in 2012—called him at the time of the molestation allegation to say "that's where Mia got the story line for her concocted tale."

Before Linda Fairstein became a best-selling author, she was director of the first sex crimes unit in the United States, appointed in 1976 by New York City District Attorney Robert M. Morgenthau. Until 2002 she oversaw the investigation of thousands of allegations of child and sexual abuse, and she has an informed opinion on this one.

"Once there was the suggestion that Woody Allen was involved with Soon-Yi, then there's every reason for Mia Farrow to be doing something from angry to insane, and there's no better weapon than your children. So take the weakest link—the youngest, the girl—and whatever you want to say that would make the public believe you are dealing with a monster, is to make this claim.

"When the story came out that Mia had videotaped Dylan"—in eleven segments shot at different times in different places, one nude in a bathtub, others outside showing her topless—"it sounded to me like one of the craziest things I'd ever heard. On every level, it's the last thing you would do. First of all, videotaping her naked while asking again and again about what happened. Why are you exposing your child to these videos that someday will possibly be in the hands of the public or in the courtroom? That fact alone set off every alarm."

In regard to Farrow's telling Woody, "You took my child, I'm going to take yours," Fairstein adds, "That sounds so real to me. That's the kind of venom I'm used to seeing in this kind of case: You've ruined my life, I'm going to hit you where it hurts most. The idea of saying to a public figure just about the worst thing you could have as a newspaper headline about them is totally in keeping with how these cases are used in matrimonial matters."

Fairstein cites studies that have been done over the past twenty years on "how suggestible children are. Dylan's been told a story, and there's only one person left to please. Daddy's already been thrown out of the picture. How frightening. Like any kid, you are wanting to be with, if not two parents, the one parent. So I don't imagine from that point on she was free to tell any other story. If you believe as I do that the allegation is false, then it is the fault of the woman who created the allegation, who has mortally wounded this child.

"I was in the district attorney's office thirty years, and this was my specialty for twenty-eight of them, so there were thousands of abuse cases in which I had a direct or supervisory role. I have no reason to believe this event happened."

2

"I am surrounded by disaster."

As the first week of filming progresses, what to do in place of having Jill and Ellie on horseback is often on Woody's mind. He wants to get away from people talking in restaurants or being inside. A walk on the cliffs is one idea, but the sun is an issue—the actors would be in the open, and unless the day is overcast, the light would be too harsh.

Scene A84 is Abe in voice-over as he stands by the ocean at sunset, his back to the camera:

I'm Abe Lucas and I've murdered. I've had many experiences and now a unique one. I've taken a human life—not in battle or self-defense but I made a choice I believed in and saw it through. I feel like an authentic human being.

His demeanor two scenes later is completely different. Rather than morose and depressed, he is full of energy as he and Jill have a celebratory and romantic dinner after they've heard that Judge Spangler has died of an apparent heart attack. The waiter brings two martinis.

JILL

I love it that you order for me.

ABE

Tonight I feel great—relaxed—happy. I want to enjoy myself.

JILL

Well, this is supposed to be a kind of celebration. Although it is a little macabre celebrating someone's death.

ABE

Yes, life's ironic, isn't it? One day a person has a morass of complicated, unsolvable problems and the world seems black and her troubles seem overwhelming—and then, in the batting of an eye, the dark clouds part and she can enjoy a decent life again. Sometimes just a little thing.

JILL

Like a sudden heart attack.

ABE

Or hitting the lottery.

The scene, which takes all of a Friday to shoot, continues through his giving her a book of Edna St. Vincent Millay's poems for her recent birthday, which she disappointedly thought he forgot. "You can do better than me," he tells her, but she responds, "Can't I make that decision?" It ends with her cajoling him into taking her to his apartment and to bed rather than ordering dinner. It is a long and emotional scene. After a perfect take of a close-up on Jill, Woody calls out in jest, "Let's move on. She'll never get it."

But not all is so simple.

"I am surrounded by disaster," he reports on Monday morning. The romantic dinner needs to be reshot. After seeing the dailies he feels that Jill's dress and hair are too sophisticated and that Abe needs to be looser and more upbeat. And there is still the horse scene problem.

The day's scenes spread over the last third of the script. Scene 87: Jill and Abe in bed after making love for the first time; 105: Jill gets into Abe's house through an unlocked window; 108: Jill rummaging in Abe's apartment; 110: Jill finds a handwritten note about Spangler in one of Abe's books; 112: Jill hears Abe return to his house; 114: Jill quickly undresses and jumps into bed as an apparent surprise to cover up her growing suspicion that Abe may have murdered the judge.

The video village is in a room across the narrow landing where the stairs come up from the first floor and offers access to the four rooms on the second. Until several years ago, Woody always looked through the camera before a shot and stood near it while the take was made. He would not see how the shot turned out until the dailies were delivered. He was leery of using a monitor long after it became commonplace because he worried that having looked at a scene framed in its proper format, he would want to shoot it again and again. When finally he tried using the screen, he found he could resist the temptation to keep shooting and that in fact it made his work easier. Now, he says, "I don't have to go behind the still photographer and six guys to get a little peek. I can just be in the corner and watch it on the monitor. It's so comfortable and simple. But what I've resisted one hundred percent is, when scenes are over, saying, 'Okay, let's look at it on the monitor and make sure we have the take,' that kind of thing you see where the actors and the cameraman come over to look at it and the actor says, 'Oh, can I do one more? I can do it much better than that.' Sometimes the cameraman will look to see, say, if the sun is streaking in, but I never watch. I want my own judgment when I'm editing a month or two later. I've seen the scene. But even when I can't see it, you can see with your ears. I hear the actor, I think: 'I've got it.' I just can't work the other way. But all this technology has been positive." Although actors are not allowed to see takes, whenever one asks for another because he or she is dissatisfied with what they have just done, Woody obliges. Over the years he has often found that the take an actor thinks is terrible is the one he likes, but many times the actor has been right.

On occasion an actor will come over to ask a question while he is at the monitor, and although he answers politely and often with humor, he notoriously keeps them at arm's length and does not engage in extraneous conversation. Over the years there have been only a few with whom he happily hangs out between setups—Diane Keaton, Tony Roberts, and Scarlett Johansson among them, and recently Emma Stone. The two struck up a cordial and teasing relationship on the set of *Magic,* and their ease with each other continues here. After Woody has the take he wants, Stone comes and sits in a chair beside him. They start considering ways to replace the scene that previously included horses. He says that Jill could narrate a sequence in which she goes shopping and runs into Ellie. That could speed up the action. Stone thinks for a moment, then suggests they could be in a yoga class.

"Can you stand on your head?" he asks.

She can. He is taken by the idea. "The two of you doing headstands against a wall and talking would be a great and funny visual. Can the other girl stand on her head as well?" (He knows the names of only the principal actors and a very few of the crew.) Stone says she's sure she can.

As Jill's stand-in goes through a camera rehearsal of 108, looking in drawers and elsewhere for some hint about Abe's involvement with the judge's murder, Woody does a mock play-by-play as he watches her on the monitor. "She walks to the door. . . . Senses something horrible. . . . She is imagining the grosses of the picture."

Loquasto looks into the monitor and sees that the white crown molding is the same color as the ceiling but not of the doors, and he winces. "I did not think it would be visible. We should have painted the molding the same cream color as the doors so they wouldn't contrast. You want a uniform glow in how the light bounces off things; you don't want it broken up unnecessarily." He has been at the house since 5:45 a.m. "It's important for the house to have its look," he says, and over the preceding days he and the set dressers changed it in small and large ways. The credo is to do as much as needed at the least expense necessary, and a location that requires little work is chosen whenever possible. Here, furniture was removed and replaced. Books were bought by the yard—all literature and philosophy—to fill the bookcases. The walls that the camera will catch have been painted taupe rather than the white used by the owner (the first floor is in real

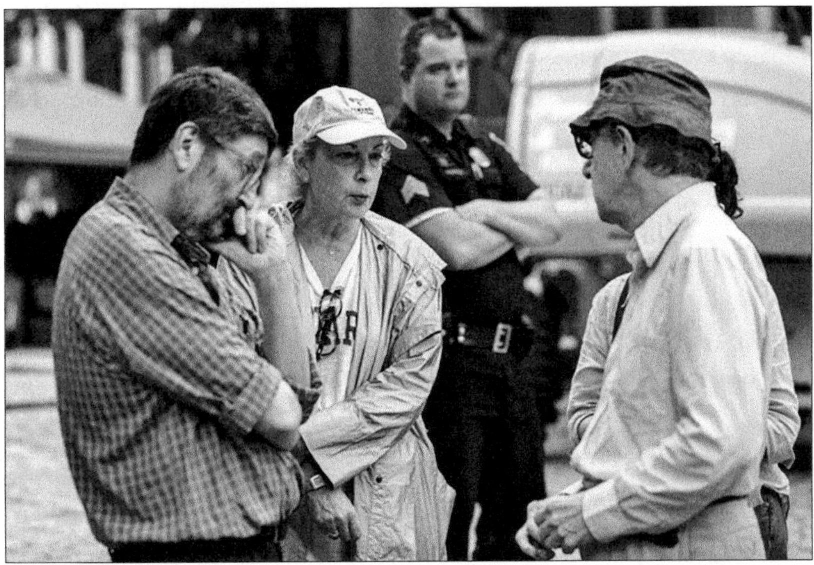

Sorting out one of several daily dilemmas with production designer Santo Loquasto and associate producer Helen Robin, who keeps the daily shoot moving. Each has been with Woody for more than thirty films.

life a Pilates studio). When Woody visited the set a few days earlier to be sure it was to his liking, he asked Loquasto to remove several pieces of wicker furniture that he thought made the house look "too beachy." ("He trusts what is true," Loquasto says. "You can't show him an empty room.")

Once the shot has been decided, Stone does the prowl through the bedroom. "Don't wander rapidly into the shot," Woody calls out. "Slowly, like a sylph."

Even though these scenes are indoors, the outside lights are set to augment the ambient sunlight. A while ago, a cloud settled over the house as a take was ready to go, and to avoid differences in light, shooting was halted until it passed by. Now, Rigby says, they are waiting on another cloud.

Woody rolls his eyes. "A fast moving cloud?" he asks. It isn't.

Shooting resumes at last. Afterward, Stone and Woody continue the discussion of Jill and Ellie in a yoga class.

"Can you *really* stand on your head?" he asks.

"Yes, but I do it better in a handstand against a wall."

"Would others in the studio be doing the same thing?"

"No." This pleases Woody, who is relieved that everyone would not need to be exercising in unison. "So while you're doing that, someone could be in the enchanted reef knot position?"

The crew are ready to shoot 110C: a close-up on Jill's hand holding Abe's book (*Crime and Punishment,* fittingly), opened to a page in the margin of which he has written a list of murderers: "Spangler—see Hannah Arendt—the banality of evil. Raskolnikov, Stavrogin, Verkhovensky, Lucas."

Stone, seeing a flaw in herself not observable by others, says, "My hands don't look great."

Woody nods his head and tells her, "I bet you're sorry you used that harsh detergent all those years."

On the monitor the book appears to have been pressed too heavily in order to flatten the pages at the spine and the names are a bit hard to read, although they will look better on the big screen. Woody shrugs. "If it doesn't work we'll shoot it again—it's just an insert." This and the next several shots are visual wheels to move the action along to 114, a critical encounter between Jill and Abe. She has to convince him that she is in his bed as a romantic surprise rather than covering up having snuck in to look for incriminating evidence against him. He opens the door to his bedroom and is duly startled as well as pleased to find her with the sheets pulled up, exuding desire.

Once Jill is under the covers, Woody goes over to her.

"You are in bed as a sensual surprise. He comes in and says, 'What are you doing here?'

" 'I thought you'd like it,' you say.

" 'No,' he says. 'Thursday is the day I make my bed and now it's messed.' "

She laughs. The camera rolls.

JILL

Surprise. I thought I'd make up for being such a stick in the mud out at the lake the other day.

(That scene, 103, is the first with Abe in which she feels he might have been involved with the judge's death.)

ABE

My goodness, this flair for theatre is so unlike you.

JILL

I don't want you to think I'm one of those middle-class drones who lacks erotic imagination.

ABE

I have you down for wild and up for anything.

(He embraces her.)

Woody says to Abe, "That had good authority. I believed you."

It is past six thirty p.m. Shooting ends for the day, but the lighting and blocking of scene 87, Jill and Abe in bed for the first time, need to be sorted out so that it can be filmed in the morning. Abe and Jill leave and their stand-ins take over. "This is the dullest shot in the world," Woody says. "There's no way to shoot people in bed and have it mean much." He muses that Abe could be in bed while Jill dresses, but that doesn't seem right. To limit the number of camera angles, he arranges the pair so that it can frame them both by coming in over a shoulder. Immediately, Woody leaves for Newport. Just after his car disappears, Loquasto comes out of the house holding up Woody's waxed canvas hat, limp from wear, which Woody has inadvertently left behind.

"I have our Shroud of Turin," he announces.

The next morning comes the scene of Abe and Jill in his bed after their dinner to celebrate the seemingly natural death of Judge Spangler. Despite Jill saying, "Dancing on someone's grave is really what we're doing," she feels the judge's death can only mean better luck for the mother whose case was before him. The camera pans up from legs under the blankets to Abe over Jill's left shoulder to avoid a conventional and boring shot of two people in bed.

ABE

I swore I wouldn't [start a sexual relationship with you] but I don't know what's come over me.

JILL

What's come over you is that for the first time since I've known you, you're embracing life instead of romanticizing death—with your crazy Russian roulette.

Half a dozen crew members surround the actors. Frans Wetterings, the gaffer (head electrician, who supervises the positioning of the lights), is just off camera by Jill's head holding an eye light—it looks like a long mini ice cube tray with tiny bulbs—that he put diffusion over to give a little kick to the eyes. There is a birdcage—an incandescent light with a soft cloth for diffusion—directly above Abe, a spotlight at the end of the bed. With all this equipment and all these people, some within inches of their faces, the actors make convincing intimate pillow talk.

It seems paradoxical to use so many lights to achieve a soft look, but as Khondji explains, "The beauty of lighting is to bring in bigger light and cut it, cut it, soften it until you have the remains of light. It's like the end of day. If you bring a big source—I jokingly call it German style—you light with a lot of exposure but all the beauty and subtleness is really with the remains."

When it is time to shoot, Woody comes in and says to Jill, "Keep it light, even 'Dancing on someone's grave.'" To Abe he says, "You want to be teasing her all the way when you say, 'I swore . . .' You're a new man and you're sincere when you say you didn't mean this to happen. You're the more experienced and so you're not as over the moon as Jill, who has wanted this." He thinks Abe will look better resting on his elbow—more in control—while Jill should look more spent. "The audience has been waiting for this all through the picture," he reminds them. Each listens intently then nods.

"Okay," he adds. "Now I've exercised my duties as a film director. You two work out what's comfortable for you," and he heads to the video village. He already has in his mind how he will piece this together in the editing room, and as he settles in front of the monitor he says, "I have to remember the cuts so if anything goes wrong, I don't have to be upset."

Khondji, as with nearly every take, has a few small adjustments to make. Woody says, "When Gordon Willis would light a scene like this he'd have cutters [pieces of fabric to diffuse and soften the light] and lights everywhere and it would take from eight in the morning until four in the afternoon—and another cameraman will spend an hour and it won't look much different to my untrained eye."

Loquasto asks about the bedsheets, which are light neutral beige, and says he has something fancier. Woody is fine with these. "Our white," Loquasto says of the color.

After the first take, in which the actors don't have the conversational tone Woody wants, he suddenly turns into T. S. Eliot as he pulls off his headphones and jumps off his chair, loudly reciting lines from "The Love Song of J. Alfred Prufrock": "That is not it at all, / That is not what I meant, at all."

Two more takes follow. During take 4, Woody gives the thumbs-down sign to Virginia McCarthy. "Tell me when it's over," he says. He is laughing as he repeats, "That is not what I meant, at all," more emphatically, then adds: "I know exactly what that is, to be misunderstood."

One take is a more intimate shot of Abe bare chested, and another is closer so Woody can vary things in the cutting room. There is just a touch of Jill's shoulder in the tighter shot. Every shot requires a new camera setup and lighting adjustments, and over a day the hours mount up. Despite Woody's deep regard for Khondji, there is unavoidable tension between his desire to move immediately to the next shot and Khondji's need to make the shot look as good as possible. This dichotomy is on Woody's mind as he waits for the next setup, which will take more than an hour. "In [Elia] Kazan's letters there is one to [cinematographer] Boris Kaufman, explaining why he is not hiring him. Kazan wants another take immediately after his instructions to the actors, but Kaufman always tinkered. I have the same problem—I want to go right away but all the best cameramen tweak. He did hire Kaufman again, for *Splendor in the Grass* [1961]. And in the end, I always defer to deep genius."

"Everything I learned about filmmaking I learned from Gordon Willis and [the late film editor] Ralph Rosenblum," Woody has told me several times. He and Willis worked together on eight films between 1977 (*Annie Hall*) and 1985 (*The Purple Rose of Cairo*).

"When I would line up a shot or suggest things, Gordon would say to me, 'You don't need that' or 'There's no reason to move the camera there, so why are you moving it?' or 'The shot has too much head on it, you're going to throw it away later.' 'Shoe leather,' he would call it. He liked Kurosawa's camera work, where the actors move the camera with their action rather than the camera move arbitrarily. He showed me how simply you can shoot. I thought he was going to use all kinds of long lenses and tricks, yet he practically always shot every picture with a forty millimeter, the most unromantic lens there is. Shot by shot I would say, 'Gee, do I have the nerve to do that?' And he would answer, 'Yes, we should': people talking off camera [Woody and Diane Keaton walking in and out of the frame in *Annie Hall*] or things being so dark you don't see their faces [the pair walking through the moonscape at the American Museum of Natural History in *Manhattan*]; people far away, the camera not moving until they walked closer; making sure that in his head the next cut will be to what we were shooting. He made sure—this is a simplistic example—if two people were across town making phone calls, that Keaton was on the right of frame and when you cut to me I was on the left. But before that I might have been on the right and cut to Keaton and cut back to me. And it would work—it's a phone call, we're across town—but it didn't look as pretty. He showed me how to light romantically when that was the mood. And he understood the script. He was with me on it and knew what I wanted. After a couple of pictures with him I became a know-it-all."

Rosenblum edited six of Woody's early pictures, beginning with saving *Take the Money and Run* by coming on to re-edit it and ending with *Interiors* in 1978. "Ralph showed me the value of music, the value of cutting not literally but actually cutting. Here's a good example: in *Bananas,* they're kidnapping me and stuffing me in a car, and he just pulled out the middle of a continuous scene—he'd been doing this forever—and he explained to me that just in the motion it's not going to bother you, and it didn't. Ralph always tried to use a piece of every angle I made. If I made six angles, he'd try to use a piece of every one."

Scene 30: Abe can't perform with Rita. They are in his bed after Rita has dropped by on a rainy night with a bottle of single-malt scotch in the hope of seducing him. It is a stormy night and the sound of rain during this scene ties it in time to 28 (Rita arriving with the scotch and making a play for him), and 29 (Jill and Roy having dinner with her parents at their house), also with the sound of rain.

ABE

I'm sorry. I know it must have been a disappointment, to say the least.

RITA

Have you tried any of the impotence drugs?

ABE

It's not physical. And don't take it personally. I haven't been able to perform in nearly a year.

RITA

Have you been to a shrink? Because I know one for that problem.

ABE

I keep hoping it will come back as mysteriously as it left. I'm sorry I let you down.

RITA

I'm sorry. I'm sure it's hell for you.

ABE

Thanks for the scotch.

This is their first scene since day one of shooting, and when Posey and Phoenix are together, she recalled later, Woody tells them, "Neither of you is going to be fired," which she found both "a relief and of course very funny. He carries a sardonic wit—and all kinds of wit—and it's really fun to be around." But there is an underlying reason for her relief because Woody is known for changing actors after shooting has begun, including a main actor in *The Purple Rose of Cairo* (he found him too contemporary for a film set in the 1930s) and *Another Woman* and several cast members when he completely reshot *September* (1987). But he cut Vanessa Redgrave's character from *Celebrity* because he disliked how he wrote the part: "She's as fine an actress as there is in the world. Obviously it had nothing to do with her acting." The number of changes he has made is small in comparison to the number of films he has made, but it is enough to make actors, by nature insecure, worry that they might be the next to go. At the beginning of *Magic in the Moonlight,* Stone was "catatonic": "I thought the first week that I absolutely was going to be fired. I was certain of it. I had heard stories of him firing people or him casting someone and then when he saw them perform and being shocked at what they looked like or they were too modern or looked the wrong way or sounded the wrong way. I was sure everything they claimed ever happened would happen to me. I was resigned to being fired."

There are occasions Woody is explicit in telling an actor there needs to be a change in performance. During a film shot many years ago, he saw the first batch of dailies at the end of the second day of shooting. The next morning he took one of the leads aside and said, "Now, you know I think you are a marvelous actor and you mustn't misunderstand and you may feel strongly about the choice you've made in this character, but if you want to continue this way we're just going to have to replace you."

The actor, completely collected, replied, "Just tell me what you have in mind." Which, as always, Woody had not done to anyone in the cast beforehand but rather trusted in their inherent ability to come to the set and perform to his satisfaction, and that meant then, and does now, to act without seeming actorly. "You're a terrific actor, you're great, you can do whatever you want," he once told another performer, "but I don't want any acting in the movie." The paradox is, by not acting, you act. Woody got the performance he wanted.

But firing anyone is not on his mind here.

"What is the scene before this?" he asks as the shot is being set up. When told it involves Jill's parents he says, "Good, not downstairs here." He likes adjacent scenes to have different locales, and, when possible, for an indoor scene to be followed by one outside because, he says, "I like to change from light to dark, indoors and out; I like the contrast of light."

He talks over the shot with Khondji and the grips and decides that the dolly track should go along Abe's side of the bed. The track is on plywood leveled with shims, called a dance floor, so that the camera, on the dolly, will always be even and keep the frame straight. Woody positions Abe on his right shoulder, looking away from Rita, who is behind him, her hands on his shoulder and hip, comforting him. He has aligned the two so both faces are in the shot, sparing him having to cut back and forth in the editing room. The gaffers set a birdcage by each actor, a spot at the foot of the bed, a flag behind Rita, and turn on the three table lamps in the room, from which the light seems to come. The shot begins with the camera dollied across the dance floor and then moves in on the couple. The take is realistic but more subdued than emotional. For the second and third, Woody suggests that Abe be "bitterer," and that gives the scene more edge.

While he waits, Woody, as he often does, flips a quarter across the knuckles of his right hand by rolling his fingers. On other occasions he manipulates three quarters hidden in his right palm between the thumb and forefinger. It is a habit he developed with his preteenage proclivity for magic and prestidigitation. It is harder to work with coins than cards but easier to do spontaneously; people always have change on them but seldom carry playing cards.

Scene 50—Abe in bed unable to sleep—and A50, him awakening in the morning after hearing the mother's lament, are a turning point in the story as they are the start of Abe's transformation from a purposeless to a purposeful man. The idea of killing the judge at first made him reel, but no longer.

ABE (V.O.)

The dizziness and anxiety I had disappeared and I accepted completely, in fact embraced, my freedom to choose action. I was too excited to fall asleep. My mind was racing with ideas—plans to kill Judge Spangler. Thanks to a serendipitous encounter with an unknown woman my life suddenly had a purpose. When I finally did fall asleep, I slept the sleep of the just.

McCarthy reads the voice-over to herself and times it at thirty-two seconds while Woody, in the bedroom with Khondji, plans the shot. "We have a few choices here to cover up this much narration," he says. "One is he gets out of bed, walks around. Or we can start him in the bedroom mirror then walk him back here, he gets back into bed and pulls up the covers, lying there. Or he can sit on the edge of the bed. We're not just confined to him lying in bed. The choice is ours."

Khondji films Abe in bed and they move on to a close-up of him. The script reads: "Sleeps, wakes up the next morning—a gorgeous day—birds tweeting, sun up." A seven-second voice-over as he stretches contentedly in bed:

> The next day I woke up feeling like a new man. I didn't have that listless, no appetite lethargy.

The following few short scenes show the manifestations of Abe's renewal. We see him eating a huge breakfast with gusto; then, walking briskly across campus, he meets Rita, who immediately notices he is "full of energy this morning" and asks what prompted it: "You have a religious epiphany?" He replies, "I just decided it was time to stop whining, to take matters into my own hands and make something happen." In scene 55, he and Jill drive to a lighthouse on a cliff that overlooks the sea and he tells her, "I can't help thinking of that phrase by Emily Dickinson—'inebriate of air am I'—to be drunk on air and not have to rely only on single-malt scotch." She tells him, "You know that I'm in love with you," and he answers, "You think you are but what you are is in love with the romantic concept of falling in love with your college professor. . . . I'll always be your friend."

All this sets the stage for scene 56, Abe and Rita making vigorous love. When Woody sees dailies the next afternoon he is concerned that cutting from Abe with Jill to Abe with Rita might confuse the audience as to which woman he is with because—looking at this on an iPad—he is not sure the distinction between Jill and Rita will be immediately clear. He asks Khondji to look. "No problem," he answers. "We see her face immediately before it disappears into a kiss and then a few seconds later."

"Are you confident?" Woody asks.

"I am completely confident."

"Okay, if you're completely confident."

The equipment is taken downstairs for scene 57: Abe and Rita postcoitus in a shot seen from the sitting room into the kitchen. Woody has moved the action to the first floor "to avoid more pillow talk. The time cut gets rid of another bed scene." He begins to work out the choreography—Abe walks into the frame and goes to the kitchen counter, Rita comes in and walks toward the camera in the sitting room, Abe comes in and puts his hands on her shoulders and kisses her.

While the equipment is set up, Woody taps out texts to Soon-Yi, something he does several times a day to her and to his assistant, Ginevra Tamberi. (This is a relatively new endeavor for him, and he does not have an email account.) With every one, immediately after hitting the send button, he gives the screen the hex sign with his right hand, as if that is necessary for the text to travel.

The scene, shot in a full-medium master, begins:

RITA

You were fantastic. What have you been eating for breakfast?

ABE

You are hot stuff, lady.

RITA

What happened to the philosophy professor?—Christ, you were like a caveman.

ABE

For the first time in so long I felt free. Just a limitless freedom.

RITA

Run away with me.

ABE

Where? To Tahiti? Like Gauguin? To make love in the tropics?

Rita asks Abe if he is sleeping with Jill. "No, never," he answers, "we're only friends" (true at this point) and says of the talk around the campus that they are more than that:

> It's just talk. People fill their lonely hours with gossip. Now put it out of your mind and let me hold you until you have to go back home.

Before the first take, Woody tells Abe and Rita: "Say it with raw candor and energy—no mercy." They laugh but he means it. He returns to the video monitor and says softly, "Now it's time for them to deliver." The first two takes are flat. "It's like they're not talking to each other, just saying lines," he says, then tells them to go again. They improve. The seventh take is very good, as the actors have added their own natural touches. Abe puts his hands on Rita's shoulders, massages them, bends over and kisses her on the mouth. "I like this staging," Woody says. "The take of him kissing her at the end is much better." As the eighth take rolls he says, as if this will make it happen, "This is the good one." Actually, it *is* very good. "That was a very good take. Correcting one nuance and then we're moving on," he calls out. Take 9 is cut just before the end because of a missed line, but much of it could

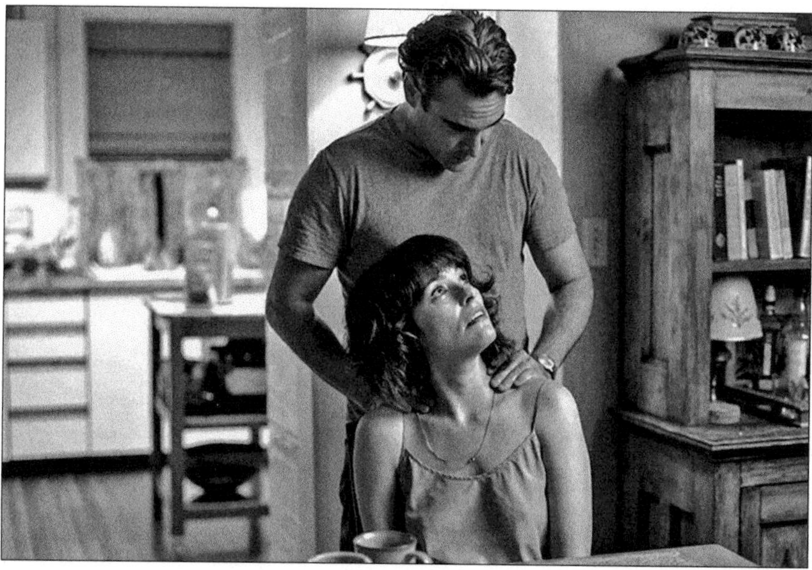

Abe and Rita postcoitus. To keep the story moving, Woody set the scene in the kitchen "to avoid more pillow talk. The time cut gets rid of another bed scene." He liked the added intimacy the actors gave the shot.

be useful. "Print that," Woody says. "We'll do another." Everyone gets set for take 10. "This is the last one coming up," Woody says. When it ends he tells McCarthy, "Print this one and not the one before." He goes to the actors and says, "Here's another brilliant twist," suggesting more nuanced kissing. The take that follows seems perfect. "We'll print that," he says after it cuts.

There are still several scenes inside Abe's house to make, more in a series of what for the past few days have been all indoors.

"I want to get out in the open air—the streets and stores—and surf the rocks!" Woody says to Helen Robin as they talk about the upcoming schedule. "I'm tired of being in these dark places. I've had too much time away from the Carlyle." He and his band play many Monday evenings at the Carlyle hotel on Madison Avenue.

"I told you to stay in New York," she tells him.

Woody assumes the part of the college president's assistant who shows Abe around his house: "We put our faculty up in the Carlyle." Then, in his own voice he adds, "That would be funny—the philosophy department gets free room service from the Carlyle."

3

"For me, the weak spot in every situation is always the writing."

Over the past several days, Woody has been enthusiastically reading the advance galleys of Richard Zoglin's biography of Bob Hope, *Hope: Entertainer of the Century,* and each morning he has come to the set with a new story or a quip from the book. He has recently slowed his reading to two or three pages a day because he is nearing the end and wants to forestall finishing. For people unfamiliar with Hope's genius as a stand-up comedian and his great films of the 1940s and 1950s—the best, according to Woody, being *Monsieur Beaucaire* (1946), *Casanova's Big Night* (1954), *Road to Rio* (1947), *The Great*

Lover (1949), and *Road to Bali* (1952)—Woody's devotion might seem odd, but at his peak, and that peak lasted a good twenty years, Hope was the embodiment of funny. He was America's most popular stand-up comedian, its most popular radio host, a number-one film box-office draw, and often host of the Academy Awards. His combination of insouciance, faux cowardliness, and delusions as a ladies' man made for a character that Woody idolized and imitated. In his early films especially (*Love and Death* and *Sleeper* are good examples), but even in one as late as *To Rome with Love,* if you take off Woody's black glasses and implant a ski-jump nose, Hope easily could be delivering those lines.

"Hope and I are both monologists, and as characters we both think we're great with women, and we play as both vain and cowardly," Woody said early in his directing career. "Both of us have the exact same wellspring of humor. It's hard to tell because I'm so unlike him physically and in tone of voice. There are certain moments when I think he's the best thing I've ever seen. Sometimes it's everything I can do to not actually mimic him." In *Love and Death,* the scene in which Boris is arranging to meet the countess could have been in *Monsieur Beaucaire*.

COUNTESS

My bedroom at midnight?

BORIS

Perfect. Will you be there too?

COUNTESS

Naturally.

BORIS

Until midnight then.

COUNTESS

(pressing his hand to her bosom)

Midnight.

BORIS

Make it quarter to twelve.

COUNTESS

Midnight.

BORIS

But of course.

An instance where Woody miscalculated by not channeling Hope more completely is *The Curse of the Jade Scorpion,* in which he plays C. W. Briggs, an insurance investigator who has a sparring relationship with efficiency expert Betty Ann Fitzgerald (Helen Hunt). Both of them fall under the spell of a crooked hypnotist (David Ogden Stiers). Woody had lined up an actor for Briggs who at the last minute could not get free from another obligation. Unable to find a replacement on short notice, he took it on himself but a week or two into shooting realized, "It was not going to work with me playing him." In many of Hope's best films, either by design or accident, he is mistaken for someone he is not, just as Boris is not who people think he is. C.W. has Hope's sound in many of his lines, Woody says, but "the tone of the picture was wrong. If you're going to make a picture where I'm the investigator, it's got to be more Bob Hope–ish, where I'm not really the investigator but I'm mistaken for being him." He considers the film perhaps his worst and feels he let down the "great players" he assembled: Hunt, Dan Aykroyd, Wallace Shawn, and Charlize Theron, among others. "They were all terrific. I could see that it wasn't coming out as I wanted it, that I was just not believable." North American ticket sales were only $7.5 million, but as proof of how different audiences react differently, it was the most successful film he had to that time in Japan and Spain.

Woody's command over the set, like any director's, is total but he exercises it quietly: no raised voice, no demands other than to get the shot right. While the last touches to the lighting are made, he recalls seeing the power of a director for the first time.

"Charlie Joffe [with Jack Rollins, his longtime manager] and I went on the set of [*What's New*] *Pussycat?* [1965] and were amazed. Clive Donner, who was a mild-mannered and lovely guy, would say, 'I need a platform over there,' and the crew sprang to work and hammered it together. He asked me if I wanted anything and I said, 'Well, a chocolate bar.' And he said to one of the crew"—Woody snaps his fingers—"'Bring Mr. Allen a chocolate bar.'"

There are still shots to be made, but the day has gone slowly. Nine scenes are scheduled; six have been done. Robin, hoping though not really expecting to keep to the production timetable, optimistically put them into the day's work, and dinner was ordered for the crew. But at 6:45 p.m., with another long setup ahead and the working day already twelve hours long, Rigby tells Woody that it will be at least 9:30 before they wrap, and he will have a forty-five-minute trip home after that. He blanches, in part because the next day is already scheduled to last until that hour, and looks over at Robin. She shrugs and says, "It's your movie. We already aren't going to finish here on time." He quickly calls an end to the day and scoots to his car. Robin tells Rigby to cancel dinner.

This second week of filming is only three and a half days because the premiere of *Magic in the Moonlight* is in New York Thursday night and in Chicago on Friday. Ronald Chez, one of the film's financial backers, lives there. Woody's enthusiasm of a week ago is already tempered.

"I'm glum," he says between shots on Wednesday. "To me the shots that I see seem dull, not how they look but how they play. It's too early to tell much but the picture does not feel exciting. I don't think it's coming together." This is not an uncommon feeling—the last time he felt this glum was on *Blue Jasmine*. Before it was released he said, "I'm never happy. I'm thrilled with Cate, and I was thrilled with the cast generally—Bobby Cannavale and Louis C.K. and Sally Hawkins of course and Alec Baldwin, who is relentlessly great since he started in the business. Whether it's comedy or serious stuff, he's amazing. So I was blessed with this wonderful cast and they all came through. For me, the weak spot in every situation is always the writing."

His script received a raft of award nominations, including for an Oscar, but considering his long-held belief that art cannot be judged, that is of little import to him: "If you accept an award when they say your film is good, then you have to agree with them when they say it's bad," he says, acknowledging the genesis of the line in Ernest Hemingway's *Green Hills of Africa,* and that is not something he is willing to do. "Sometimes I'm right" about a film not working, he says, laughing again, though it would be difficult to find many who would agree that *Blue Jasmine* didn't work, no matter how much he worried about it not coming together.

Still, that was then and there are fresher worries. Now, "I have a picture that's premiering tomorrow and opening in a week and I have that feeling that *it's* never come together."

Because of Woody's yearly shooting schedule, by the time a film comes out he has long ago emotionally moved past it and is wholly invested in the current story. He was in France shooting *Magic in the Moonlight* when *Blue Jasmine* was released in the United States in July 2013 and so was too far away to attend the premiere and do the attendant interviews. This year, however, he is a half-hour flight from New York. The cast and crew will break around noon on Thursday so Woody, Soon-Yi, and Emma Stone can be on the red carpet at the Paris theater on West Fifty-Eighth Street before the screening. There was a time that his absorption in the film at hand was so total that no break of any kind was welcome. Now, however, the interlude has its bright spots.

"Normally it would kill me," he says. "For years I hated every interruption at all, even the weekend. I don't think it will bother me this time only because it will give me another weekend not here. The weekdays are fine. I work all day and go to sleep at night so it's okay. But the weekends when you get up and [*tired voice*] it's Saturday *and* Sunday. I wish we were shooting six days a week; years ago I would have been happy with seven because I was so into the picture."

In two days, the first reviews of *Magic* will be out. Early in his career he read reviews, but since the early 1970s he has refrained from following what critics say, although he does gather their general tone from conversations with his sister and others involved with the film. He says he has "an affection" for *Magic* because he "*did* it and I have an affection for the people. Now, you have to have a taste for this kind of upper-class . . . drawing room—I don't know what to call it—comedy, because that's what it is. It's Colin Firth with this uncouth American girl. It's a combination of Merchant Ivory and Masterpiece Theatre and not as good [*laughing*] as either of them. Colin and Emma and everyone in the picture are so good that I have an affection for it. But that doesn't mean anything. The audience can feel it's not funny enough; they can feel it's too verbal—and it deliberately *is* verbal, I wanted to make that kind of a picture. Coming on the heels of *Blue Jasmine* may be a handicap. I'm sure they'd be very happy if this was another *Blue Jasmine*–style picture, but that's not what I wanted to do. It's a lose-lose proposition all the time. If you do the same thing they say, 'Ah, you're doing the same thing,' and if you do something different, they don't like that either. So you tend to ignore that because if you listen you go crazy. For the director, it's serious business—it's what you do. But for people who watch movies, it's, 'What do you want to do tonight? Let's go to the movies. We'll go eat after.'"

For him the film is the result of a year's concentrated work, but for the audience it is "an hour and a half of relative unimportance. They sit through it and they hope they're entertained. Then if they are, when it's over they say, 'Boy that was terrific, where do you want to eat?' Or they say, 'God, I'm bored stiff, where do you want to eat?'

"Once a girl said to me about somebody else's film, 'It was a noble failure.' And I thought, 'You wouldn't know if it was a success or failure or noble or ignoble,'" he said a dozen years ago. "She was a nice person but people throw out terms that they hear. It's film talk. You turn on television and people are talking and it's mostly what Norman Mailer years ago called 'polluting the intellectual waters.' It's prattling. They set that structure with [Gene] Siskel and [Roger] Ebert talking about film, the notion that two honorable men may disagree. Now wherever you turn on television you see people talking about films. Some people are more qualified, others are totally unqualified, but they're all entitled to an opinion. It bears very little or no relation to the real film world where people make pictures and participate in a serious, ongoing, life-dedicated way. And this is true of many critics who have dedicated their life to film. It is very hard to separate what Gore Vidal talked about as the difference between criticism and mere opinion, because criticism is basically mere opinion. A critic who was a wonderful writer like Pauline Kael could write about a film and it could be junk, but she liked it, and in her writing she gave good reasons why you should like it and she made it sound exciting. She followed her arguments, they were sound, but then you see the film and it's no good. And it's no good because you didn't like it."

Critics were evenly divided on *Magic.* There were some raves and some pans with the majority feeling the film was a pleasant diversion but not among Woody's best. He is in an odd position. Because his movies are as annual as the summer solstice, there is not the same excitement that comes with a great director who makes a film every five years. Last year's picture has barely receded in the mind when this year's comes along. But coming on the heels of *Blue Jasmine,* which was wildly appreciated and grossed about $100 million worldwide with a third of it in the United States, *Magic* opened to very big business in 17 theaters—his films traditionally open first in New York and Los Angeles and then in other cities—with growth to 964 in the weeks ahead. The wide release would prove to be half that: total ticket sales worldwide came to $51 million.

On the Monday morning after the premieres, Woody is back in Providence with the fate of *Magic* gone from his mind, the benefit of being absorbed by the film at hand. His concern at the moment is how to make the most interesting shot of Abe being shown his home the day he moves in, scene 9. The house, built in the 1930s, is in a pleasant middle-class neighborhood with cozy homes and small yards. A half-dozen stairs lead from the sidewalk to the verandah and front door. The shot needs to take Abe and the college president's assistant from his car into the house. It is tagged A9 to differentiate it from the portion inside. A dolly track has been laid out on the street at a forty-five-degree angle to the house. The first thought is to have the camera on Abe and the assistant (played by Nancy Giles) as they get out of the car and then pull back to pick them up and track them in a wide shot to the door. But after looking at the run-through, Woody thinks the widest portion is the nicest part of the shot. He suggests cutting the car and having them walk instead: "If you were wide and they come and go up the stairs—no car—we follow them." After more thought, however, he decides to start on the car and moves the assistant's lines about the house and neighborhood, written to be said inside the house, to be spoken during the walk, so there is no dead air.

The first two takes look boring. For the third, he suggests Abe and the assistant drive up in the car and get out—"The car should pull in a bit otherwise it looks tacky"—but he doesn't like this either. He again wants to lose the car, but McCarthy reminds him that Abe's bags are in it and he holds them in the interior shot. Woody shakes his head, thinking. "I want to get the dead weight off this shot," he says. His solution is to start on the porch and have the camera pan down at the sound of the car door closing, then pick up the pair as they walk and climb the stairs. But two takes produce nothing he likes and he tells McCarthy not to print either. She points to her iPad with the details of all that has been filmed. "See that? All red. Bloody." Two more useless takes follow. Then, finally, a good one, followed by another. Satisfaction.

The afternoon will be spent at another house for the faculty party welcoming Abe to the college, scene 10. Loquasto is about to go to the new location but first checks to be sure all is okay here for the interior shots that follow. It is.

"Everything going smoothly?" Woody asks of the next location.

"Yes, absolutely."

"Smooth as silk?" he asks further.

"The silk is polyester," Loquasto quickly replies, referring to the film's budget.

For the interior shots of Abe's home, the need to establish the house is hampered by its small rooms. Because it is impossible to get much into a shot, there can be no master that incorporates it all. So there will be one of Abe and the assistant as they enter from the right into the foyer, then another from the landing in the stairwell. Woody asks assistant director Rigby to tell Giles to add to her lines, "It's a small but comfortable house," and to say where all the rooms are, upstairs and down, to get around the problem of not being able to clearly show the layout on camera. He also tells her to pass along that she should come inside and close the door before speaking. This spreads out the dialogue through the various takes, which end with Abe offering the assistant a drink from the flask we have seen him drink from earlier. "Oh, no," she says, taken aback but polite and setting up what follows, "there's a little cocktail party to welcome you at six."

The need for so many setups is slowing production. The film requires the variety, but there are only twenty-eight shooting days to get it. Shots scheduled but not made must be added to other days but not randomly; every day of shooting is already planned for one location or another, which often means that the location cannot be returned to the owner as scheduled, which then means more money has to be paid for its use, which also means that the date for one or more subsequent locations has to be moved, which invariably means that extra shooting days are needed at a cost of about $175,000 per, which finally and most importantly means that the budget balloons. As the first dollars over budget are deducted from Woody's fees, only he can make the decision of how long to go on because it is money from his pocket. Abe's house already is being kept longer than allotted. There is a shot he wants to make of Abe in the bedroom after the cocktail party, but there is no way there will be enough time today. Asked if he really needs it, he replies, "I'd rather make it and throw it away if it turns out we don't need it." Khondji says, "The day we come back and finish the scene upstairs we can do this." It does not make the final cut.

No location in an Allen film has been held longer than the three blocks in Long Island City made to look like it was the late 1930s for *Sweet and Lowdown*. For such a location to work, every person who lives on the blocks has to cooperate, in exchange for some tidy cash: in this case, air conditioners had to be removed from windows, awnings had to remain where the set designer placed them, fruit stands were erected, the elevated subway signs had to be changed, street lines were painted out, buses rerouted. Christie Mullen, in her first job in the locations department, had to deal with fifty-one separate parties for a shot that was scheduled to be made the first morning of filming, as Sean Penn comes down from the El and walks past a newsstand. The morning dawns, it is a bright sunny day—anathema for Woody, who likes an overcast sky because sun washes out color. He drives up, gets out of the car, takes a look at the readied set, and says, "Okay, let's move on to the next location." Several times over the next sixteen weeks, word would come that the neighborhood was on the next day's schedule. The crew scrambled to get everything back to 1938, but either because it was another sunny day or because a different location needed to be used, the shot was not made until the last day of filming. Even then there was trouble. It was sunny yet again and the shot had to be changed so that the action took place under an awning and beneath the El.

Radio Days had locations that show a favored period of Woody's. Anyone who has seen his fond recollection of growing up in 1940s Brooklyn has a bit of an idea of his home life: an extended family of aunts and uncles share a house, as was the case with Woody and Letty, who arrived when he was seven and was not subject to as much strictness from her parents. Over lunch one day, the talk turned to their childhood and a favorite bakery, Ebinger's, from which their mother, Nettie, bought half a cake every day. By Letty's account, she was a good if predictable cook: Monday fish; Tuesday lamb chops; Wednesday steak; Thursday liver; Friday candles were lit for a Shabbat dinner with chicken but no prayers. There were always extra people that night, making perhaps a dozen in all around the table. The housekeeper who came on Fridays would answer the phone, "You coming tonight? Just tell me your name." Saturday, leftovers; Sunday, Chinese.

Scenes 10 and 11 are exteriors of the faculty cocktail party to welcome Abe, to be filmed at a Victorian house with a sweeping verandah. Two grey twenty-by-twenty-by-three-foot helium-filled balloons float off the side of the house like alien spacecraft to block the sun and provide

Helium-filled balloons over the verandah of the house for Abe's welcome party.

Darius Khondji instructing camera operator Maceo Bishop, wearing a Steadicam, on the camera movement for the next shot on the verandah at Abe's welcome party.

an even light. Woody and Khondji walk around, considering possible shots, and finally Woody says, "No continuity, three shots on the porch and then one inside. Or two and two," meaning the shots do not have to follow in real time but rather serve as bits of party conversation.

In scene 10, done with a Steadicam (a stabilized mount worn by the camera operator that allows him to follow the actors and keep the frame even), Abe exchanges small talk on the verandah with three professors who are local hires for the day. (In the ensuing small talk we hear that Abe has come from Adair College, from which Woody's character in *Deconstructing Harry* was kicked out as a student but that later honors him once he's a famous novelist. Also, Scarlett Johansson's character in *Scoop* is a student at Adair, an institution named by Woody in admiration of Allison Adair's poems.) Just before the first take, Woody goes to them. "I told them to talk about anything until they heard the cue line. That's what I *told* them. Let's see what they do."

They do as instructed. "They are very good," Woody says, pleasantly surprised by their capability. They move on to 11, a vignette of two faculty members talking about Abe. This and an earlier collection of reactions by Braylin College faculty and students to Abe's hiring in scenes 2, 3, and 4, plus two instances of seeing him with a flask, are meant to establish Abe as someone with deep problems who cares little about what others think of him.

DOUG

You think he's attractive? Harriet finds him sexy.

LAURA

He's interesting looking. Clearly he's paid his dues.

Kenneth Edelson, Woody's dermatologist, is ready for his annual cameo, as a faculty member listening to a colleague's gossip about Abe. Several of Woody's friends regularly show up in scenes, sometimes with lines. He likes putting them in but marvels at their enthusiasm: "They come by plane, boat, and dogsled to do their parts."

Scene 14, inside the house: Abe with Rita and her husband, Paul, introducing themselves by the staircase in the foyer. Party guests mingle. The video village is in the cramped kitchen, stuffed with equipment and people. Many electrical cables snake along the floor going through the doorway. The light is low, and each time Woody goes out to talk to the actors and returns, his feet wobble a bit on the uneven tangle; he is rather like Lillian Gish on an ice floe heading for the cataract in D. W. Griffith's silent film *Way Down East* (1920). Worry mounts that eventually he will fall, but no one wants to seem to patronize him by offering a hand. After surviving several of these missteps he then starts what appears will be a calamitous stumble, but he immediately rights himself. He points his right index finger toward the ceiling as if instructing students and says, "I trip but I don't fall. That's the secret of comedy." Eventually someone does the sensible thing and tapes a rubber mat over the cables.

A bit actor in the scene is not as good as the ones on the porch were, and Woody, despairing of getting a usable reading, moans, "This person is hopeless." But after a couple more poor attempts, the line is delivered naturally, and he relaxes. An apparently simple scene like this—a husband and wife introducing themselves to a newcomer—is filled with nuance, and if the dialogue is off even a bit, it will make the conversation seem stagy instead of spontaneous. Sometimes the difference is only a word or two, for instance Rita talking to Abe after her husband leaves to refresh their drinks and the dolly pushes in on the pair.

RITA

> Rita Richards. I'm in the science department. If you ever get bored and want someone to give you the real lowdown on who's fucking who, let me know.

But she says it, "I'm Rita Richards of the science department," and Woody stops the action; both his writing and her reading are slightly off because they are not conversational enough. He goes back to the actors. "Not 'I'm Rita Richards of the science department'—that's too formal. 'I'm Rita Richards, I teach science,'" he instructs, deprepositioning the line.

4

"What seems right weeks ago often doesn't when you are ready to shoot."

Week three of production begins in the early morning light as Judge Spangler walks on the street by his house (scene A59, a tracking shot without dialogue) and by nine thirty the company has moved a block away to the Hope Club, a gracious antebellum red brick building located in a leafy area near Brown University, different parts of which will serve as four locations in the film: the bridge club where Spangler plays cards with friends; the Braylin College president's office; a college hallway where Jill and her boyfriend, Roy, walk and talk; and a campus outdoor café where he breaks up with her.

Scene B59 establishes the building as Spangler arrives at his club, without dialogue. The camera tilts down from the sky to the entrance as two men walk out of the club and exit right. It is a bright summer's day, and although the front of the building is generally in shade, there is more sun to the left of the entrance than when Woody and Khondji scouted the building three weeks earlier. Their idea then was to make the shot from the right side, but this morning the left looks better to Woody, so the crew who came ahead to get the camera properly located change its position and the paraphernalia for diffusing the light; yet another example of why he dislikes planning shots ahead. "What seems right weeks ago often doesn't when you are ready to shoot," he says.

The crew moves inside to set up scene 8: Abe meets the college president. While he waits, Woody bemoans that because of his myopic right eye, he can no longer easily catch a baseball; the loss of depth perception makes it difficult to track the ball into his left hand. An avid baller as a boy and into his thirties, he played hour after hour throughout his childhood in Brooklyn and then in the Broadway show league; he stood out among the players but was even better as a teenager. He was second baseman for the *Play It Again, Sam* team in the late 1960s, and for the Schlissel Schleppers, a team put together by producer David Merrick's general manager, Jack Schlissel. He also played against Major League players in a televised game at Dodger Stadium in 1967, in the First Annual All-Star Celebrity Softball Game, with show-business celebrities against such baseball all-stars as Willie Mays, Roberto Clemente, Jimmy Piersall, and Willie McCovey. Vin Scully and Jerry Lewis were the announcers. Don Drysdale, the great Dodger pitcher with a penchant for throwing at batters he felt were too close to the plate, hit Woody, the leadoff batter. He was not hurt, and Mays flied out to him later in the game.

"I was a very good fielder, ran fast, and we spent hours shagging flies. I played second base and also the outfield," he says in fond recollection, seeming to re-experience it. "If I could go back in time for a day it wouldn't be a day of sex or going to the movies but playing baseball in my teens when I was at my zenith."

In the club bar, prop master Jen Gerbino unwraps two new decks of Bicycle playing cards for use in the next scene, in which Judge Spangler is seen playing bridge with friends. Woody takes a deck from its box, fans it perfectly, spreads it evenly on the table, gathers it, shuffles it, cuts it several times. The top card is the ace of hearts. He keeps control of it while cutting, shuffling, and doing one-hand cuts; each time the ace pops up on top. Then the two of hearts appears. He continues cutting and shuffling. The three of hearts comes up. More cuts, additional shuffles. The king of diamonds appears and returns each time. He takes it from the deck and rubs it facedown on his left sleeve. When he turns the card over, it has become the king of clubs. He says he has not touched a deck in two or three years. "It would take me a few weeks to get my hands back in shape."

Magic, illusions, time travel, and characters visible only to one person in the room are a staple of Woody Allen movies: a character in a film comes off the screen in *The Purple Rose of Cairo;* a writer is transported from 2010 to the 1920s and earlier in *Midnight in Paris;* a woman is made invisible by enchanted herbs and thus able to be in a room and listen to what people are saying in *Alice;* a writer is feted by his characters in *Deconstructing Harry;* a kibitzing architect is seen and heard by only one character in *To Rome with Love;* and a mother who truly vanishes from a magician's box meant to make her disappear and then reappear materializes as a sky-filling nag who is constantly critical of her son in his "Oedipus Wrecks" segment of *New York Stories.* "You know where this is going to resonate?" Woody said while casting the mother. "Israel. It's going to be the *Gone with the Wind* of Israel."

Loquasto comes by and asks Woody what should be on the table the next day for the two different dinner table scenes at Jill's parents.

"Desserts," he says immediately.

"It's always starters or desserts," Loquasto says, "never entrées." They are easier to set up.

Over lunch Woody and Letty talk about the current anti-Semitic rallies in France and Germany. *Magic in the Moonlight* will open in France toward the end of next month, not long after shooting ends, and he has plans to be there. She is cautious about whether he should go and suggests they check how public the animus is at the time as Woody, despite his popularity there, could be a target simply for being Jewish.

He returns to do scene 59—the judge playing bridge—a thirty-second wide shot (also called an establishing shot; it shows the scene in relation to the surroundings) with Spangler and his buddies at the card table with the dolly slowly moving in and no dialogue, which is filmed in a snap. Scene 96, in which Roy breaks up with Jill, is equally easy, but in a couple of takes there are noises from airplanes and cars honking. Rigby comes to Woody at the monitor and says that the sound technicians want to know if they can turn it up a bit to counteract ambient noises.

"Sure," Woody tells her. After she leaves he says, "How's *that* for directing?"

He is more sanguine about the film now. The actors are comfortably settled into their roles and the local players used for bit parts have come through splendidly. He finds Jamie Blackley, fresh on the set, "excellent" as the boyfriend, Roy. And he says as with every film Khondji shoots, it looks beautiful.

All the action for the day is in Jill's parents' home—two scenes at the dining room table, the third in the living room where Jill opens birthday presents from her parents and Roy.

In scene 29, Roy and Jill are having dinner with her parents. She has become friends with Abe, who is the talk of the campus, and is eager to share what she knows about him without concern for how her parents and Roy might view this new friendship. Her enthusiasm sets off a distant warning in Roy that he is meant to display in an easy, bantering manner with Jill; at this point nothing of significance has occurred between Abe and her. Woody wants Roy to be loose and amusingly irritated yet also show that underneath he senses a potential threat that while improbable is not impossible.

In scene 115, it is Abe who has dinner with Jill and her parents. Woody does not want the two dining scenes to be similarly staged, however far apart in the film they are. He has decided that in 115 the participants will stay seated, so he wants 29 to be the more active, with people coming to and getting up from the table. Jill walks in from the living room, talking all the way; then her father gets up and takes dishes to the kitchen and returns followed by her mother doing the same to, as Woody says, "infuse it with a bit of specious energy. There's not much you can do without it seeming forced. You *can* force stuff, but I don't want to do that. I've found over the years it's best to do what would be natural in the situation."

Like any filmmaker, Woody has stored in his mind favorite scenes from other directors' pictures that can be brought into play, often unconsciously but sometimes purposely, as he did in *Manhattan Murder Mystery* in homage to the shootout in a house of mirrors in Orson Welles's *The Lady from Shanghai.*

In this case, there are two table scenes that have stayed with him: one, a flashback in which a man relives an extended family lunch in Bergman's 1957 *Wild Strawberries* ("Marty Landau [in *Crimes and Misdemeanors*] seeing his family at a seder maybe would not have been possible if I hadn't seen *Wild Strawberries*"); the other in Welles's *The Stranger* (1946), in which Welles and the family sit around a table; there's tension because he's a soon-to-be-exposed Nazi war criminal. Woody was reminded of it as he wrote the dinner scene "because it has a deep psychological component to it and this one is about psychology—I mean shallow psychology but still psychology. It's not the same thing at all, but there's a similarity. So if you play it a certain way then it should work because it has a certain structural similarity. I felt if Welles could make that scene of people sitting around the table gabbing work, then I should be able to make this work. Now, he may have started with better material and a better situation. But it's the best I can do. I'm going along with the assumption that the audience will be involved with the characters, the characters will be involved with each other, and to see them interact in a kind of teasingly tense way will hold your interest—and in the editing room I won't want to say, 'Oh, god, let's cut this dinner scene down to two speeches.'" Often there is no conscious consideration of a memorable shot; rather, he says, "you feel it from having grown up with these films that this is the way a scene is going to work. In *Dr. Strangelove* [1964], [Stanley] Kubrick is manipulating all those switches in the airplane, and without thinking I'm going to copy Kubrick, it's become part of the DNA of filmmaking.

"Scenes always stick in your mind, and if you are doing something that even approximates one you go there for guidance. In *Small Time Crooks* I remembered films by [Billy] Wilder and [Ernst] Lubitsch where they always try to get a punch at the very end of the picture. I tried for one because mine was in the genre of what they had done. The end of the movie is a debt—theft—to the curtain of *Trouble in Paradise* [1932]. Watch [Vittorio De Sica's] *Shoeshine* [1946] and then see the opening and closing of *Cassandra's Dream,* and look at the ending of *Sweet and Lowdown,* and then the ending of [Fellini's] *La strada* [1954]. Influence! I only recently saw *The Lady Eve* [1941] for the first time. I came in for the last ten minutes and [Preston] Sturges had a wonderful punch ending that was right up there with the best."

He says there are many beloved movies that he has yet to see. "Contrary to what people may think, I'm not overly film literate. You'd be surprised by my film ignorance. I didn't see *The Wizard of Oz* [1939] until I was in my fifties. I've never seen [Buster Keaton's] *The Navigator* [1924] nor [Chaplin's] *The Circus* [1928] or his war movie, *Shoulder Arms* [1918]. When Aljean Harmetz phoned me while she was writing her book on *Casablanca,* thinking that the author of *Play It Again, Sam* would be an expert, she was taken aback that I had seen only moments of it but never the whole film, and I was in my late forties or early fifties. I didn't see [John Ford's] *Stagecoach* [1939], [Ford's] *How Green Was My Valley* [1941], [Howard Hawks's] *Red River* [1948], or [William Wellman's] *The Ox-Bow Incident* [1943] until I was in my late thirties or forties, but loved many when I finally saw them." (Orson Welles said that he watched *Stagecoach* dozens and dozens of times while making *Citizen Kane,* the first film he directed.) "I do not mention all this with pride—or shame—just as brute facts. Interestingly, I've seen all of Bergman, Fellini, Truffaut, De Sica, etc."

Scenes from Bergman's films often come to his mind. When Woody was making *Wonder Wheel* in 2016, he said a scene in which Kate Winslet and James Belushi eat silently in their kitchen was influenced by one in *Cries and Whispers* in which the husband and wife are not speaking. "You can see the same roots, but of course his is a masterpiece scene and mine has to serve a different purpose—it has to be in the 1950s with a different class of people. He was dealing with people in a Victorian house in the Swedish countryside and I was dealing with a brash couple in Coney Island, so the requirements are different. But you hear the footsteps in the back of your mind of the scenes you've seen."

It is, he adds, the singular artistic sense of how a scene will work best that makes for the best films. "*Grand Illusion* [the prisoner-of-war story of World War I French soldiers of differing rank and class who plot an escape, and an argument for the futility of national conflict] is a mature work, a great story told with the director not worried about pleasing his audience, and so he pleases them. [Jean] Renoir tells it beautifully but very simply by the pace and the detail within the frame and the detail within the performances. If Welles had shot that during the period of his life when he was making *Citizen Kane,* you might have seen very expressionistic or stylized shots such as high and low angles, and shadows. But Renoir, like Satyajit Ray or John Huston, just gives you very basic, bread-and-butter filmmaking. He uses common sense in telling the story: I want the audience to feel frightened here; I want them to feel sad or moved or tense. When I directed my first film, someone asked me if I was worried about being responsible for a million dollars. And I thought to myself, 'No. It doesn't mean anything that I've never directed a film. It's common sense. I know what I want to see up there.'"

He uses a jazz analogy: "For the clarinet player, it's irrelevant what the proper fingering is. New Orleans players, for example, will finger it however they want. Their attitude is, 'This is what I want to hear. It doesn't matter to me that you make a D with these fingers that way. I want to make my D this way because it sings out more, it's more squishy, because I'm playing by what I hear.' It's the same thing with the film. Someone standing next to me could have gone to film school and say, 'Well, you can't do this.' And I'd say, 'This is what I want the audience to laugh at and they're not going to laugh if I make the shot longer or shorter. Can't you see that it's not going to be funny if he says those two lines before the punch line?' Groucho [Marx] once told [Dick] Cavett, 'People just don't understand that an extra syllable totally destroys the joke.' Making a terrific film is of course very hard because you need a terrific piece of material. *Take the Money and Run* was a light, jokey script. But let's say I had the script of *Citizen Kane*. I would have made it so you were interested in that story and in those characters. It would never have had that superb flair or genius of Welles, but my common sense would have told me that, for instance, you want Welles and his wife to be tense at the breakfast table and you're not going to get that sense if you put the camera over their heads like Hitchcock does. You will get it if you can see her face. You either know or you don't."

Still, he is always on the lookout for something by another director that he is "happy to copy and steal and fob it off as influence. I've never had any compunction about that." While surfing TV channels he may see an interesting shot in a picture whose title he does not know ("the movie can be terrible, releasable only on cable") and think that it would be good if applied to something substantial. The Brazilian film *City of God,* directed by Fernando Meirelles and Kátia Lund, which takes place in the eponymous Rio de Janeiro slum and is dizzying in its camera work and visual bravura, was a pleasant surprise to him. The lens seems to look everywhere, darting quickly from one place to another. A flashback from the slum to the soccer field of the narrator's youth snaps the colors from vibrant darkness to sunbaked brown. The fast cuts and instability of the handheld camera give the action the sense of urgency and danger that is part of life in such surroundings.

"A *fabulous* film," he says. "It made me think I would like that herky-jerky graphic technique to make a relationship film, not a film about crime with those sort of exciting scenes, but a scene between a married couple that isn't the sedate way we usually see it. *Husbands and Wives* was in that direction, but I liked the extreme they went to." For those who found the handheld camera work in that film unsteadying, this would require a double dose of Dramamine.

Occasionally as Woody writes a scene he thinks to himself that it would look best if done in moving cuts, but those times are rare. As is his custom, when he stepped onto the set this morning, he had no thoughts of what he was going to do; however, the dining room immediately gave him ideas. When Rigby told him that Khondji was thinking of making the shot from a corner, Woody quickly said no, regardless of how pretty it would look. He admires how Khondji is able to make any shot gorgeous, and he often gives him opportunity for splendor, but there are times when just the physical beauty of a scene is not enough, and this is one. "The key thing here is to infuse the scene with some movement so it isn't just another around-the-table scene," he says after the camera is set behind the mother and father.

This is the scene that bookends and ties in by the rain to Rita coming to Abe's house with the bottle of scotch and their being in bed after Abe has been unable to perform:

JILL

(starting in the living room)

> When the hurricane hit in New Orleans, Abe went down there and stayed six weeks. He said the problems were overwhelming and the political red tape and corruption were just a scandal. He couldn't believe the stupidity and greed. (She is seated by now.)

DAD

It was a scandal for George Bush.

(Gets up and clears some of the plates as he says this.)

JILL

Well, Abe was in the thick of it trying to get something accomplished. Meanwhile his wife was falling in love with his best friend.

MOM

Uh-huh . . .

JILL

Abe really loved his wife. He met her on a trip to Machu Picchu to see the ruins—and they both experimented with mescaline. He's tried everything—hates drugs—actually he's very conservative in a kind of liberal way.

MOM

It seems he's really opened up to you. Everyone says he's not easy to get to know.

(Dad is back in his place and now she clears. The camera stays on Roy and Jill for the remainder of the scene.)

JILL

I haven't found that.

ROY

Hey, can we get off the topic of Abe Lucas? And I must say I'm not thrilled you invited him to come out with us tomorrow night without asking me first.

JILL

He needs to have some contact. Otherwise he sits in his room and broods. He's at a low point.

ROY

But you *can* see where it might make me jealous.

JILL

Well, that's silly.

ROY

Famous last words.

Woody hoped to do the scene as a master but there are too many problems with the action. A single shot will spend too much time on Jill and Roy without anything happening, so instead there will be three: one that starts on Jill in the living room and tracks back with her to reveal Roy, Mom, and Dad already seated as she comes to the dining table—first Dad (Ethan Phillips) and then Mom (Betsy Aidem) exit from the right; one that starts on Roy and then includes Jill as she enters from the right; and one of Mom. The first of the shots is ready. "Unfortunately," Woody laments, still wishing there was a way to get this in one go. He tells Jill to time her walk so that it ends with her saying, "He couldn't believe the stupidity and greed," which is the cue for her father to get up, and for her to take her seat on his line "It was a scandal for George Bush."

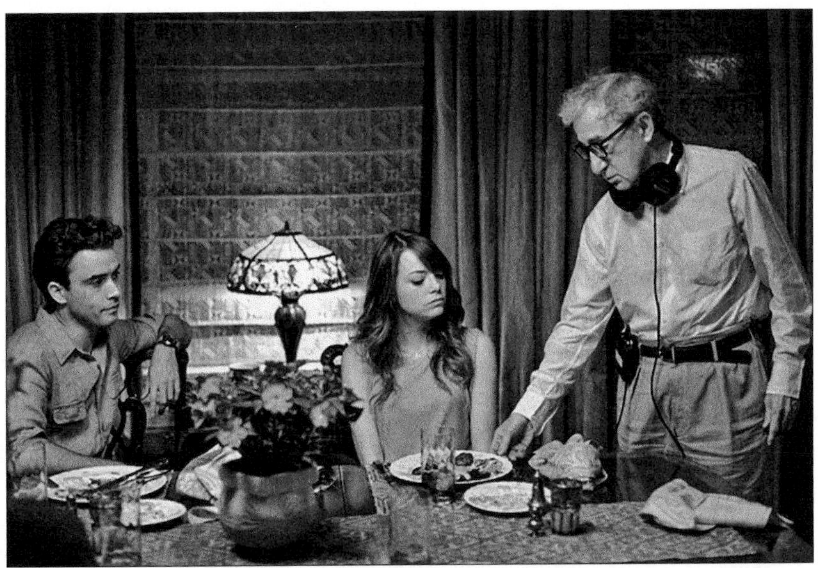

Working on the choreography of when first Jill's father and then her mother take plates from the table to provide movement in a long dinner scene.

Like all the actors except Stone and Phoenix, Blackley has only his sides. His entire knowledge of the film is what he has read in them and seen while on the set. He says he likes it that way "because especially with my character I have no real reason to know what's going on. My character's very paranoid with what's going on with Abe, so it kind of helps me not to know. You're only working off your interpretation. It takes you away from the place where you were before in a way that's great."

Woody tells him to play it not angry but "more 'enough already' " when talking of Abe, but he struggles with Roy's tone through a few takes because, he says afterward, "I found that tough to do. I was trying to infer the note and it didn't just seem to come across. There was a line about him saying, 'You're inviting him out a lot without asking me first,' and I was stuck with how to get that out without being too questioning."

Woody was patient and even joking, which kept Blackley at ease, especially after he completely flubbed a take: "I was waiting for a cue and Emma had switched the lines around, so I was waiting for a line that wasn't going to come. I panicked and just said my dialogue. Woody came over afterward and said, 'What, did you have a stroke?' It was great."

While the next scene is set up, Woody elaborates on the problems of shooting this one in a master. "I had to get Emma to the table early enough so we could see her father get up and take dishes to the kitchen, otherwise there would be an empty chair at the table. So if she gets there early enough for the rise, then she has a lot of stuff to say at the table, so you're hanging on her sitting on her chair for a long time. If I didn't have the problem of the father rising and leaving to keep the scene moving, she could have spoken slowly on the walk from the living room and come to the table significantly later, and when she sat I could have had much less hang time on her. But she had to get there early in order for the audience to see him leave. So it was annoying. I had to change the blocking in the middle and that meant two more shots in order to make it work."

The dinner conversation in scene 115 requires none of the choreography of 29, but it is a long conversation and it comes at a turning point for Jill. Slowly and against her best defenses, the idea that Abe is a murderer is seeping in. Rita's explanation of her "crackpot theory" of Abe's involvement in the murder when they meet in the bar in scene 101 (filmed the first day of shooting) kindled her misgivings, no matter how hard she tried to smother it:

RITA

I was just thinking about you.

JILL

Me?

RITA

Yes, it's ironic, we both have a crush on the same man.

JILL

Oh—well—I ran into Ellie Tanner, who said you had a theory about Abe.

RITA

Oh my god—don't get me started . . . you want some single-malt scotch?

JILL

(orders a glass of white wine)

She said your theory was very funny.

RITA

Yes, it's what's called a crackpot theory but it's not totally off the wall.

JILL

I'm all ears.

RITA

Promise you won't tell?

JILL

You have my word.

RITA

You've been following that judge that got poisoned in the papers?

JILL

Oh yes—Spangler—Spangler, isn't it?

RITA

(half-joking delivery)

Spangler, right. They don't know who did it—my theory is one live possibility—of the philosophy department—our mutual crush.

JILL

(joking back in kind)

Well, now this is intriguing.

RITA

Well, it's crazy and yet not.

JILL

But why Abe?

RITA

Once or twice when I was alone with Abe, let us say in a moment of post passionate intimacy—on the pillow—

JILL

Yes, I get the picture—you don't have to be too graphic—

RITA

We both said we had experienced many things in life and Abe said one thing he'd never experienced, but wondered what it would be like to actually kill.

JILL

Yes, but that sounds like random silly talk. Y'know how Abe gets especially when he's had a few.

RITA

He said it would be a stimulating artistic challenge to plan and carry out a perfect murder. This was before the judge was poisoned.

JILL

Yes, but everyone at one time or another fantasizes about some perfect crime.

RITA

When I talked with him about the immorality of taking someone's life he said there are no rules—we're all free to choose, to make our own moral decisions.

JILL

Okay, but Abe is a philosophy teacher—all this talk is so dramatic—that's his bread and butter.

RITA

Exactly what I thought. It's just Abe being Abe. But then my husband saw him leaving the campus very early the morning the judge was killed. Very early—six thirty. Now have you ever known Abe to get up at six thirty? He barely makes it to class on time.

JILL

So what's your theory? That Abe visited Lippitt Park, went up to a total stranger, and somehow dropped poison in his juice? He doesn't know the judge to get close enough to do that, plus he'd never do it. Abe's radical but he's not nuts.

RITA

Let me give you the final tidbit.

JILL

Yes?

RITA

A few weeks ago I lost my lab key. Now I never lose anything—but that key was missing from my bag and it opens all the lab doors to the rooms that keep the dangerous chemicals and the poisons.

JILL

I'm sorry, it's too crazy.

RITA

I started by saying it's a crackpot theory but you must admit the facts are fun and tantalizing.

The dinner conversation in 115 is lighthearted and serves as a counterpoint to what is going on beneath the surface with Abe and Jill. It will require many cuts in the editing room to pull the scene together; Woody wants five separate shots to vary its look.

The dinner table is set with—what else?—dessert (strawberry rhubarb pie), and Woody wants many candles on the table and around the room for the relaxed ambience that overlays the drama. While the last touches on the lighting are done for the first take, Woody says to Loquasto with mock seriousness, "This will be my greatest film."

"Or most complex," he replies. Then, looking at all the candles, "It is going to look like *Barry Lyndon*," referring to Stanley Kubrick's picture that relies heavily on candlelight.

In the sequence immediately leading to this dinner, Jill discovers Abe's annotated list of murderers in the copy of *Crime and Punishment* on the desk in his apartment, which enflames her suspicion. Still, she can't bring herself to believe he really is guilty. The scene is written in a way that puts Abe's delusional, narcissistic, sociopathic pathology on

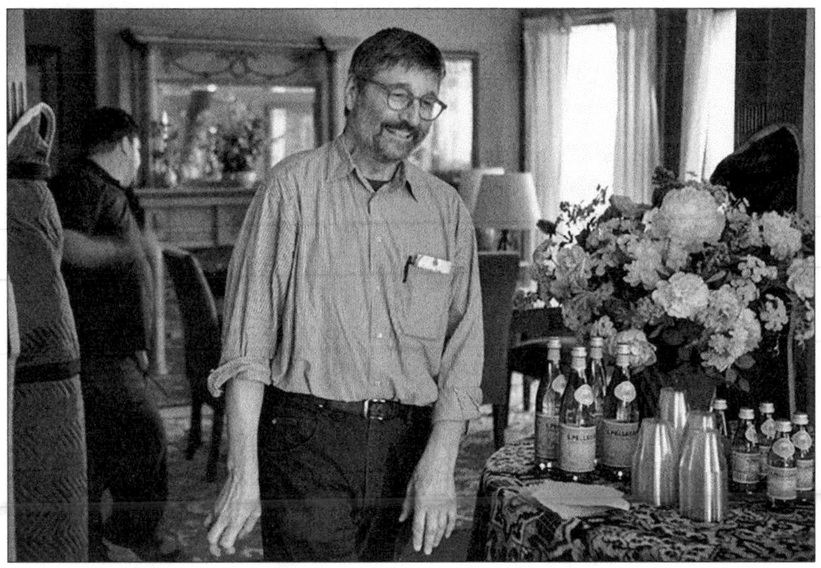

Production designer Santo Loquasto arranging the look of a dinner scene. He is known as the "Woody Whisperer" for his ability to anticipate what Allen needs, and because of their close understanding and appreciation, he is often sent to deliver bad news to him.

full display. He savors joining in the discussion of how a murder that he committed could have been carried out. It is Jill who eventually suggests exactly how the murder (scene 79) was accomplished.

ABE

Dinner is delicious. It's so nice of you to have me over.

MOM

Well, we're happy to—particularly since Jill always speaks so highly of you.

ABE

You okay, Jill?

JILL

Oh, yes—sure—

ABE

You've been so distracted lately.

MOM

She's trying too hard to finish a term paper on Marcel Proust.

ABE

Yes, well, Proust can be a chore. But well worth it. Have I been taking too much of your study time?

JILL

No, not at all.

DAD

Have you been following this Judge Spangler murder?

ABE

(looking at Jill)

Have we? We have a special attachment to Judge Spangler because we heard some people talking about him and what a rotten judge he was and we kind of rooted for him to have a coronary or get run over.

MOM

I've jogged in that park with Sally Kelly.

DAD

When I first heard it, I thought someone poisoned him at breakfast and it kicked in when he was in the park, but when I read it was cyanide in his drink, my theory unraveled.

JILL

You were right, Abe. It was cyanide. You guessed that early on.

DAD

That's what they said it was.

ABE

I always think cyanide. Cyanide's the cliché—because it's so quick and fatal. Arsenic takes time and is very painful. None of the herbicides are quick and dispositive.

MOM

I don't know anything about poisons.

ABE

I don't either. Just what I read.

MOM

Who'd want to kill a judge?

DAD

Only everybody—every person he ever ruled against.

JILL

But they questioned all the obvious suspects, including that woman—and they ruled them all out.

MOM

That's why they think it might be a sick prank or intended for someone else.

JILL

If it was a quick-acting poison the person had to slip it into his juice right there in the park.

DAD

That makes sense.

ABE

Not an easy thing to do with a total stranger in broad daylight in a public place.

MOM

Unless he was there with someone he knew and trusted—a friend.

DAD

A weekend—early in the morning—not many people around.

ABE

It had to be someone he knew.

JILL

I'm sure they checked out everyone who knew him.

DAD

It was a regular orange juice. They said he'd buy an orange juice there every weekend and he'd read the paper after jogging.

JILL

So that means if somebody knew his routine they could come by and drop the poison in his container.

ABE

He wouldn't be on a park bench reading the paper unless he was alone. It rules out a friend.

MOM

How do we know it was a man? Maybe it was a woman.

ABE

Good point.

DAD

Maybe he turned his back.

ABE

And someone appeared out of the blue and dropped something in his drink.

MOM

Aren't those takeout juices covered? With a straw?

JILL

Or someone could have bought a juice at Pascal's, poisoned it, and then switched it with the judge's.

ABE

I'm sure the police have run through every theory.

JILL

The judge is there with his O.J. Along comes someone with a container of juice with poison in it.

ABE

But who comes along? Someone that wants to kill the judge. Whoever it was had to get the judge to look away long enough to make the switch. He'd be taking a huge risk.

JILL

He sits down on the same bench. He doesn't even know the judge—he sits innocently—the judge reads his paper—he sips the juice, puts it down, opens the paper—he's blocked off just long enough . . .

MOM

If he didn't know the judge why does he want to go to all that trouble to kill him?

DAD

He'd have to be familiar with the judge's routine, the details.

JILL

He could have stalked him, this was obviously his Saturday morning ritual.

ABE

I like it. What she says makes sense. It's a well thought out concept. The judge reads the paper, blocks his eye-line, a quick switch. If someone sits next to you on a bench you often turn away.

DAD

I'm sure the police are way ahead of us on all of this.

Although Woody is rarely hesitant to ask an actor to change a reading, he has decided not to correct Phoenix, whose distinctive manner is an asset for Abe. "He's such an unusual actor," Woody says after the scene, "he's just got a great natural gift and he speaks in his own rhythm and has his own timing and his own nuances and idiosyncrasies. And the trick, I think, is to go with him rather than force him to do exactly what I hear. By going with him I mean just correct him when there's really a fatal error that hurts the story or looks terrible. But that doesn't happen. He's just a great natural actor. So it's different. These two kids I'm directing, Emma and Jamie, it's simple. I say, 'a little more of this,' 'a little less of this,' 'a little faster,' and they do it. They're in the realm vocally and emotionally that I recognize. But Joaquin is his own eccentric, unique character, and I think the way to get the most out of him, because he's been brilliant in so many pictures, is to go instinctively with what he wants to do and forget getting scenes that sound like I want them to sound."

It is a bit of irony that Woody has found Phoenix not in the least insistent on doing things his natural way. In general, he says, "I try not to direct the actors very much and let them be very free, and I thought this would please him, but it doesn't. He likes to be directed, so I'm trying to give him a certain amount of guidance without getting in the way of his personality."

The day ends with 73, a straightforward scene. Jill's parents and Roy are in the living room to celebrate her birthday. Presents are opened, then Jill goes into the next room to check her messages to see if Abe has remembered the day and is disappointed to find nothing from him. It is past six p.m. when Woody has what he wants.

"That's enough filmmaking for one day," he says. As he does every evening, he tears his sides into eight squares to be tossed, then hurries out to his waiting car for the drive to Newport.

5

"I'm starting to see some of the scenes I wrote look like I wanted them to look like."

One of the four most dramatic scenes of the film is an exchange between Jill and Abe (117). It is set up by 116, in which Jill runs into her friend April in the student lounge and finds that her growing suspicions about Abe are all too true.

JILL

How's your paper on Kant coming?

APRIL

Going well, actually, finally—thanks to Abe Lucas. I ran into him in the chem lab and he was so nice and gave me a list of people to read. So yeah, it's going well now.

JILL

Abe was in the chem lab?

APRIL

Yeah. It was so funny. I startled him after hours, I felt really bad. I came up and he freaked out, you would have thought he was stealing something.

JILL

What was he doing after hours?

APRIL

I think he was researching some book or essay that he's writing. I don't know. That's what he said.

JILL

About what?

APRIL

Chemistry, poison or something like that.

JILL

But isn't that all locked away in the lab?

APRIL

Well, yeah, but he had a key. I think he said he borrowed it from someone. (*beat*) You look so concerned.

The note in the script for where the confrontation is to be filmed is purposely vague: "After class the next day. Jill has taken Abe off to a private spot. Either a café or a secluded exterior place. Note: this could also be an empty schoolroom or empty parked car, whatever we can find." He will shoot it on the patio of Jill's parents' house, in part because he can knock off two scenes in one place.

The large stones that pave the patio are uneven, and dollying the camera on them will make the shot bouncy, so while the crew spend an hour setting inch-thick plywood atop two-by-fours to make a dance floor, Woody ambles across the street from the house and sits in a canvas-seated chair in the shade under an open plastic tent, a script in hand, to rewrite Abe's and Jill's several voice-overs that they will record on Saturday.

He is lost in the work and does not notice Manzie as she comes from behind his right side and gives him a kiss. He jumps in surprise, then smiles when he sees her.

Scene 117 is emotionally explosive as well as intricate. Jill, who has fallen in love with Abe only to find he is a monster, is bereft and furious but also rational. Her once fascinating philosopher has shown

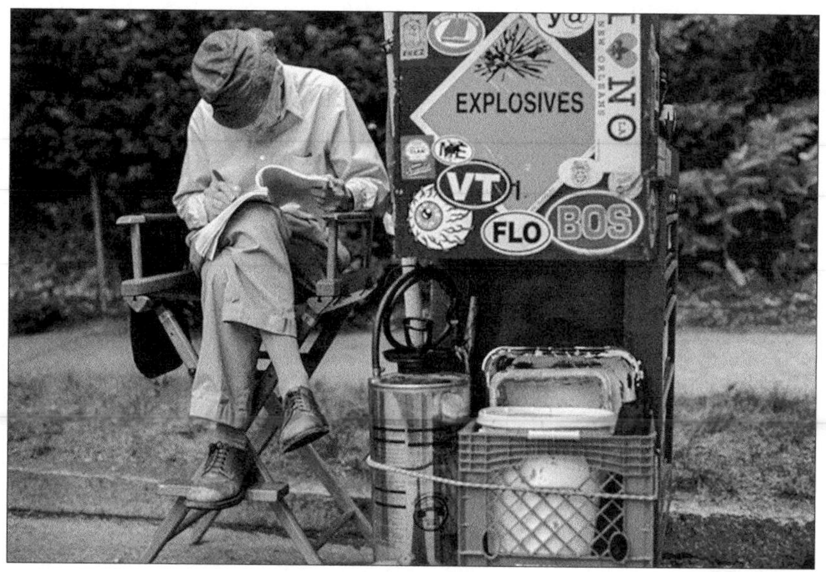

Woody rewriting . . .

and with Manzie.

himself to be conscienceless as well as crazy. The scene requires Abe to demonstrate that his intellectual justification for what he has done makes perfect sense—at least to him. It takes six minutes to play and will be shot from five different angles that alternately favor one character over the other, and one that is equal for both. It is a workout for the actors and begins with Jill coming from the kitchen door down the steps to the patio, where Abe is seated, clueless about what awaits him.

ABE

Why are you acting so strangely and what's on your mind that's so important that we have to go over it right now? Are you pregnant?

JILL

You killed Spangler, didn't you?

ABE

Why do you say that?

JILL

You went to the chem lab and stole cyanide. You didn't get an MRI—you went to Lippitt Park and somehow you slipped it into Spangler's juice.

ABE

Are you nuts?

JILL

Don't tap-dance. There was a note in your drawer—Spangler—the banality of evil—you decided he deserved to die. You stole Rita's key—April surprised you.

ABE

(pause)

I made the choice to help that woman. You figured it out the other night. You always had a first-rate intelligence.

JILL

I felt it. The whole business with the park bench and the newspaper blocking his vision—it all came to me and it felt right—but I didn't want to believe it.

ABE

I've always taught you to trust your instincts. Not everything is grasped by the intellect—if it feels right it often is. This was the meaningful act I was searching for.

JILL

Oh god, Abe—what a crazy thing to do.

ABE

I thought it was a very reasonable thing to do. She hoped he'd get cancer. But what the hell is hoping—hoping is bullshit—you have to act.

JILL

You can't just take it upon yourself to take someone's life.

ABE

You're talking rules but there are no god-given rules. Each choice has to be made on a case by case basis.

JILL

You can't believe in the morality of what you did.

ABE

Of course I do. I consider myself a moral man who's lived a moral life—who came to the aid of a woman suffering a great injustice.

JILL

And you're willing to go to prison for the rest of your life?

ABE

The police are not thinking of me and they never will because I'm a total stranger with no motive. This will be just another unsolved crime.

JILL

You know Rita Richards has a theory you did it.

ABE

Yes, she told me. We had a big laugh over it.

JILL

How could you do it, Abe?

ABE

Is the world a better place without this rotten judge?

JILL

Oh Abe—

ABE

I ask you—is the world a better place without Judge Spangler?

JILL

I'm so crushed. I'm lost. What do I do?

ABE

Meaning?

JILL

Meaning I care so much about you but I could never go on seeing you again—it's unforgivable.

ABE

Are you thinking of turning me in?

JILL

That's what I should do but I can't bring myself to do it. Christ, if I don't I'm an accessory to murder, but I don't want to see you go to prison. This is crazy.

ABE

I'm asking you to put your everyday assumptions aside and trust your experience of life. In order to really see the world we have to break with our familiar acceptance of it. The second I decided to take this action, my world changed. You noticed it. I suddenly found reason to live. Everything became brighter—I could make love—I could experience feelings for you—because to do the deed for this woman gave my life meaning.

JILL

Just leave here, Abe. I don't want to see you again. I won't say anything. I believe you actually thought you were doing something morally worthwhile even though it's reprehensible no matter what kind of bullshit romantic spin you use to distort all that postwar French coffeehouse rationalizing—it's murder and murder opens the door to more murder. I don't have the intellect to refute your arguments but you taught me to go with my instinct, and without having to think, I feel it's no good.

ABE

Okay—I'll finish off my last weeks here and go. You won't see me again.

JILL

Go where? What will happen to you?

ABE

I don't know. But away. Europe.

JILL

That will be hard for me, Abe. I really fell in love with you.

ABE

(goes to kiss her)

Jill—

JILL

Don't. It's over. I'll keep your awful secret.

ABE

I'm sorry I disappointed you. Someday you'll understand that as counterintuitive as it seems. I made a choice and I take full responsibility for it.

The video village is in the kitchen, from where Jill makes her entrance through the screen door to a small landing at the top of the stairs; the camera picks her up as she comes out and walks down to the patio, where Abe stands. Stone and Woody talk before the start of every take but the conversation is low-key so as not to interfere with the emotionally difficult work at hand. Eleven of the twelve takes of the five different shots of the scene are filmed all the way through and printed. The first three are good, but Woody is sure the actors can do better. Before take 4 he says to her, "Go all out, get angry, trust your instincts. Play it all angry and hurt." He assures her that he already has much good footage and that these takes will be cut up to assemble the scene. She follows the suggestion: her performance is sensational, by turns angry, hurt, confused, steely, and tearful—a young woman whose life has been turned upside down, and whose knowledge of human nature has suddenly and painfully deepened.

As she did the takes, Stone knew exactly what Woody wanted from her. "He was pretty concise," she says afterward. "I always see

Woody as very to the point and calm, no matter what the scene is. He doesn't seem to get wrapped up in the emotion. He knows what he wants and what he's looking for. He's always able to articulate it, and although he has a specific viewpoint he also wants the actors to feel free. So if ever there is a time you disagree with something, he's completely understanding. Probably because he's an actor, he understands if it doesn't feel natural, and if it doesn't make sense to you in the moment, then it's going to feel false. So he doesn't push for anything that doesn't feel natural.

"When it comes to a working relationship with someone creatively, there is some sort of intangible type of communication. I think I understand his rhythm and his writing and I think, I *think,* his intention. There's something I relate to in his storytelling and his dialogue and in the characters he's written."

He says of her, "Emma is an actress of limitless ability. Great range, great beauty, great intelligence. I really think she can do anything, and do it brilliantly. Her only drawback is, if you listen closely, she sounds like Sylvester Pussycat."

When Woody watches the monitor as a scene is filmed, he is feeling not the emotion of an audience member but rather that of a director who waits until he can say, "Oh, good, I've got it, and later when I'm editing it the screen is alive with emotion." Occasionally a take he thought was a lesser one turns out to be the best. "Sometimes," he says, "the one you like is overacted or it's not consistent with what's gone before it. But generally when they act it well you can see it in the moment. When I was doing *Blue Jasmine,* Cate Blanchett would do something and I'd say, 'That was great,' and it *was* later when I saw it."

The crew break for lunch after 117 is finished. All told, the scene required nearly an hour of repeated dialogue. Fortunately the afternoon shoot, scene 38, in which Jill's parents lightly question her about her budding friendship with Abe, also on the patio, is relatively easy, and even more so by comparison. Again Jill comes out the kitchen door and down the stairs to meet her parents, who are sitting on a garden sofa. Her first take is very natural. Woody tells her to do one a little lighter: "Natural but not lugubrious." She laughs.

Woody expects the take to go right away, but there are lighting adjustments to make. Stone is waiting by the door. He kids her about the paleness of her legs.

"It is like trying to light a ghost," she tells him.

"My kitchen isn't as white," Woody replies. "Should we spray some beige on you?"

"I'm already beige," she says, pointing to her costume of standard Allen taupe, tan, or beige.

Woody is annoyed by the delay. "I'm going to go and kick some ass," he announces as he gets out of his chair and sticks his head out the door. "Are we ready?" he calls out into the yard; this is his version of kicking ass. Not yet. Besides the technical delays, nearly every take is being polluted with extraneous sounds—airplanes three times (after one interruption he says, "That was very good. This time, without the plane"); a siren that revs up in the middle of the shot; people talking loudly on the street; a lawnmower; shouting, laughing children in a neighboring yard.

At last, quiet. Jill prepares to make her entrance.

"Fast and energetic," Woody says.

There is a school of thought that holds that the director has to fall in love with his leading lady through the camera so the audience will as well. Woody's version of this, where it is important to establish the allure or character of the actress in her first appearance on the screen, is to make sure he's sold her to the audience in the way he imagined her. Barbara Hershey in *Hannah and Her Sisters* is a good example. First there is a card on an otherwise black screen that reads, "God, she's beautiful," and in the smiling close-up of her face she is so stunning you want to reach for the thesaurus to find a more hyperbolic word than "beautiful," the very thing Woody aimed for: "You have to know why guys are attracted to her." He will take as much time as necessary to get exactly the look he wants—he spent a lot of it to be sure the audience would immediately understand why Jason Biggs would be so obsessed with Christina Ricci in *Anything Else,* why he would put up with her sleeping around and living with her neurotic mother. The first time the audience sees her—getting out of a taxi in the rain and then draped on a living room chair wearing a satin robe, her legs bare to nearly her waist—it is completely evident that, as Woody says, "Christina had a kind of compelling, pretty, sexy quality, and she could get a guy hung up on her."

To get the same effect with Scarlett Johansson in *Match Point* he shot the scene in which she meets Jonathan Rhys Meyers at the Ping-Pong table three separate times so as to immediately establish her beauty and dangerous sexuality, which are central to the story. "I changed her hair," Woody says, "I changed her costume [she appears in a low-cut, tight white dress], I changed the way I shot it; the cameraman [Remi Adefarasin] and I talked about it. It was very important for me to present the vision of her as I felt her in that character." But in *Scoop,* the film he made with her the following year, she plays what he calls "a semi-nerd," and he devoted no attention to making her sexy. "What little attention I devoted was so she would look like a potentially attractive college kid."

He was "conflicted" over what to do for Emma Stone's initial appearance in *Magic*. Sophie is dressed in plain clothes when she and her mother are introduced, but among the many reveals in this film about the difference between appearance and reality is how gorgeous she turns out to be when dressed for the ball toward the end of the movie, in the same way that Eliza Doolittle is breathtaking at the ball in *Pygmalion* and *My Fair Lady*. (The latter film, he says, was an influence on this one.) He struggled through editing to get it just right but was not satisfied. "I blew that a little bit. I wanted her to have a great entrance, but I also felt she shouldn't look too good, she should look like a bedraggled little thing so later when she comes to the ball she can become more spectacular looking. That's why I had Brice [the scion of the wealthy family who is so infatuated by Sophie, played by Hamish Linklater] buy her all those dresses. But then I was caught in the middle because I wanted her to have a good entrance, but I didn't want her [*laughs*] to look great. I had the same problem with Penelope Cruz in *Vicky Cristina.* The first time you see her is when Javier Bardem brings her home from the hospital. I wanted her to look spectacular, but also like she had just tried to commit suicide. It's a hard balance to get. Now, I think Emma does look very cute when she comes on the screen. But I got neither fish nor fowl with her. I didn't get, you know, a kind of mudlark entrance or a spectacular entrance. This was hard with Emma, who is startlingly beautiful in a totally unique way. Her face is beyond beautiful, by which I mean her face is so damn interesting. She projects wit and intelligence plus those great features. I was coasting on costumes and Emma's natural beauty and appeal. But I didn't handle it well."

An example of when the first shot is intended not to make the actress desirable but rather to show her personality is when we first see Diane Keaton in *Sleeper.* In this case, Woody wanted to present her character as someone interested only in her looks and the easy life brought to her by her robot valet, and so when she opens the door we see her in a white caftan and towel around her freshly washed hair, her face covered in a lime mudpack save for circles around her eyes and mouth; vaudevillian greenface rather than blackface.

That is not his intent here. Jill is seen first among the vignettes in scene 1, walking on the campus as her voice-over plays, a back-

The audience's first view of Jill. Woody makes sure that his leading ladies are introduced in a way that flatters as well as establishes the character.

pack strapped on and a computer in hand: a serious and attractive student. Then in scene 5 we see her closely at home, in a twenty-eight-second shot talking with her parents, wearing shorts and a light blouse: an intelligent, idealistic college senior. Woody says before the shot, "It's not only beauty but her face says something—it's different in its beauty and I want to show it."

Midway through filming, Woody remains vaguely upbeat. "After the first traumatic few days, which are always terrible, I'm starting to see some of the scenes I wrote look like I wanted them to look like," he says one afternoon while the crew ready the next shot. For him, this is almost satisfaction. "And I like the people. Joaquin is a very nice person to work with and Emma is a delight, plus I've known her from the last picture. I always enjoy working with people more than once, provided they are right for the role. I've worked with great actors who have said, 'You never worked with me again.' But that was only because there was never a role they were right for."

He is waiting to film scenes 95 and 103, which take place some days apart in the same spot by a lake; 95 is the start of the arc of Jill's discovery of Abe's guilt. Woody had originally scouted this location not for the lake but for a barn that houses a restaurant with a large floor for line dancing where there could be a party scene, but he found the barn too big and rewrote it as the smaller party in the home of the student's parents who have just bought the de Kooning. Although the barn did not work for him, he liked the look of the lake with its decaying wooden dock and the shoreline of tall trees and heavy foliage as another place to have lovers not in bed after sex. The day is an example of how he is instantly willing to make a change to something he has given the various department heads to carry out as written in the script.

"I could visualize the scene playing there," he explained after making the technical scout shortly before filming began. "If you're the author you can see things with more meaning, more open-mindedness than people who are working on something. Whether they're the actors with the script or the art department or Juliet Taylor, they feel obliged to give you what you asked for and they want to help you realize it. But sometimes when we're casting Juliet will come in and I'll say, 'Why couldn't *this* person play the doctor and Wally Shawn play Rocky Marciano?' I believe in a second that this doctor or this college professor is right and she wouldn't have thought that, because she was trying to give me something that appears in the script. The same with Santo. Many times over the years Santo has had helpful opinions. He'll say, 'Why can't you do that scene in an amusement park?' I do that all the time and now *he* does that. The same with the actors. The actors want to give you what you wrote, and I always say, '*Don't* give me what I wrote. You can improvise, make up your own words,' and they often are reluctant to do that."

An eight-foot-tall lifeguard chair constructed of chipped, faded hospital green iron pipes rises above the ground by the path to the crumbling dock. The wooden seat is weathered; the entirety is in disrepair, a relic of a more useful past when children frolicked in the water. Khondji and Woody wonder whether to move it. Loquasto, astonished, says, "No, it's cemented in. Besides, it looks romantic." Woody, who is generally in sync with Loquasto, turns and cocks his head, eyeing him quizzically. "Romantic," he repeats firmly.

"I thought, 'He can't be serious,'" Loquasto says later. "For me, the whole point was that dilapidated lifeguard chair! When Abe stands on the wharf, it's all beautiful."

But Woody is adamant and Loquasto, though he has grown more forceful with Woody over the years, knows that this discussion is over. "There's that moment you think, 'We'll take out the saw and cut it down,'" he continues. But that won't be necessary. Shots can be made around it.

What went unnoticed when scouting the location and making the scene changes was how loud the traffic is on Interstate 95, just beyond the trees across the lake, perhaps half a mile away. Now that quiet is needed, the steady hum is all too noticeable. This creates a problem for soundman David Schwartz to minimize the noise while capturing the dialogue, but whatever cannot be compensated for can be eliminated almost entirely during the mix with routine if complicated technology. He asks Woody if it is okay to turn up the mikes on Abe and Jill. Woody, unfazed by the ambient noise, says sure: "We can drop a piece of music in there." He had to deal with far worse in the making of *Magic;* the seventeen-year cicadas in the French countryside, cacophonous in virtually every outdoor scene, were erased during the mix.

Abe has a voice-over in 95 and Jill in 103. Woody and Khondji walk around to decide how to stage them differently. The decrepit low wooden dock extends fifteen yards into the water, one side diving into it where it has collapsed at the end. The characters will be nicely separated if one is at the end of the dock, staring off while the voice-over plays.

"My question to you is," Woody says, "does it bother you that in the first shot we see her on the dock and in the second we see him?" After more discussion he says, "There is a voice-over, so we have to have something in the shot to hold the attention and not repeat." He decides to save the dock for Abe. Jill will walk a few feet from the blanket they are on to between two trees, and take a sweater from her bag by them to give distance for her voice-over. A discussion of whether it is possible to do the scene as a master quickly ends when Woody says, "It's pointless to do much of this scene at this width, we'll never use it." There will have to be four shots. Their postcoital talk turns to her saying lightly, "Today for one comic moment I thought it would be ironic if you had poisoned Judge Spangler." In talking about Spangler's murder, Abe says, "If I had to eliminate someone I'd use a gun or run him over. Cyanide's a whole other deal." Jill, puzzled, says that cyanide has not been mentioned in any of the reports. Abe covers by saying he just assumed it, and Jill, her suspicion mollified, goes back to speculating: "It had to be someone who knew him—someone he felt comfortable enough with to get close to him to poison his coffee. No, it was orange juice."

As they sit romantically together, Abe says in a bemused but chilling voice-over: "I enjoyed the whole conversation. It was like sitting at a tense poker table holding a full house and chatting innocently, confident I had the winning hand but getting a thrill out of the chance I could be beaten with a straight flush or four of a kind."

The scene concludes with her telling Abe that her feelings for him have led to an argument with Roy, who will break up with her in the next scene.

ABE

Just what I didn't want to do—come between you and Roy.

JILL

You tried to discourage it but it happened so now here we are making love.

ABE

I must say you were special from that first day.

JILL

You read my paper and were attracted to my mind. That was such a turn-on.

ABE

Your mind and your eyes.

JILL

And I set my sights on you right off.

ABE

Aha—now the truth comes out.

JILL

I remember the day you started to change—it was exactly one day after we overheard the Judge Spangler story in that diner—as if overhearing the terrible injustice that poor woman was going through motivated you to shape up and maybe see how lucky you were.

• • •

As the scenes are shot, and again when he watches dailies, Woody is editing the film in his head: "I'm thinking to myself, 'I've got it, because I can use the close-up from this take and the third line from this take and the fifth line from this take and when he's just coming on and saying, "Hello, George" I can pull those two lines from the sound track of the third take and put them in the fifth, so that take is good except for those first two words that I'll steal from another take.'" When he knows he has all the bits in place he can move to the next scene.

Scene 103 has a completely different mood. Jill, recently having heard Rita's "crackpot theory" about Abe in the bar, now has to fight her new suspicion, as the audience hears in her voice-over:

> Why was I so goddamned rattled by Rita's outrageous theory? My psychology teacher would say Abe disappointed her romantically and so she cast him in the role of a mad killer. I knew Abe had a very emotional reaction to the woman's plight and what was he doing out at six thirty on a Saturday morning? My thoughts were very mixed up and uneasy and more devastating revelations were to come but for the moment I lapsed into complete denial and told myself this was too absurd to even contemplate. I must not get carried away with my usual overactive imagination, but a dark cloud had crossed the moon, resist it as I did.

The shot begins on Abe, then dollies back to reveal Jill in the left foreground, leaning against a tree. After the voice-over, Abe comes to her. Below the camera's frame, a black cloth covers her body to prevent reflections off her clothes. There follow a pair of mirror over-the-shoulder medium close-ups.

Once the technical details have been set, the shots go quickly. Of more importance to Woody is the depth Stone is giving Jill in all her scenes. The script was written with the idea that Abe would overwhelmingly be the most compelling character and that Jill would be more of a foil, but that is not what is happening. Stone has brought unanticipated nuance to each of Jill's scenes.

"Emma is even better than I expected," he says after the last take, with obvious pleasure. "I don't say this just because it's my movie or I like her, I mean this in the most objective way. She's exceeded my expectations. I knew she'd be *good.* Joaquin is older than her, he's been around for years, he's done dramatic things, and I expected him—like I expected Cate Blanchett or Marion Cotillard—to be a kind of noncommercial genius, because I think that's what he is. Emma has been around a very short time and I figured, 'Well, she's a very good actress,' and I worked with her in one movie but I haven't seen her in a dozen movies where she's played drama. She's played comedy, and I'm thinking, 'She'll be a pretty little college girl and I know she'll do this part well; she's perfect casting for it.' I wasn't prepared for *how* good she is. She's surprised me. And I think that some of the axis of the story is going to shift because she's so strong. I thought that nobody would be able to stay with Joaquin. But she's a twenty-five-year-old kid who's just now really beginning to emerge. She's matching him all the way in terms of emotional impact and strength and effectiveness on the screen. I feel that although a lot of the focus will naturally be on Joaquin, the audience will go equally to her and it will be not a two-hander between a forty-year-old experienced great master actor and an upcoming star, it's going to be a two-hander between two very strong people."

"Being in *Magic,*" Stone said a few days later, "changed the trajectory of what I wanted to do with my life, with work, because I loved to watch comedies growing up and I loved *Saturday Night Live.* I think when I saw *Annie Hall* and subsequent films of Woody's I realized there was a way to marry all of these concepts into one, and I was hooked. I never thought I would get to work with the actual person who made me feel that way or to play two characters written by him. Being in the film changed my life because it felt like a combination of an actual dream come true, and it happened when I was young—I know a lot of actors who waited thirty years to get a call.

Colin [Firth] said he waited all that time to ever hear from Woody." What most appealed to her about doing this film, she continued, "is simply the unique experience. Everyone is here for just one reason, and it's Woody." She paused. "And the paycheck," she added with a huge laugh. "Having that as a kind of anchor in a storm is hugely comforting and satisfying. You know that you're within the confines of a Woody Allen movie, you're in a world he created playing a person that he created, and you trust this man who's done forty-five movies."

"All these pretty, funny, talented women," Woody says of the actresses in his films, and how rarely he has easygoing banter with them. "I must have done at least five movies with Judy Davis by now [*Alice, Husbands and Wives, Deconstructing Harry, Celebrity,* and *To Rome with Love*]. I'm not saying that maybe she doesn't do this to somebody else, but she doesn't seem to me ever to invite chitchat. Cate Blanchett, I wouldn't have dared; I was intimidated by Cate. I've been intimidated by many of the people I've worked with over the years because they're not just movie stars, they're great actors and amazing women: Geraldine Page, Maureen Stapleton, Keaton, Gena Rowlands, Judy Davis, Marion Cotillard, Scarlett Johansson, Cate Blanchett, Penelope Cruz, Naomi Watts, Emma, Eileen Atkins, and, briefly, Meryl Streep, just to name some. One after the other they keep coming in."

Scene 37, the party at the home of Jill's friend April, a student whose parents have just purchased a large de Kooning painting, will take two nights to film. It is the first of the four most dramatic scenes in the film. It begins calmly enough—Jill has persuaded Abe to come to the party with Roy and her in the hope of drawing him out of his melancholy—but events build until we see just how irrational Abe is. This scene, originally meant to be at the barn by the lake where Abe and Jill have their romantic interlude, has changed in many ways. Woody expanded April's part because he was so impressed by Sophie von Haselberg in her audition.

"She's ready to do big stuff. She's one of those actresses I feel that anything she's right for in a film of mine, I would call her in a minute. And I knew that fifteen seconds after she came in and so did Juliet. She's great, she's service with a smile, she gets it, she can do it, she can execute."

The scene is changed in other ways than the character. In the first versions of the script, there were the barn party, the house party, and two car process shots of Abe, Jill, and Roy driving to and from the house. Now rather than four scenes, everything takes place in one location; Woody, echoing Gordon Willis's view of shots that do nothing to advance the story, says that the car scenes were "shoe leather." Although he made the changes to benefit the flow of the action rather than for economy, he saved hundreds of thousands of dollars rolling four scenes into one and needing only 50 extras rather than the 150 or 200 who would have been required to fill the barn properly.

When Woody arrives at the house at dusk—filming will not commence until after nine p.m., when night has completely fallen—he wanders around the large open room with a fireplace that separates the living and dining areas, checking on how the set is dressed. The sofa on which Jill and Abe will sit is flush against a wall. Woody wants it pulled out. A long, narrow table is placed between the sofa and the wall and a lamp placed on each of the side tables so that light will get behind the sofa and improve the overall ambience.

"These things are always a problem," he says. "It usually doesn't look good to photograph flat against the wall. We could have them standing up, but that doesn't seem quite as natural. Actually," he adds, turning his head from side to side, "the room looks better. Tonight I'm just trying to get rid of the introductory material and tomorrow we'll get into the meat of it. But I don't really know what I'm going to do. I see the beginning as the shot of the de Kooning and pulling back and having the conversation. This is the kind of scene—it is so annoying—that needs a lot of coverage. You want to cut to this person, cut to that person to build up the tension, which means long hours, a lot of setups. I want to make the thrust that way [from right to left, the action covering 270 degrees in two shots] so I can cut into this room where the painting hangs."

The establishing shot will show guests in the indoor swimming pool that is just off the living room and students standing and smoking marijuana. Helen Robin comes over to Woody.

"Do you want drugs to be visible?" she asks.

He thinks a moment. "Yes."

"Just to remind you that you are guaranteed an R rating if they are visible."

"We'll have one anyway, though, won't we?"

"Probably."

Woody shrugs and goes back to inspecting the set. (The film receives an R rating.)

Jill leaves Roy at the end of the establishing shot, and the camera tracks her thirty feet to where Abe is sitting on the couch.

JILL

Are you having one of your morbid insights about the transient futility of human joy?

ABE

Is my face that grim?

JILL

Or are you checking out all the students and feeling sad for them because they don't realize yet how empty life is?

ABE

If you must know I was clocking the girls thinking not long ago I would have regarded this group as a bonanza of hot little rosebuds yearning to be gathered while I may.

JILL

And now?

ABE

Now, I couldn't handle one in bed without embarrassing myself.

ROY

(comes over)

Anyone like another drink?

ABE

Sure. To quote the great Tennessee Williams, I drink 'til I hear that click in my brain.

SANDY

(coming over)

Have you seen the de Kooning? April's parents bought it last month.

The second night of shooting the party is devoted to the heart of the scene. It also is family and friends' night on the set. Manzie is spending her last hours before going to camp the next morning, while Bechet has just come after several weeks at camp. Ron Chez and his longtime partner, Athena Marks, have arrived for a week; he will have a cameo as a professor. He also had a large part in a big and expensive scene in a Gypsy camp in *Magic*, but no matter how Woody tried to make it advance the story during editing, it did not and was cut. Even someone who fronts the money can end up on the editing room floor if his scene does not propel the story. And Pedro Chomnalez and Maria Herrera, Argentinian friends of Woody and Soon-Yi who live much of the year in New York, are staying with them for the weekend. Chomnalez, a financier who wants Woody to make a film in Buenos Aires, played a reporter in *Magic*.

The camera starts on the five-foot-tall de Kooning (a copy, meaning the production company has to pay a smaller royalty, plus give the phony to the estate after filming), then pulls back to reveal Jill, Abe, Roy, April, Danny, Mark, Jane, and five others without lines. Jill, rather awestruck, says that she has never seen a de Kooning in a private house. April answers that her parents have just started to collect—a Kitaj, a Warhol—and got this at auction.

The scene pivots here toward the start of the drama.

JANE

Aren't they afraid of being robbed?

APRIL

The house is all armed but we were broken into once—they got jewelry.

Woody tells April to respond immediately after she is asked if her parents are afraid of being robbed. "No air space," he says, and adds that she must say it loudly because there will be music playing and she needs to be heard above the din. "Fight it over the noise of the reaction to the collection," he adds. After a take he says to other actors, "You need to be loud and energetic. Get into the scene, don't just say the lines. But have a little pity on April—she needs to get above you." And to April after another take, "You have to bulldoze it in. No matter how you have to do it, do it." She does it.

April's boyfriend says she should show them what her father has hidden. "No," she says, so he goes to a cabinet and pulls out a revolver. There is nervous oohing and ahhing. After a bit of talk about the gun, April says her father shoots it in the woods. Her boyfriend says he loves the part in *War and Peace* where they play Russian roulette. After a student asks, "What's that?" he explains as he puts a bullet in a chamber and spins it. After some more chatter, Abe takes the gun, spins the chamber again, and puts the muzzle to his head. Immediately there are cries of "Be careful!" and "Don't do it!"

(Abe squeezes the trigger—a deadly silence falls on the room—everyone is stunned and scared. The click of the hammer is heard but no gunshot.)

JILL

What the hell are you doing, Abe?

ABE

The odds were in my favor.

JILL

Do you think that's funny?

MARK

Is the high worth the risk? Did you feel a high?

ABE

Not at five to one.

JILL

This is not amusing.

ABE

Here.

He spins the chamber amidst protests from everyone, puts the gun to his head, and squeezes off three clicks.

ABE (Cont'd.)

Here—fifty-fifty odds.

(More protest and shock follow. The gun is snatched away.)

ROY

Are you crazy?

ABE

What's the bottom line?

JILL

(angry and upset)

You blow your brains out. Is that what you're trying to do?

MARK

If you want to kill yourself, go to the chem lab and swallow the cyanide—that way you won't get blood on her parents' rug.

(More yelling)

ABE

Life is risk. If you're going to gamble, you want to gamble for high stakes. At this moment I feel alive—you mentioned Pierre in *War and Peace*—did you read Graham Greene's autobiography? This is an existential lesson better than in the textbooks.

JILL

You're drunk. It's time to go home. You're drinking too much, Abe.

ABE

Fifty-fifty odds is better than most people get in life.

There are eleven people around the table near the painting. Three more setups are needed to record them all. Between the takes of Abe pulling the trigger, Woody says to the group: "You're terrified by the first pull and really upset by the second [Abe's three pulls]. You've never seen a gun before and when he does the first you are shocked and react. Then when he does three, this is not a shenanigan but truly upsetting. You should be calling out, 'That's dangerous,' 'Put it back,' 'I

Woody instructing the students at the party how to react to Abe taking a revolver and playing Russian roulette. Sophie von Haselberg, whose audition he liked so much that he enlarged her part, is fourth from left.

hate guns.' It should all be a negative feeling. When he does it the first time there is some talk, but the second should be really unpleasant."

The camera rolls again, but the voices of the group are still too tame. "You guys are not getting upset enough," Woody tells them. "When he does the one you need to be upset. It's like you're saving it for when you know he will do three, but you don't know that when he does the one."

During the evening word arrives that Morgan Neville, Woody's assistant film editor in New York, has noticed that scenes in the bathroom and another on the stairs in Abe's house are slightly out of focus, because one of the Panavision lenses is out of kilter. The problem is so slight that Khondji had not seen this on the large TV he uses to screen dailies; Woody had caught it when he watched on his own but it did not bother him. The question, however, is not how it looks on a TV or iPad but how it will look on a fifty-foot screen. Khondji's first thought is that the lab can fix it, but he will watch the scenes again over the weekend. Woody, though he appreciates the close attention paid, is almost completely unconcerned. "If you're creative you don't care," he says. "Those things just don't matter very often. But for technical people they are very important."

More important to him at this moment is getting the shots he wants. At one a.m., the end of the night is in sight. "One more and we can check the gate," Woody says. "Get my Ambien ready." (The gate is the place in a camera where film is exposed to light. If a mote of dust or a strand of hair falls in, it will scratch the negative.)

Loquasto, sitting in the chair behind him says, "I thought you had already taken it."

"This is positively the last take," Woody announces, but a gel that provides tone to the light slips off a fixture above the actors and dangles into the frame. The next is good; Woody and Letty slip out the back door, leaving Khondji and Rigby to make the insert of the boyfriend taking the gun from the cabinet.

6

"No air space at all! It's dead! You can't do it! You've gotta keep it going!"

After a weekend to sleep off two long night shoots, the fifth week begins with scene 69: Abe takes cyanide from the locked chemistry lab storage room, entering with the master key that he surreptitiously took from Rita's purse during a visit to his apartment for a tryst. The partygoer in scene 37 who yelled at Abe, "If you want to kill yourself, go to the chem lab and swallow the cyanide," neatly identified where Abe can find the poison to kill the judge. He has come after class hours believing he will not be noticed and is startled by April coming into the room.

The location is the chemistry lab at Salve Regina University. The school had removed much of the scientific equipment, but Woody told Loquasto to put some back, though not too much. "Don't get all Jekyll and Hyde on me," he warned. A chartreuse wall that will be seen in the shot has been painted a mossy green because Khondji wants it to look like a shadow. Abe enters the lab from the hallway; while he is inside, April will be seen walking down it toward the door. A glass-encased bulletin board on the wall near the door will be in the shot, and even though its contents will almost certainly not be visible, Loquasto and his crew have put up wonderfully nonsensical academic announcements on Braylin College stationery. One heralds that on July 10, 2014, at noon, the Department of Sociology Colloquium Series will feature Professor H. Carlyle Vento of the Universidade Umberto delivering the talk "Nihilism and Protostasis in the Best of All Possible Worlds." Another lists the Summer 2014 colloquia for the Department of Medieval Studies. Among the topics: Legerdemain and Pluranatural Behavior in Charlemagne's Court; Preening and Prancer: The Chamber Aesthetic in Statecraft; Change Is Good: Specie and Coinage as Royal Portraiture; and Merovingian Microbiae: From Germs to Germans.

Woody and Khondji work out the camera moves to show Abe unlock and enter the small storeroom in the lab, pull on rubber gloves, find the cyanide, and pour a small amount into an empty spice bottle he has brought. Just as he is about to pocket it, April enters the lab and is surprised to see him in the storeroom.

APRIL

Professor Lucas, what are you doing here? It's April.

(Caught off guard, Abe searches for a response.)

ABE

I'm doing research for a book I'm working on.

APRIL

I'm glad you're wearing gloves because a lot of those poisons are very dangerous.

ABE

Oh, yes, I know.

APRIL

How did you get in here? This room is always locked.

ABE

I borrowed a key.

APRIL

Say, while I've got you here—can I ask you a question about the paper I'm writing on Kant?

ABE

Sure. Can we talk as we walk?

(Abe pockets the spice bottle with the poison when April turns her back on him.)

APRIL

(as they walk toward the door)

So my paper's due Friday and I'm having real trouble with Kant's [*Lectures on*] *Ethics.*

Short as the scene is, it is complicated to film. There is a yellow CAUTION sticker on the door to the storeroom that Woody wants in the frame, and he and Khondji discuss whether to have it in the first or second shot as well as how it might be cut in editing. The second shot has the camera behind the door to the lab itself, which picks up Abe and follows him as he turns left and opens the storeroom door. The third is from Abe's back so the door is plainly seen, then a fourth from inside the storeroom as we see him through the rectangular window in the door. Once inside the storeroom, they discuss how he will look around before finding the cyanide and how to light him from above. Khondji asks if there should be a shot of April at the door to the storeroom as long as it is lit. Woody says to make the shot first of Abe and then see. (They do a shot of her.) For Abe looking for the poison, Khondji suggests a wide shot, but Woody answers, "Not that wide. We need a usable two-shot of April and Abe between the shelves of the chemicals." The scene ends with April walking out followed by Abe. Woody tells the actors to time their dialogue so that it ends in the storeroom.

He has reluctantly finished the Bob Hope biography, but Hope is still on his mind. While waiting in the hall outside the lab for the next setup, he talks about being in the running to be a writer for Hope when he was seventeen. In 1952 he was working after school for David Alber, a public relations man who placed one-liners and bon mots in newspaper celebrity columns for his clients. Alber thought Woody was his best writer, and he sent a letter of recommendation to James L. Saphier, Hope's agent-manager, with a selection of Woody's jokes that he thought matched Hope's style. (Hope worked from his home in the San Fernando Valley suburb of Toluca Lake, California.)

"These are very good jokes," Saphier wrote back. But "we're not doing anything here now. Maybe in the fall there could be something."

"Well, that was all I had to hear," Woody says, laughing all through this tale. "You would have thought I had hit the lottery for Mega Millions. There was no living with me. I thought I was going to be living in Toluca Lake." A year or so later, Woody, now working in the NBC Writers Development Program, was sent to Los Angeles to team with Danny Simon, Neil Simon's older brother. (Woody has said on several occasions, "Everything I learned about comedy writing I learned from Danny Simon.") The program set up a meeting with Saphier, who told Woody to come to a rehearsal for one of Hope's TV specials, but nothing came from it. "I don't know how or why," he says. "For all I know he finished that special and flew to Saigon the next hour."

He returned to New York and before long was writing for Sid Caesar, among many others. A few years later he turned to performing stand-up and got his break in the movies by being hired to write the script for *What's New Pussycat?,* leaving the question of what might have happened to his career had Hope offered him a job. He thinks he might have made the jump to writing and directing his own films, but says, "I don't know if I would have made the jump to being a comic if I hadn't seen Mort Sahl. If Lester Colodny [the head of the NBC Writers Development Program] had not sent me to the Blue Angel to see him, I'm not sure I would have ever become a comic."

Sahl was a tremendous influence on Woody. His style and the content of his act were revolutionary. "People talked about him the way musicians talked about Charlie Parker. He fused a way of performing that doesn't seem like performing. He was a vibrant young intellectual talking to you in a funny way; his jokes were so skillfully told. He was such a funny guy but a different kind of funny. He wasn't like comedians who came before." Nearing ninety, Sahl still performs, and Woody finds that "his greatness sustains." So much so that over the past few years, he has talked several times of being inspired to go back onstage himself.

"I keep telling people, 'Luck, luck, luck,' and they say, 'Well, you're very modest, you're talented, it's not luck,' but such a *huge* element of it *is* luck. If Danny Simon had seen my jokes and had brushed me off with, 'Yeah, they're good and I'll call you,' I don't know what would have happened. But the exact opposite happened. He said, 'These are great. You have a big future. I want to work with you.' It was such a boost to me."

At the start of his career, Woody's writing strictly favored the male comic lead. Among the samples of Woody's work that Alber sent Saphier was a sketch for Hope and Kathryn Grayson that was admired for the lines given to Hope but rejected, Woody recalls, because "they said, "There's just not enough for Kathryn Grayson.' I think it was a cowboy sketch in a barroom. But I gave nearly everything to Hope. In my early movies, I never wrote anything for the women. It was all me, and if I was working with a strong woman like Louise [Lasser, his second wife] or Keaton, they would make something happen, but I never helped."

His love affair with Keaton in the late 1960s and early 1970s changed how he writes for women. They lived together for a couple of years and remain the closest of friends.

"I played the jokes like Hope—it was always the guy looking at the girls and striking out with beautiful women and the standard Hope armory of comedy tricks: being the coward, being the braggart; always from the guy's point of view. Then when I was living with Keaton, she was so funny and so smart that she opened my eyes to so much by experiencing things with her. When I was writing *Annie Hall* with Marshall [Brickman], the film originally reflected my point of view, but we kept making Annie Hall a bigger and bigger character part and she did such a great job with it. [It brought her the Best Actress Oscar in 1977.] I started to look at the world through her eyes. I think it may have been William Gibson, the playwright, who said that when you love someone you have experiences through their eyes. And this was true with Keaton. I was crazy about her and have had nothing but admiration and respect for her to this day. I still look at things through her eyes. I can empathize with her seeing the same bridge or the same movie or the same sunset or the same two characters talking over dinner. I can see it through her. And because of her I started writing for women."

Now in his sixth decade of writing and directing films, Woody has created dozens of deeply drawn women characters. A few: Cate Blanchett's emotionally disintegrating Jasmine in *Blue Jasmine;* Scarlett Johansson's smoldering Nola in *Match Point;* Samantha Morton's mute Hattie in *Sweet and Lowdown;* Judy Davis's vituperative Lucy in *Deconstructing Harry;* Mira Sorvino's sweet, helium-voiced hooker Linda in *Mighty Aphrodite;* Dianne Wiest's Broadway diva Helen Sinclair in *Bullets over Broadway;* the three siblings in *Hannah and Her Sisters;* Mia Farrow's escapist Cecilia in *The Purple Rose of Cairo;* Mariel Hemingway's wise-beyond-her-years Tracy in *Manhattan;* and of course Keaton's la-dee-dah Annie Hall.

It hasn't hurt that two of his greatest idols, Ingmar Bergman and Tennessee Williams, created complex female roles. He learned that women make more interesting characters. "Guys tend to see things more black and white—at least when I was growing up. They were more macho, personal things embarrassed them, certain attitudes were important for them to feel masculine, whereas the women had more complicated feelings. Take a play like *Streetcar.* Stanley wants his essential pleasures and everything to be as it is: his poker game, his sex, his food. But Blanche is much more complicated. She has desires and fears; she feels guilty about the death she caused; she has feelings about life and culture and refinement and the complexity of expression in hypersexuality. Bergman's movies were frequently female centered because they had complex feelings about life and sexuality and love and children. When they were human problems they were very feminine. An existential problem could be more masculine because then it had a more life-and-death struggle, it had a simpler kernel, even though it had complex ramifications. In *The Seventh Seal* the knight wants to know the meaning of life. You get into complex philosophy, yet basically it's a simple thing. But *Persona* deals with the emotions of the women and the identification with the woman who has a nervous breakdown and her feelings about having children. Those emotions are more tantalizing to me." (On a wall in a sitting room in Woody's home is a framed work by Ed Ruscha, white letters on a green background that reads: "HE ENJOYS THE CO. OF WOMEN.")

He says he finds it more fun to work with actresses "because it's always a hassle getting guys; there are a lot of great actresses around, but people aren't writing for them and they're happy to work. Actors are always more difficult to pin down, to get. It's always a macho thing about the money. And it's generally true with American films that men are heroes, they have guns, they get shot, they shoot the bad guys. Once in a while you get a brilliant character like Willy Loman, but it's a rarity. Look at *Hamlet* or any of Shakespeare's plays—then the stories were almost always men and the women always played highly subsidiary roles. But the modern world isn't such an utterly male-dominated society like England in the sixteenth century. As you come into modern society where the women are assertive, developed, complex, equal beings—except in pay—they become very interesting; to me, more interesting. So when I have an idea I always think, 'Can this be done with a woman? Can it be told through a woman better than a man?' If it can, I'm always happy."

Scene 120: Jill and Rita in the chemistry lab after Jill has confronted Abe about his involvement in the murder. Rita has heard he is leaving Braylin and asks Jill if it is true. "Yes," she says, adding that he's thinking of moving to Europe. Seeing her chance for a new life evaporating, Rita says matter-of-factly, "I wish he would go to Spain and take me with him."

JILL

Really? He said you two had a good laugh over your theory that he was the Lippitt Park killer.

RITA

We did have a good laugh over it. And yet, if it turned out to be that he did it, I'd be surprised but

> not stunned, not flabbergasted. And I'd still let him
> take me to Spain.

Woody wants to do the scene in a master to accomplish several things: the audience needs to have a sense of the lab; he wants them to see the women in full face rather than in profile over the shoulder because there is important emotional information to be given; and he wants the most flattering view of Jill before slightly swinging the camera to get Rita on her last line as she walks to where Jill is standing.

Apart from Khondji, the camera crew have not worked with Woody before, but they all know and appreciate his sensibilities. Faith Brewer, the first assistant, says as the setup progresses, "Woody has established a style. His masters go on and on and can make you uncomfortable, which is a good thing because you are out of control; he has control of you. You feel something should be happening but you are only a spectator. For instance, the shot in *Match Point* when Jonathan Rhys Meyers is just sitting at the table and watching while everyone else is talking, and we know that he has committed murder. It makes the audience focus on what is the intent of the story."

Khondji later explains that this shot had extra considerations for him. "We had these two actresses and we had two different layers of concern. No matter what, in cinema, actresses have to be beautiful. There are very few instances where we don't want that. I think Woody has this immaculate image of Emma that he wants to preserve. I think he uses her also not only because of her incredible talent as an actress—I think she is one of the greatest actresses I have ever worked with—but Woody wants her to look really good all the time. Some actresses you want them to look rough, but even when she looks rough and when she cries and is really angry, we want her always to look her best. So we are always working on that. When he knows you are lighting the main actress, he is always very helpful. All great directors I work with are like this, too."

Woody instructs Jill and Rita on their movements and says to their amusement as he leaves, "I'll go to the monitor so I can clock your mistakes." In the first take, Rita veers from the script slightly; it works, and the dialogue is kept in for the following takes.

In the script, the opening of the film is a montage of shots around the campus that establish the story's locale. But as shooting has gone on, the most picturesque parts have been used, and Woody finds himself looking for three new shots for the montage, so far without success. Khondji suggests that as the campus runs to the ocean, one shot could be out to sea, but Woody says, "It's very pretty but it doesn't say anything, it's not tied in to the buildings." Khondji tries to work out a shot that pans from the sea to the back of the college's administration building, which from the front is a gracious redstone Gilded Age mansion but from the rear is monolithic and, with its window shades down, looks ready for Edward Hopper to paint. Woody considers it a moment then says, "Does this remind you of a mental hospital?" The scouting crew laugh, as does Khondji, who says, "I was trying not to think of that."

The problem is still unresolved the next day. At eight a.m. Woody is practicing his clarinet in the backseat of the Chevy while scene 100 is set up:

Abe gives Jill poems he has written for her in what the script calls "a romantic spot," which in this case is a vine-covered pergola. When Woody emerges, Helen Robin greets him with the suggestion that at the start of the picture we see Abe driving toward Newport over the Claiborne Pell suspension bridge that spans the East Passage of Narragansett Bay. Woody immediately likes the idea and without hesitation says he envisions three shots. This will add at least half a day to the shooting schedule, a minimum of $85,000.

The bulk of the day is spent a block away doing three scenes in the Athenaeum library, a Greek Revival gem that, apart from a computer on the librarian's desk and the lights hanging by long cords from the ceiling, has seemingly not changed since it opened in 1838.

The brightness from more than a dozen 18,000-watt HMI lights set up on the roof of the library shines through the opaque skylight into the room. All this is for a walk between bookshelves by Abe as

Woody practices on his clarinet daily. Sometimes when a scene requires a lengthy setup, he does it in the car that takes him to and from the set, the windows up to keep the sound in.

he goes into an alcove to find a book on poisons, scene A67. The light that reaches into the alcove has been cut many times over so that it is soft and natural. The action takes place both at the library and in his house. It is filmed without sound and needs to run thirty-eight seconds for Abe's accompanying voice-over.

ABE

I was right in thinking the killing would be an act of creativity. It was artistically challenging to plan how to do away with Spangler and bring it off perfectly. Weighing all the options I came to the conclusion the only practical way I could do it was to poison him. Careful not to leave any record on my computer, I researched all the poisons and it was clear why cyanide had become the popular cliché of mystery writers and spies. Cyanide would be quick and painless.

CUT TO: INT. ABE HOUSE—NIGHT

Abe watching Rita putting her keys in her bag.

ABE (V.O.)

And while it would be impossible to obtain any legally, I knew where I might get some without having to fill out any forms. Every stage of the way was a risk and I must admit, exhilarating.

The stacks are washed a rich golden brown. The shot starts as a full on Abe as he enters from the left, then walks toward the camera, turns into the alcove, and picks his books. On one take the focus is soft as Abe turns the corner. Woody says to print it anyway; it doesn't bother him. His only worry is that from the way it looks on the monitor, it is being shot too dark: "I just don't want it to look sinister." (The darkness, however, is not in how it is being shot but simply that the brightness on the monitor needs turning up.)

Scene 26 has Jill and Roy in the Athenaeum earlier in the film, he not wanting to hear more about Abe. When Woody scouted the location in June, he thought that a shot of Jill and Roy at a desk and table, made from the second floor looking down at them from a balcony opening, would look "very Hitchcockian." Seeing it again today, however, he finds "nothing there" and so puts them by an alcove in the main reading room.

JILL

I had an interesting talk with Abe Lucas the other day—he's got a lot going on inside.

ROY

Uh-huh.

JILL

He thought my paper was well organized and original.

ROY

I can see where this is going.

JILL

Oh, stop—he's fascinating because he's bright but a sufferer.

ROY

Perfect. You always become attracted to sufferers. That's how we met.

JILL

But he's a real sufferer. You had shingles. He was traumatized when he lost his closest friend. He was a journalist killed in Iraq.

ROY

He had his head cut off, right?

JILL

No, that's not true. It was an explosion. It's amazing how stories get embellished. Abe says people need whatever drama they can manufacture. Their lives are so empty.

ROY

Can we change the subject of Abe Lucas? You've been singing his praises for half an hour.

JILL

Then I'll sing yours. I love the way you look in that cardigan.

ROY

Of course you love it, you bought it for me.

JILL

But you look great in dark colors. Y'know Abe's mother committed suicide.

ROY

Abe again.

JILL

When he was twelve. She drank bleach. He's charming and he hides it but the anger comes out.

ROY

Help. Somebody.

A bust of horror fiction author H. P. Lovecraft stands on a pedestal by the nook, which might be incongruous were he not a Providence native. Woody wants the movements of Roy and Jill to be choreographed so that each of their best lines is close to the camera and that the most intimate part of the scene be done in the alcove, itself the most intimate place in the room. At the start, Roy looks for a book on a shelf.

Woody says to Roy: "You're not angry but a little annoyed—enough already."

And to Jill: "You're impervious to Roy's complaint."

He stands beside them as they rehearse their movements, his left hand mimicking the camera as he sorts out the blocking. To Jill: "Say your line." To Roy: "Now you come in." They switch places. Roy joins her. Roy walks back. Woody is looking for one more crossover.

To Khondji he says, "Start with her, bring him with the wide shot," then leans back on the Lovecraft statue base and strikes an insouciant pose. The actors laugh. He says to Stone, "Can you lean on this? Is it too disgusting?" After she does, with her head a bit turned, he says, "If it were me I would put the whole face right on the camera." Then he adds, "You'll have to work this out." Stone suggests that they reverse Woody's moves, that she do Blackley's and he do hers, and it works perfectly. The shot is done in a master.

The basement of the Athenaeum has windows at the top of the wall level with the street. It has been easily transformed into a faculty meeting room: Loquasto only had to add "lights and more lights" to the bookcases and plug in a few table lamps, plus put a little paint on a wall. Library tables, one of which is used for the meeting, were already in the room. "Small room layering in lights all goes back to Gordon and his sense of composition," he explains. "He taught Woody a lot about foreground architecture."

In scene 79, Abe switches juice containers with Judge Spangler as he sits on a park bench following his Saturday jog, then quietly walks away, his twisted philosophical theory of improving the world transformed into a deadly reality. Now in scene 80 he is at a weekend faculty meeting (one of the professors is played by Woody's friend Maurice Sonnenberg, another cameo regular), the humdrum nature of it in stark contrast to the dreadful act he has just committed.

ABE (V.O.)

I got out of the park and no one saw me. I never saw Spangler drink the juice and while I tried to stay focused at our weekend faculty meeting, my mind was a million miles away.

Shot of meeting going on. Ad-lib school curriculum topics to cover the above voice-over. We then pick up a snatch of conversation wherein Abe is distracted.

KEVIN

What do you think, Abe? Funny?

ABE

Huh?

KEVIN

What did you think of Greenberg's pun?

ABE

His pun?

KEVIN

Cheer, cheer for old Alma Mahler. Lovely, no? Did you not get it?

The actors playing the faculty need to respond to Kevin with nods and laughter. "You guys are having fun, so this comes out naturally," Woody instructs them. Take 1 is cut almost immediately; too much time was spent waiting for the other person to deliver his line—too much time literally being less than one-tenth of a second—and a comedy master class ensues. Woody says the lines of dialogue at the speed he wants them to do it: "'Did you not get it? Abe, you are so out of it today.'" They try again but a minute amount of air between the lines again spoils the joke and take 2 is a cut. Woody goes over to the actor and says the lines again: "What did you think of *Greenberg's* pun? Cheer, cheer . . ." But take 3 is another no-go. "No pause between 'His pun' and 'Cheer, cheer.' And no pause *after,*" Woody calls out. Take 4 is printed but 5 and 6 are cut midstream. "No air space!" he yells. "No air space at all! It's dead! You can't do it! You've gotta keep it going!" After the sixth: "You can't wait for an answer! Take over!" The seventh brings luck. "That was much better. One more and we're there." As the camera starts to roll he calls out, "Everybody up!" But it is still another cut. "No pause—it all has to come out at once! Don't wait on Abe." Nine and 10 leave no air space and are printed. Class dismissed.

To keep the film going at the pace he wanted, Woody cut the scene in editing.

This scene and other instances when Woody has coaxed actors to use a more conversational tone highlight why comedians are often very good actors. To win over an audience they have to seem completely natural, and that is difficult. "Stand-up is grueling," Woody says from experience. "You're up there by yourself, you've got to get laughs, laughs, laughs for an hour, one after the other. It's very tough. You're talking directly to the audience, they're not bystanders like where you're having a conversation with Tony Roberts or Diane Keaton onstage; you're talking to them, the involvement is with them. It's a completely different dynamic, a more demanding one. Comics make good dates. I remember from my late adolescence when I saw *Lunatics and Lovers* [1954] by Sidney Kingsley on Broadway.

They gave an important part in it to Buddy Hackett, who was broad, and [*snaps fingers*] instantly he won an award for best debut. He just was automatically terrific. Alan King could always act. They put Red Buttons in the movies and he won an Academy Award, for *Sayonara* [1957]. Ed Wynn was very good in films. [He received a Best Supporting Actor Oscar nomination for his work in *The Diary of Anne Frank* (1959).] And of course Hope and [Jackie] Gleason and Chaplin—all first-rate actors. It's just harder to be a stand-up comic. If you can do that, there's a very good chance you can be a good actor."

It already should be evident that Woody's directorial style can be summed up in four words: "Make it sound natural." Referring to the actors in all the films he has directed rather than to those at hand, he says, "That's where they screw up. If it sounds natural, then it's fine. But if it doesn't, it always sounds actory or fake. Even fine actors will do a take and I may have to say something to them." He mentions one line in a long piece of dialogue that an actor with a small part stumbled over the other day. "Everything was great except that one line didn't sound real to me. It sounded like it was said because that's how I said to say it. So I tell them and they say, 'Oh, okay, got it,' and they make it more real the next time. But you need it to sound like real people, otherwise you notice that they're acting. I'll sometimes say, 'I don't care about my words. I don't know what to tell you, but you guys have to make this happen, I can't make it happen.' Sometimes they get it right away, sometimes I have to say something like, 'That would have been perfect if only you had not waited so long to speak, or if you had not been so angry when you came in.' " The point is that the audience should be aware of the content of the dialogue, not how it is delivered. "If it sounds tinny," he adds, "it's no good and I won't like it later.

"That's one of the problems when I do this for the actors. I'll go up to them when they're not getting a scene and I'll do the line, and they're always amazed at how well I read it. But I'm not reading it well because I'm a better actor than Joaquin, I couldn't stay with him for two seconds. It's that I wrote it, so when I wrote it I wrote it in my rhythm, my idiom. When I was doing this with Sam Shepard during *September*, I said, 'You know, it's more like this.' And he said to me,

'Yes, but if I do it that way it is so *Jewish*.' [*He laughs very hard.*] And he was one hundred percent right. I didn't see it at the time. So it may look to Joaquin or Emma like, 'God, this guy is so good, he can do his jokes, he can do his stuff so well, I wish I could do it as well.' But it's not that. He does it one hundred times better. It's that I'm doing it the way I want to hear it and that's the only difference. To me it sounds better, but it's just more what I wanted to hear."

Shepard is one of the very few actors to work with Woody who has seemed openly critical of him. Of Woody and Robert Altman he said in *Esquire* in 1988, "They're piss-poor actors' directors. They may be gifted filmmakers, but they have no respect for actors. Individually, each knows zip about acting. Allen knows even less than Altman, which is nothing."

What Shepard meant, as he clarified to Mitchell Zukoff in *Robert Altman: The Oral Biography* (2009) is that "I was spoiled to a large extent by working in the theater, by working with great directors who *do* know actors . . . who have dialogue with them, who spend weeks in rehearsal. You don't have that luxury in film. These guys want to make a movie. And they're great casting guys. They find the absolute right actors for the job. Those actors know how to do it, and they *know* that they know how to do it. But there's no dialogue, there's no discussion. It's, 'Let's shoot it.' They're making a movie! Their focus is the camera, the lights, the set, what's going to be on film. They're not interested in how the actor is approaching the character and what he's trying to investigate or anything like that. Neither one of them would sit down with an actor for six to eight weeks working on a role. There's no way . . . it certainly wasn't meant as an insult. It was meant as a perception, mainly having to do with the difference between film and theater."

After the film was completed, Shepard gave Woody some rare Sidney Bechet albums from his father's collection, and Woody says, "I always liked Sam personally, and still do."

Stone points out that although Woody constantly tells actors to use their own words, it is not always easy. "Woody's writing is so good that I feel terrible when I get nervous and flub what he wrote. What you want more than anything is to speak his words. It's why it's so funny when he comes up to you and says, 'Screw my words, don't worry about my dialogue. Say something better than what I wrote, what I wrote is garbage'—which is never true. Maybe you want to pare things down or rephrase them because they feel too foreign to you, but it is very rare that the line is not exactly what it should be. This gives you such freedom. It's what I could always see in Diane Keaton in his movies. She's one of my favorite actresses because whether she's playing a cold intellectual in *Manhattan* or a version of herself in *Annie Hall,* the way they combine, the electricity between them, she was able to have that on-point line reading of his writing and understood his style. I think when it comes to a creative working relationship there is some sort of intangible communication. There's something I relate to in his storytelling and his dialogue and his characters."

The many shots scheduled earlier in production but still unmade are a growing backlog as filming enters its last ten days. Seven exterior campus shots from every part of the script (scenes 3, 4, 31, 84, 92, and 137) somehow need to be made in a single day: one is two pages of dialogue, two are about a page each, and one, although it is only about a page, is the final scene of the film, and a long tracking shot as well. The forecast is for weather that will help—overcast in the morning, a chance of rain later, sunny toward sunset when golden-hour light will be useful. The most important shot of the morning is scene 92: Abe bumps into Rita on campus and as they walk and talk, Jill calls out to Abe from twenty-five yards away and rushes over with news: the police have announced that the judge did not die from a heart attack; he was murdered. After a few lines, Rita leaves and Abe and Jill walk toward where she started in the scene. The crew came at six thirty a.m. to set up for an early shot, but instead of cloud cover to even the light there was bright sun and there are no balloons to mask it. Clouds have come in since but keep breaking up, and the most recent forecast is for overcast with a 50 percent chance of rain. Khondji consults an app that shows the day's arc of the sun so shots can be set up and made at the optimum time.

Woody was supposed to be on set at 7:00 a.m. but arrives at 7:20. Tamberi hands him his sides. "Ah, the words," he says, and then looks around like a gawker who has stumbled onto the scene. "Where's the movie?" He asks McCarthy what the last cut is; it's of Abe watching Jill take her piano lesson.

He always asks because he doesn't want to cut from, for instance, Abe in the classroom saying, "So that's the existential motif of the story and for tomorrow . . ." to Abe in a restaurant having a cup of coffee "because it would not look nice." He is careful to ensure that if he errs, it is on the side of exterior. Like most directors, he tries not to cut interior to interior, knowing there are times that he must, but he endeavors to make as much of the picture as possible outside. He also tries to alternate the size of shots so that he does not go, say, from a very wide shot to a very wide shot. "All those things are on my mind when I'm shooting and also when I'm writing," he says. "I won't have the location but I know I'll want something outside."

An outdoor shot may be to his liking, but the way the light outdoors is behaving this morning certainly is not. It is too changeable to film anything Woody will like, so the company does what he always does when he doesn't have the light he wants: they wait. Some of the younger crew, who have not worked with him before, are stunned to see so much time pass without a shot, but this is nothing compared to waiting four months for one shot in *Sweet and Lowdown.* Sometimes a crew can chase the light and grab a shot; other times, like now, the only thing to do is wait for the light to find them.

"We shoot when the light is right, and if it's not right we don't shoot," Woody says with a shrug. "And if it takes longer to do the picture, if it costs more money and we go over, I pay the money out of my salary. We do go over almost every picture, but you do get that beauty. Later there's a certain pride. You look at *Magic in the Moonlight* and say, 'God, it looks so beautiful.' And yeah, it looks beautiful because we were shooting at six o'clock at night, seven o'clock at night, and sitting around twiddling our thumbs from three to six o'clock, trying to find a shady spot to do an insert or go inside someplace. And if nothing is available, we wait."

An outdoor scene with only two actors is hard enough to light, but one with three who each require different lighting is really difficult, Khondji explains, as he keeps trying to adjust to changing conditions.

"Joaquin has two specific lights for his face. One is a top light on his head, like a sculpture, like a Roman emperor. He has a great face. Top light is incredibly beautiful for him—at a certain height. If you go too high it's a different story. But if you light it low he becomes like a god. And the other light is a half light, to show the duality of his character. Now, when you have Emma on one side of him and Parker on the other, it becomes difficult. Emma needs a very specific light; she has to be lit evenly and very softly and very plainly from slightly higher. The light on Emma has to be very pure. You cannot have a rear-view light or other bits and pieces of light that normally are there in nature. Nature is made of bounced light and the top light of the sky. If you want to make her extremely beautiful you have to come at her with a pure light on her face. Parker is pure light too, a very simple, glamorous light. So you have three people and a different light for each." The problem is the natural light he is trying to work around is not cooperating. If the budget allowed, there would be balloons overhead on this and several other days.

The shot starts on Abe and Rita, then the camera pans left to Jill, who is calling out from afar to Abe and comes right as she approaches them. Rita exits from the left while Abe and Jill walk away from the camera, toward where she started. A couple of takes are attempted but they are no good. A noisy bird interrupts and the sun is harsh for the camera; in the third take, the light changes throughout the nearly two-minute shot.

The three actors talk about other movies while waiting to go again. Posey mentions *Babe* (1995). Woody hears her as he walks toward them and says, "*Babe.* It was on a double bill with *Grand Illusion.*"

Around nine the decision is made to forget this shot for now and do scene 4 (three co-eds on a bench under a nearby tree that will filter the light, talking about the announcement that Abe is coming to Braylin; scenes 2 and 3 are short reaction shots by faculty). Khondji leaves the camera for 92 in place for when the weather cooperates and has a second camera set up to film the students. But just as 4 is ready, the clouds return. Everyone rushes back to get 92, but the sun comes out at some point in every take. Then the sky totally clears. The weather app shows it will be at least twenty minutes before more cover, so the crew traipse back the couple of hundred feet to shoot 4.

Woody talks to the three young women, who have only this scene. "Add on to each other, step on each other, it should sound like a real conversation. Don't worry about the words in the script, just get all the information out there."

The first take is cut but Woody likes how they are keeping the conversation natural. "That was good—you got the idea of it very well. What you're doing is right so I don't want to take you down from that."

One of them says, "We'll go crazy."

"Don't go crazy," he replies. "That's the one thing you can't do." They laugh, then nail the next two takes. It has taken less than five minutes between the first take and checking the gate.

"You guys were great, absolutely perfect," Woody tells them. "There'll be something extra in your pay envelope."

It would be nice if every scene was so easy, but no others are today. It is after three p.m. before 92 is finished. This is Posey's last scene, and at its end Rigby, following the tradition of saluting a departing actor, announces, "Ladies and gentlemen, Parker Posey!" The crew applaud, there are hugs and handshakes, and Woody walks over to offer his private thanks. He is always physically undemonstrative in these moments, but they inevitably bring a smile and a look of gratitude to the actor's face.

"He warded off a hug by saying he had the Ebola virus," she said later, "and thanked me for my performance. He told me I said the words like he had written them and heard them and 'Now your parents can be proud of you.'"

It is past six p.m. when the other scenes are finished, with 137 still to be shot. That, however, cannot yet commence; the sun is still high enough to cast a bright light on the leaves of the trees and wash out the color. Sunset is at 7:57. There will be a window of forty minutes or so before the light goes from optimal to useless. This is the final scene of the picture and to be effective it requires an elegant sense of summing up. The shot is simple enough: Jill and Roy are back together, languid after the high drama of the scene before. They talk as they stroll from under a huge weeping tree onto a broad campus lawn then disappear into a clump of other trees whose leaves and branches cascade to the ground. The scene, which lasts just under fifty seconds, needs to be at once romantic and bring closure.

Fifty feet of dolly track are laid so the cameras can follow alongside Jill and Roy as they walk and talk. Each has four lines as they go over what has happened. They end with Jill moving from what might have happened to what might be:

JILL

This is not the time or place to open up a philosophical discussion.

ROY

You usually enjoy philosophical discussions.

JILL

Let's get away from all of these people and obey our instincts.

ROY

There are a lot of people around.

JILL

(pulling him into trees)

Life is risk.

Nothing goes right. After the first two takes, Woody tells them to drop the last two lines. After seven takes, he has not printed one. The light is beautiful but it is starting to fade. He and Khondji confer after every take. Khondji eventually suggests blocking the scene so that Jill and Roy come not from under the tree but across the broad lawn with part of their walk visible through the tree, then cross open ground before disappearing into the foliage. Woody likes the idea; it opens up the shot and gives it a valedictory feel. The first take shows promise. Woody says to Jill, "Don't run away from 'instincts.'" A dozen more from this new angle are done, six printed. The light has fallen considerably, but the film stock is so sensitive that color will saturate the screen. Woody, however, remains discontented; something is not right, but he can't discern what. He has the soundman record a wild track of Jill's last line, her voice without film, which might prove useful in editing. They stand face-to-face and he asks her to repeat after him: "Let's forget philosophy and obey our instincts."

"Obey our instincts."

"Obey our instincts," he says again.

"Obey our instincts," she says, mimicking his cadence.

Woody calls it a day just as dusk starts to settle.

"He was having a problem with the conception of the shot, and he couldn't find exactly the texture of the material," Khondji says the next day. "We talked about it. Sometimes it is he or I or someone on the crew who comes up with a solution, and yesterday it happened to be me. I always use something that he says. When you listen to directors, some say a lot, some say very little. Woody says very little and does not explain a lot, but once you work with him, most of the time you catch what you have to do. Yesterday he couldn't feel what was wrong. It was a difficult moment where we could not find the camera position or a shot or what the actors should do. Sometimes you are blind, you don't have any answer, you are in a state of blockage—we all are. And I feel bad because I can't help. It is the worst feeling. And then I just heard something he said about people crossing, just in passing, and I underlined it like reading a book with a pencil—*tree frames them as they walk through and then into open toward other tree.* I also heard him say, 'They could come from the field, from the other direction.' So I just said it back to him instead of saying, 'Okay, we don't have a solution, we'll do it another day.' But we are running out of days.

"I was using a daylight film stock that I've used for the whole exterior day of the film. It is a very low daylight stock that has a very nice touch and gives very beautiful skin tone. It looks very real, very organic. It also has a candid look and you can manipulate it very easily, like a sculptor uses clay. I remember we were going through those last few takes and Woody was asking if we could keep on shooting because he could see the light was going. He feels the light very well. He has this quality that is not technical but more a feeling with light."

As to how the level of light that passed into the camera was so much better than what it looked like to the eye, he continued, "It is fortunate that we are using film rather than shooting in digital. Digital creates light where there is no light and you constantly have to turn off light, you can't light. When you light a scene, imagine we are sitting here, and there is a very large window with very soft skylight but still backlighting and there's no detail inside. Still, we put a little top light here. In digital you bring a white canvas and immediately the black becomes alive. These are the good things with digital. At the moment I just want to shoot film because it's not going to last that long. I love exposing film, I love the danger of it, I love the feeling of letting your brain and emotions tell you how to expose the film. In digital, you don't have that. You watch it on a screen and that is what you get. Any idiot can do it."

Khondji and his crew are using three types of film—mostly Kodak 5219 500 tungsten because it is the most sensitive to light, but occasionally Kodak 5213 200 tungsten or Kodak 5203 50 daylight. The 50 daylight is used outside because it tends to develop very blue; as the incandescent lights are very orange, the film and the artificial light balance out to give a neutral hue. The film costs about a dollar a foot including processing and transferring to video—a thousand dollars for a thousand-foot roll, about ten minutes of viewing. The standard for shooting is twenty-four frames per second, or one and a half feet of film. The speed was established at the advent of talkies. The film stock of the time was not sensitive enough for faster, and slower dulled the sound. Slow motion requires more frames a second, faster motion fewer. More than two hundred rolls will be used during the production, but because not every foot of film on a roll is used, about 150,000 feet in all will be shot, or around a mile of film a day, not that much by most standards.

Woody has his own thoughts about the previous evening. "Well, most of it was my fault," he says while waiting for scene 128 (Roy and Jill in a coffee shop; they get back together) to be lit. "I set up a shot, but when I was looking at it with live people, it looked too forced and too cutesy and too artificial. I didn't like the staging and we were losing light and we were stuck there. And then the actors had their normal couple of takes they blew and had to be helped but it was mostly me. We were trying a few different experiments—I was trying a few aborted, terrible ones. I had the feeling that if they didn't head straight for the tree but were deceptive about it, it would be better. Then Darius had an idea that was quite good, to bring them in from the side, and it worked reasonably well."

Shortly before this scene in which Roy and Jill reunite, Jill, knowing that Abe is a murderer, confronts him and says he has until the coming Monday morning to turn himself in, otherwise she will go to the police. He agrees, but in his following voice-over we hear that he

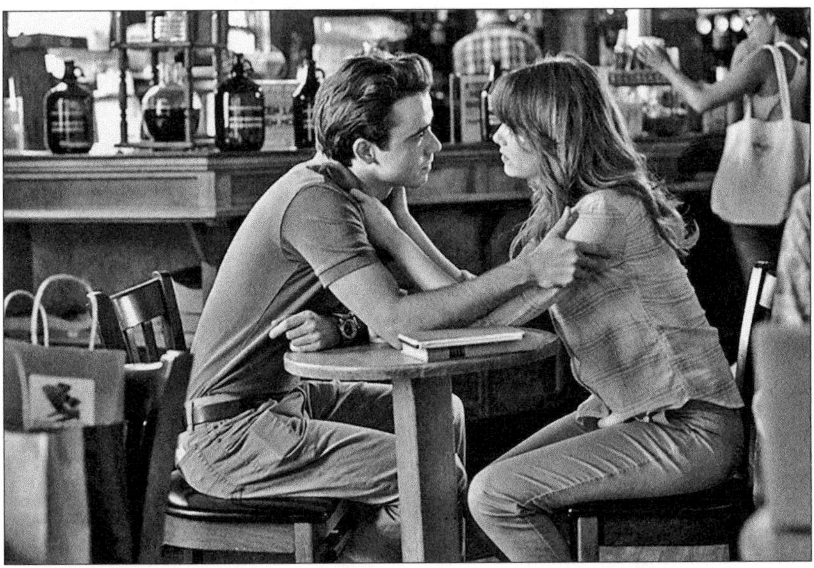

Jill tells Roy how mistaken she was to break up with him.

has no intention of doing that, although Jill is unaware that she is now imperiled. She realizes only what a terrible mistake she made falling for Abe and marvels that Roy is so understanding and accepting of her when he tells her he never stopped caring about her. She says she's been foolish but doesn't want to talk about why she changed her mind.

ROY

But I feel you're keeping something from me.

JILL

Monday. I'll tell you everything Monday.

The scene ends with a kiss, but Woody calls "cut" before it becomes a long one. "I can't take too much of the sticky stuff," he says.

7

"Everything's always disappointing."

Despite the occasional fits and starts and snafus, as filming winds down Woody is feeling slightly hopeful. "It reminds me of the Truffaut movie *Day for Night* [1973], where everything goes wrong at the beginning but then you hit a pace and you start to make the movie and things improve. And that did happen. I've had a better run and I'm starting to feel a little more comfortable." Which should not be taken to mean he is happy. "Well, everything's always disappointing," he says with a smile. "The picture doesn't look like it's shaping up to be the electrifying, groundbreaking, stunning thing you hope for—it's not going to be that. At this point I keep thinking, 'If I do this here or if I switch the narration to this, or I put this thing here, maybe I'll survive.' It metamorphoses into a fight for survival."

Woody's films often change considerably during editing. Most recently, in *Magic in the Moonlight,* information first given to the audience about Emma Stone's character was ultimately withheld, and Colin Firth's character was made to have no romantic interest in her until the end of the picture. But that is less a cause for solace than it is for fear, even though Woody is the first to say how much can be accomplished in editing. "As Ralph Rosenblum used to say, 'Directors get testy in the editing room because that is the last chance you have to make the film—and if you can't get it to work in the editing room, that's it, there's no more recourse to anything.'"

When dailies arrive by email later that day, scene 137, Jill and Roy on the lawn, looks gorgeous. But how it looks is not enough. It's what it does to the audience that matters, and the scene just does not deliver the strong closing punch Woody imagined. He knows he needs to do something more, just not what.

The Friday at the end of the fifth week is devoted to the most elaborate location of the film, a night shoot in an amusement park. The Washington County Fair is set to open soon, and Robin has rented the site and all the rides for a day and night to shoot scenes 62 (Abe, determined to win a prize for Jill, shoots at a target with such intensity that his manic and crazy side is on display), 63 (Abe picks right at a numbers wheel and wins a prize for Jill), and 64 (Abe and Jill in a fun house with distorted mirrors, where they kiss for the first time).

The reason to shoot at night is simple: the fairground will be much prettier with its gaudy lights shining brightly on the screen. In daylight the rides and concessions look cheap and tacky and the field they are in is seedy. Woody wanted an amusement park that was pretty but "they are all so cheesy looking, unless you're in the Tivoli Gardens or Playland, the one in Rye, New York. So we were going to have to make our own but Santo said, 'You're going to *think* it's cheap and cheesy, but if we shoot it at night it looks a hundred times better.' So contrary to what I'm comfortable with, I said, 'Okay, the amusement park we'll do at night.' Naturally I want the Ferris wheel—the stuff that's clichéd at an amusement park."

He will first establish the carnival. Then there will be a shot of Jill and Abe looking at a stomach-turning ride and the Ferris wheel, followed by them at the rifle booth, then at the numbers wheel. Finally, the pair walks into the hole in the wall that is purportedly the entrance to the fun house. The shots will have a host of cameos, including Bechet (Manzie is already in another shot), Woody's assistant Ginevra Tamberi, and John Doumanian, a close friend of Woody's since his Chicago days as a stand-up and now the manager of his band.

"The fun house is not a lot of fun because none of them ever are," Woody says. "This one just has some distorting mirrors in it and most of them make you short and don't otherwise distort you but we don't need a lot of elaborate mirrors, it's just the idea of it. Santo elaborated on it much more artistically than me. Visually, he's amazing. We'll start on the mirrors and see them come as if from the hole they entered, and then get to the scene. We'll want to make a shot in the mirror when they talk, so we can't do this as a one-shot. We'll do a little of the dialogue just on the mirror characters and then cut to the live actors and hope they can do the rest of the scene in a two-shot. I'd hate to have to cover it."

Several tall trees provide shade on the dusty fairground. While the crew prepare and others wait for nightfall, Woody sits in the shade in his long-legged canvas-backed chair beside the just-completed fun house, which has taken a couple of weeks to design and build. From the outside it looks to be only two-by-fours with plastic sheeting, but inside is a movie marvel of warped mirrors and bright lights. Loquasto generally is able to have a set up and running with only minor expense. This critical piece of the film, however, will likely run twice its projected cost of $10,000 because of many changes plus improvements to the interior lights. Still, it is a bargain. The inside is thirty-five by twelve feet, lined with 320 yards of black sequined fabric at three dollars a yard. To cut a few dollars from the cost, Loquasto and Suzy Benzinger specifically went the day before to shop at the local Savers because the store offers seniors 10 percent off on Thursdays.

"Another Santo special," Woody says, approvingly. He also has added red fringe to the numbers wheel booth. These seemingly little touches make a big difference.

There are several hours before it will be dark enough to shoot. Woody's job in the meantime is to look at a piece of scenery when his opinion is sought. Otherwise he has some unavoidable downtime and is reflective on this film and on other filmmakers. There are only nine days of shooting left, and he knows there is little now that he can do to change its course. "The film is rolling along, for better or worse. It's now," he says with a little laugh, "out of my control. It's like a boulder going down the mountain, completely on its own momentum."

There are American directors whose work Woody admires, but the reason for his European-style preference is the creative freedom that European directors were allowed and Hollywood studio directors were denied, no matter how successful their films, because "Americans were constantly beholden to studio heads who routinely chopped up their pictures." For instance, Orson Welles made *The Magnificent Ambersons* (1942) immediately following *Citizen Kane,* which had brought him an Oscar for Original Screenplay and nominations for directing and acting; all together the film garnered nine nominations, including Best Picture. No matter. RKO Pictures, unhappy with Welles's cut, took away the editing, changed the ending, and shortened the running time by an hour with two uncredited directors (one of them Robert Wise) doing the butchery.

"It's a great achievement when you see some of those fine Hollywood directors," he continued. "John Huston, John Ford, Welles, William Wyler, and George Stevens did such good work operating under terrible conditions and came up with many wonderful films. [Huston's] *The Treasure of the Sierra Madre* [1948] is as fine a film as some of the best European films ever made. Part of the reason is that there wasn't a lot in it for them to censor. There was no sex in the picture, no political issues or violence that would encroach on the general sense of censorship."

There is nothing in particular about Huston's style that Woody admires, but he finds the overall effect of his films admirable. "He was just a very fine director, dependent on the material. So when he had *The Dead* or *The Maltese Falcon,* he did a fantastic job. In that

Hollywood studio system you could have given those stories to fifty other directors and they would not have made such films. My guess is that if he and Stevens and Wyler could have worked freely all the time on projects they wanted, uncensored and untrammeled by overlords, they would have made consistently great movies."

Stevens's *Shane* (1953) is a particular favorite of Woody's. Even though he is not a fan of Westerns, the film transcends its milieu. "It hooks into me. It's a great fable and a thrilling story executed beautifully about a man who is an artist at what he does [gunfighting]. He tried to give it up, but there are times in life you just need somebody to go in and clean things out. The picture is human and heroic in the best sense of the word—someone saying, 'You poor people are never going to be able to handle this mess. You really need somebody who knows how to do it.' And he does it. I don't find that in other Westerns. I liked *The Ox-Bow Incident* [1943]. *High Noon* [1952] and *Red River* [1948] are excellent, but to me, none of them compare to *Shane*."

When he talks of films and directors that mean the most to him, they almost always are from his youth, the time we are all the most impressionable and have the most to learn. But there were two tiers to his appreciation. As much as he was impressed by such exceptional Hollywood films as *The Treasure of the Sierra Madre, Citizen Kane, Double Indemnity* (1944), *White Heat* (1949), and *Paths of Glory* (1957), very few American films since have equaled the impact of the movies by the European filmmakers of the 1940s, 1950s, and 1960s, including Godard, Alain Resnais, Fellini, Hitchcock, Ernst Lubitsch, and De Sica. (The only non-Europeans on his list are Akira Kurosawa and Satyajit Ray.) "Consequently, my films have been well appreciated in Europe, more than the United States—maybe because, in spite of my imitations, something seeped in."

There are several contemporary directors whose work he enjoys. "Of course I've loved Scorsese and I like David O. Russell and I like Paul Thomas Anderson. Scorsese is a natural talent with a great feel for film. He makes you feel it. A wonderful writer—Chekhov or Norman Mailer when he's writing a journalistic piece—makes you feel the tension or the terror or the joy, and with Scorsese you feel what is happening on screen. Anderson has a wonderful imagination and a great eye. Russell is a marvelous storyteller on film. You can feel his excitement. Oliver Stone. David Fincher is an excellent director who makes really good movies. Christopher Guest is an excellent comedy director whose films are better than iconic ones overly praised. David Zucker and Jerry Zucker. I loved the humor of *Airplane!* [1980] and *The Naked Gun* [1988]. Naturally, Tim Burton is a real talent—*Edward Scissorhands* [1990], *Sleepy Hollow* [1999], and *Sweeney Todd* [2007]. Also, of course, Coppola, a true master. I want to say there are ones I'm forgetting, because I hate for some hardworking artist to be left out because I'm borderline senile."

But he is most drawn to and was influenced by filmmakers of a couple of generations or more ago. "I'm awestruck by how the directors in the older films handle the actors and the pace—when you watch a [Preston] Sturges film, you're overwhelmed by how everything is at lightning speed and paced so energetically. There's not a lot of directorial pyrotechnics, and that's fine. Everything with the older directors was story oriented, rarely stylized except for Welles, and they told the stories beautifully. My favorite film by Sturges, and it's telling, is the one with Rex Harrison, *Unfaithfully Yours* [1948]. That was an example of Sturges not being midwestern with those characters played by Betty Hutton, William Demarest, Eddie Bracken, and his stock players. This was Rex Harrison and Linda Darnell. I just gravitate more to that style of sophistication, of people in tails, of champagne corks popping, of penthouses. I like that ambience more. I loved [Sturges's] *The Lady Eve,* which I saw only recently. I'm a big fan of the movie version of *Born Yesterday* [1950]. When you think of verbal, talking comedies, it's hard to think of a better one. *The Front Page* [by Charles MacArthur and Ben Hecht, produced on Broadway in 1928 and made into a film in 1931], the play, was a great comedy, and Shaw's *Pygmalion* [1938]. But it's hard to find talking comedies. I don't find a lot of the so-called screwball comedies very funny. *His Girl Friday* [1940], with Rosalind Russell and Cary Grant, based on

The Front Page, is amusing, but I can live with it or without it; it doesn't compare to the play done well. Making the man a woman was commercially successful but diluting of the tale. Lubitsch's *Trouble in Paradise* [1932] is a talking comedy that's wonderful and so is his *The Shop Around the Corner* [1940]—these are plays made into movies. He was hip and sophisticated. But if you don't count the jokey kind of talking comedies like the Marx Brothers or Bob Hope, which are hilarious but not necessarily fine film works, it's hard to name some that are funny. I never found [Howard Hawks's] *Bringing Up Baby* [1938] funny, although there are some wonderful things in [Lubitsch's] *Ninotchka* [1939]. I love Wilder but not *Some Like It Hot* [1959]. All in all, I'm cutting a lot of slack to these things. I actually laugh at the Marx Brothers, at certain Bob Hope movies, and W. C. Fields. But I don't really laugh out loud at much else. Even as a kid I could never warm up to Laurel and Hardy or the Three Stooges, they're not my kind of comedy. This isn't out of any feeling of competition or superiority, it's purely personal taste. They just don't make me laugh. Now, the Marx Brothers were low clowns but sophisticated clowns. They worked with [George S.] Kaufman, with [S. J.] Perelman. They appealed to you through their wit. For me, wit is a very pleasurable thing; you don't see much of it."

Bergman may occupy the first place in his pantheon but he says that Kurosawa "in a sense towers over everybody. He's such a visual artist. He's mature. He doesn't fool around or indulge himself. The actors move the camera. He's not fancy, yet he's stunning in every little touch. A couple of films were not worthy of his genius, but his *Macbeth—Throne of Blood* [1957]—is the best *Macbeth* I ever saw, and his version of *King Lear* [*Ran,* 1985] is terrific. Some of his others, such as *Seven Samurai* [1954], you're overcome with the greatness of how he makes films, but they're really Westerns. It's as if Rembrandt came and drew clowns.

"De Sica was another who was very simple. There are practically no pictures to compare to *The Bicycle Thief* [1948] or *Shoeshine* [1946] or *The Garden of the Finzi-Continis* [1970]. They're not like Fellini's films. When I first saw *La dolce vita* [1960] and *8½* [1963],

I admired them, but I wasn't sucked into them. Then when I saw his earlier films, like *La strada* and *I vitelloni,* I was very taken. The early films before he hit his baroque period were human stories told beautifully. As the years progressed I saw films I like very much, others I can admire, like *Amarcord,* which I can watch once a year, every year. I had great fun watching *Juliet of the Spirits* [1965]. Some of those that came later, I could admire them but I didn't get involved with them. I loved *Roma* [1972] and *The Clowns* [1970], his documentary, and I liked *Ginger and Fred* [1986], that was fun. I could say, 'This guy is an artist with film,' but I wasn't that interested in the story.

"Truffaut was always interesting. When I first saw *The 400 Blows* [1959], I was aware of his enormous energy. It was like I had never seen a movie, it was so fresh and bouncy. Later on I saw *Breathless* [1960], the Godard film. It was a great time in filmmaking. I liked *The Man from Rio* [1964] and *Weekend* [1967]. *Weekend* wasn't so much a story; it was just so imaginative. There were tour de force things like that traffic jam shot. Who would have thought of that?" The nearly seven-and-a-half-minute master shot tracks along a French country road lined with cars backed up bumper to bumper while a heedless, selfish couple cut around and through the mayhem that, after about seven minutes, is revealed by bloodied bodies at the side of the road, victims of the accident that has caused the traffic jam.

Woody has an interesting way to gauge a director's ability. "I've always felt Sidney Lumet is underrated. You can handicap a director by his best films. Very often an actor's best performance is in a Lumet film; he was a first-rate actors' director. The best I ever saw Sean Connery was in *The Hill* [1965], the best I ever saw Chris Sarandon and Al Pacino was in *Dog Day Afternoon* [1975]. Of course I have always been a great admirer of Coppola. There's so much feeling in his work, like a jazz musician plays a couple of notes and there's a feeling in them. You can't codify it; it's talent. Picasso draws a line with a pencil, I draw a line. Whose do you think is going to jump off the page? It's only a line, and yet because he's a genius and I'm not, his breathes."

Since he began directing, Woody has had credited appearances in five films by other directors, each with a different style. Herbert Ross "was very professional, a bread-and-butter guy you could hire and he would give you a nice-looking, very professional, well-put-together upscale movie. If you look at *The Sunshine Boys* [1975], it is excellent, and he did a good job with *Play It Again, Sam* [1972], such as one could do with that material. He was conscientious and had a sense of trying to do things in a classy way. He didn't take shortcuts. When he felt the makeup wasn't good on Keaton, he sent for Dick Smith [*The Godfather, The Exorcist,* an Oscar for *Amadeus*] to fly in and set it straight. If a take had a little something in it that would not annoy me for a second, it did annoy him. He was more meticulous and fastidious, more dedicated.

"Marty Ritt [*The Front,* 1976] rehearsed. You read the script and you rehearsed, but he was also fine in letting me ad-lib when I wanted to. But Marty wasn't a filmic guy so much as he was a stage guy. I could see when we were shooting, he would start a scene and the camera would take a long pan and then the people would start talking. And I'm thinking, 'I know you're going to cut the pan out later,' and he would because when you see a picture cut together you don't want to wait to hear them speak, you want [*snaps fingers*] to get to it and move. But he was very committed to social issues in all his pictures. [Ritt was blacklisted for five years in the 1950s. In the film, Woody plays a man who is the front—the supposed author—for blacklisted writers.] He was very easy to work with as a performer. He'd be on the sidelines rooting you on. He was a very nice guy, a great, larger-than-life character. I loved Marty for many reasons. He'd say, 'I did make a mistake in that picture. A woman in Idaho caught it and sent me a letter saying, "The sports jacket wasn't the same color in that scene."' I said, 'What did you do?' He said, 'I didn't answer it.'

"He covered as much as Mazursky did. Paul [who directed Woody in *Scenes from a Mall,* 1991] covered every speech because he liked doing that. He liked to be in the cutting room later and have all those options. I don't have his patience. When I worked with him he rehearsed us and he went to the locations we were going to work in and he marked off stuff and he taped on the floor where we were to stand. And that's an admirable way to work, he made good movies, but I just don't have the dedication he had. Most of the guys I've worked with did a sensible amount of coverage. They were not wrong for doing it or unimaginative, they were doing it correctly, because you can always throw the coverage away and not use it. But they had it. I didn't have it, and by not having it I've had to tap-dance when there was a problem. They didn't. If a scene was too long, they could shorten it. I've had to figure out ways to do it, and it was not so easy—but I had an easier time on the set because I didn't work as hard as them on the set. I guess I worked harder in the editing room, but you're sitting down."

In the interval between finishing *To Rome with Love* and starting *Blue Jasmine,* Woody acted in John Turturro's *Fading Gigolo* (2013). He says Turturro demanded "no preparation at all. He knew the way I like to work—he's a fine actor himself. [He played a writer in *Hannah and Her Sisters.*] He gave me carte blanche to ad-lib, and if I was ad-libbing with him, he was ad-libbing back as well. He had a very good cameraman on that picture, Marco Pontecorvo, and the picture looks very nice. He was easy to work with and closer to my kind of thing, where it's loose and easy. He did cover more scenes [shoot them from different angles] than I would have, but he did fine work."

With no disrespect to the directors he's worked with, Woody has not taken as his own something any of them did. One reason is that he started with broad comedy that relied on his comedic predisposition. "When I was making *Take the Money and Run,* I was flying by the seat of my pants. I did instinctively what I wanted to do in *Bananas* and then in all my films. I learned a little by watching films. I could see what the great filmmakers were doing, but it was hard to apply that because I was doing these very broad, silly comedies. When you come back from watching [Antonioni's] *L'avventura* [1960] and nothing that you ever need in your picture has to look so amazingly beautiful and passionate and meaningful, how am I going to apply that to me getting hit with a cake? It doesn't work."

Where he did mimic other directors early in his career was in

Everything You Always Wanted to Know About Sex But Were Afraid to Ask* (1972), particularly in the Italian sequence. His first thought was to channel De Sica and make it a black-and-white segment in the peasant style of Roberto Rossellini's *Open City* (1945) and De Sica's *The Bicycle Thief*. But after more thought, Louise Lasser, who played in the segment with him, suggested he switch to the modernist style of Bernardo Bertolucci and Antonioni, using dense colors and shadows contrasted with light. He found it "fun to fool around and make those kind of pretentious shots because that sketch supported them. I had only wished that I could do a real picture like that where it wasn't the comedy version. In *Interiors* [1978] I got to make a lot of [Bergmanesque] shots that were the kind I wanted to make—but then very few people saw the movie and even fewer liked it.

"I always have remembered a review of *Love and Death,* I think it was in the *New Republic.* It's interesting. Stanley Kauffmann and John Simon are two critics who rapped me a lot over the years, and I still have great respect for both of them. There are critics who have rapped me that I have no respect for because they rapped me for the wrong reasons. [This was before he stopped reading reviews.] Kauffmann pointed out that *Love and Death* was gorgeous and it didn't require so much gorgeousness. I think that was a reasonable point, but it's debatable. I happen to think that it was nicer and I didn't *lose* anything from that. But it didn't require the effort we made.

"And then in *Everything You Always Wanted to Know About Sex,* Kauffmann said the camera was always in the wrong place. I felt that was not valid because there *is* no automatic right place; it's subjective. What's right is where the director wants to put it, and the proof of the pudding is with the audience: if it works, it works. It's like someone seeing a picture and saying, 'Well, that joke's not funny.' What they mean is that joke's not funny to *them.* I do that all the time. The writer of some hit movie will say, 'Well, I think Woody's wrong. I think if I write these toilet jokes he finds unfunny they will convulse an audience'—and they do. So when I don't laugh at them, it's only my taste. With critics it has the imprimatur of print and the logo of a newspaper or a magazine, and you get the feeling that a professional who knows more than you has made a pronunciamento. But it's not an objective truth, even though it comes across as one."

When darkness falls, filming begins. Scene 62 starts as a wide shot of a ride, which establishes the amusement park, then dollies back and tilts down to reveal Abe and Jill.

JILL

I never thought I could get you to go to an amusement park.

ABE

Where's Roy tonight?

JILL

Studying.

ABE

Well, I'm mellowing in my old age and now we're here, I'm determined to win you a prize.

(Abe and Jill buy popcorn.)

JILL

Ever think about that poor woman and that judge?

ABE

Yes, of course.

JILL

I still get mad when I think about it. If I was that woman I'd also have taken the kids and fled to Europe—even if I had to live in Iran—rather than lose my kids.

(A shooting concession. He begins squeezing off shots with an intensity that she notices.)

JILL

Easy, Abe, I don't need the stuffed panda that badly.

ABE

You were right—that judge was a vermin.

In 63, Jill and Abe enter from the right and stop in front of a numbers wheel. There, Abe picks the number on which the wheel will stop, and Jill makes a choice that will have an effect on the end of the film.

ABE

Unbelievable—I won.

VENDOR

You're a lucky man.

ABE

Luck rules the universe.

JILL

You think so?

ABE

Correction, not luck—chance. We're all at the mercy of chance. What prize would you like?

JILL

How about the flashlight. *(It is a small red one that fits in a purse.)*

ABE

A nice practical choice.

JILL

I'm not practical—I like the color and the compact little design.

ABE

Remember, you can never really know the object—only our perception of it.

JILL

I'll keep that in mind—no pun intended.

ABE

(shines flashlight)

May this torch be the eternal symbol of chance in the universe.

JILL

I hate that you think of me as practical. I'm much freer than you think.

Afterward, Woody wrote a voice-over for Jill that was intended to follow, but it was not used:

JILL (Cont'd. V.O.)

I loved my little red flashlight. Abe said I brought him luck and he picked the winning number because it was in a fortune cookie at the Chinese restaurant we had dinner at. All I knew was that I would always carry the flashlight and treasure it as the souvenir of a wonderfully romantic evening—even if the romance was a little one-sided.

The following scene, 64, has them in the fun house, where Jill initiates a kiss. Abe responds but then pulls away and tells her it's not a good idea.

ABE

You don't want to get involved with a radical extremist like me.

JILL

Why not? I can be as risk-taking as you.

ABE

We got carried away. Forget the kiss, okay?

JILL

And what if I can't forget it?

ABE

Then I have to be the responsible one and keep things from getting out of hand.

In the next scene, 66, Abe watches as Jill takes a piano lesson (65 was omitted). The original voice-over by Jill:

> He warned me. He wasn't even hinting—he was explicit—I think differently, he said. But it didn't matter. I was in love. As much as I cared for Roy, and I really did, I was swept off my feet by Abe Lucas. The more he tried not to let anything serious happen, the more I wanted something to.

This was later changed to include a reference to the policy on most college campuses that forbids a relationship between a teacher and a student:

> I was sure Abe had feelings for me but maybe it was just that he wasn't in love with me the way I was with him. I tried telling myself the reason he wasn't letting anything go too far was because a relationship between a professor and a student was against Braylin's rules, but I knew in my heart Abe was too romantic to shy away from risks. All I was sure of was that as much as I cared for Roy, and I really did, I was swept off my feet by Abe Lucas—the more he tried not to let anything serious happen, the more I wanted something to.

Woody, it should be clear by now, is not prone to overt enthusiasm, but a couple of days later he arrives on the set bursting with it. While practicing his clarinet the day before by playing along to old New Orleans jazz recordings, he came upon a George Lewis rendition of "Sheik of Araby" on a record of old jam sessions released in 1991 that he had not heard before. (The actual recordings were made decades earlier.) Lewis has been a seminal influence on Woody's playing.

"You have to hear this," he says excitedly, handing over his phone and earbuds. "This is a perfect piece of New Orleans jazz. The polyphony, the crude sound, the soaring high notes, the way he swings it, the rhythm, the clear notes—they're perfect. I turned on this Bunk Johnson thing so I could play with it and there it was, it just came on. I found myself playing to it before I was listening, but soon I was so overwhelmed I stopped and just listened. It's just *beautiful*, it's just amazing playing. It's so full of feeling—that's of course the main thing with all of them—and the rhythm is so sensational, the tone is so beautiful, the tonguing, the articulation, and his ideas are so *pretty*; he's such a pretty player. Usually he's playing soft and lyrically and soulfully and very often religiously, because he *was* very religious, but here he's playing just rough whorehouse music. It's a very crude kind of jazz. His style derived from parade music, just tons of arpeggios. But they're so beautiful in the way they resolve themselves and what they say and how he says it. He was a genius, absolutely a genius." In the song, Lewis hits notes from the very high to the very low registers. "He liked that. Every note is so beautiful. In that record he's going pretty rapidly, and the musical line just keeps flowing into another pretty part of it. These things are still just as meaningful to me as when I was fifteen and sixteen years old."

The day, the beginning of the sixth week of shooting, is devoted to the eleven scenes in Abe's classroom that are spread through the movie. Two are about a page of dialogue, but the remainder are half a page or less, some just a line or two. They will be filmed in block shooting—the camera films everything in the various scenes from one side and then again from the other to save setups and make the day shorter, or at least less long. A condor, a crane, and a scissor lift outside the second-floor windows blast light that is diffused by blinds and silks.

Billy Weberg, the key grip and a thirty-year veteran of filmmaking, hustles his crew to get everything set up. "With great cameramen like Darius or Bob Richardson or Janusz Kaminski [Steven

Lights for Abe's classroom, second story, left. Air-conditioning tubes are connected to keep the interior, where there are more lights, cool.

Spielberg's longtime cinematographer], it's the quality of light they want to get—to keep it as natural as possible, bring out the level of what exists," he says when they're done. "Woody is a true director. I've worked with [Robert] Altman, [Sidney] Lumet, and now him: the trifecta. These guys are the last frontier of real film directors. They can write, direct, even produce, and have final control. They know their craft. I did *Amistad* [1997] with Steven Spielberg. There was no camera movement. It stuck to the period and was static. On the other hand, there was *War of the Worlds* [2005]. He lights big. Janusz has to light three hundred sixty degrees because Spielberg never knows which direction he wants to shoot. It's ten times more lighting than we do here. And it's broad-stroke lighting as well, using three cameras, not the one we have. Ridley Scott in *American Gangster* [2007] used five cameras at once, covering everything, because he knew how he wanted to cut it together. With Woody, with anybody, you have to be nimble. Deck out the patio at Jill's house, fly balloons, you need to do it quickly—that's why sometimes you see people on Friday but not on Monday"—if you're not fast enough, you're replaced. "There's a saying that there are three movies: the one you rehearse, the one you shoot, the one you edit."

As Woody does not rehearse his, he has only two. (Of course he does block out where the actors should go, and the camera crew does rehearse its moves. Tape is placed on the floor as marks for where the dolly stops, and the focus puller carefully measures the distance from the camera to the actors.)

Scene 22, in which Abe tells Jill that her paper is both good and original, is their first scene together in the finished picture. As opposed to Jill's introduction in the film, Woody says he wants it "unhighlighted."

Between scenes he says that he is thinking of calling the movie *Crazy Abe.* The title has been in his mind since he began writing, but he has not mentioned it to anyone. His sister, Letty, is not sure, feeling people might think it is a comedy. Woody is unconcerned. "They always do anyway," he says, and reminds her that *Merton of the Movies* (1924, remade in 1947) is about trying to make a drama that ends up a smash comedy.

Crazy Abe has an amusing corollary. In *Take the Money and Run,* there is a minor character with that name played by Minnow Moskowitz—his brother's name was Fishy—a pal of Woody's from his days as a stand-up at Mister Kelly's in Chicago in the 1960s. "He was very nice. He was a mug who sold a couple of jokes, and he had delusions of being a comedy writer. I didn't think that was his future. He came to San Francisco when we were shooting, and I used him in the scene when we all get together in a room and look at a film of the bank we're going to rob. [But first there is a travelogue, *Trout Fishing in Quebec.*] He's the guy who says, 'Ah, there's always a boring short.' I had a lot of laughs with him. We hung out for years. Every time I came to Chicago he always showed up. We shot a lot of pool together. I remember when I was striking out with these pretty girls he was saying, 'I can't believe you're striking out. I go to bed with them just because I know you!'"

Each day's call sheet has a few-word summary of the scenes to be shot. Today's: "17 Abe teaching Kant; 19 Lecturing on Kierkegaard; 22 Abe thought Jill's paper was good; 32 Abe is late, tells class he's hungover; 53 Discussing existential choice; 61 Discussing continental philosophy; 88 Abe talks about *Shane;* 106 Abe finishes lecture, 'Being in itself'; 107 Abe finishes class; sets out for home; 124 Jill confronts Abe. He should give himself up; 127 Abe thinking about murdering Jill."

For the most part these scenes are vignettes that serve to show Abe making points in class and as bridges to other action in the story. For instance, here is the whole of 53:

ABE

Today we are going to discuss existential choice—
that life has the meaning you choose to give it—and
we'll examine Jean-Paul Sartre's wonderful insight—
hell is other people.

Woody prints the first two takes but in the third Phoenix makes a mush of his lines. Woody, watching on the monitor in a classroom across the hall, laughs, says, "Cut," and calls out, "Go get some sea air. Take an ocean voyage and you'll be okay." Phoenix laughs in return. Later, filming a different classroom scene, he asks for another take. "I wasn't speaking English," he tells Woody. "Not a word of that was English."

"Well," he answers, "try to make sense. They're selling tickets."

All levity vanishes in the afternoon when word comes that Robin Williams is dead by suicide. Woody and Williams had shared the same managers, Jack Rollins and Charles Joffe. Williams gave a memorable performance in *Deconstructing Harry* as a man who not only feels out of focus but actually *is* out of focus in every scene. Woody is deeply saddened, and for several days will ask again and again, How could this have happened?

The next day is still somber, but there is a movie to be made and postponed scenes are piling up. Everyone knew that getting all eleven scenes scheduled the day before would be close to impossible, and three are left over. Woody has been thinking for a few days of cutting one of those remaining, 88.

BECKY

We saw you at the Campus Cinema Society last night. What did you think about the movie?

ABE

I'm not usually a fan of Westerns but *Shane* is special. Why is it special? Because it resolves itself with the hero riding into town and killing three men—men who deserved killing. He is putting his own life on the line to help others—it's killing but it's moral—

BECKY

What's more moral is passive resistance—what Gandhi preached.

ABE

Martin Buber asked Gandhi if he thought passive resistance would have worked against the Nazis.

Woody's very favoritism for the film has caused him to think about dropping it: "I felt I didn't want to pause in the picture that much and I felt that people would associate it with me personally because I've been so outspoken about how good it is." When Woody casually asks Phoenix if he is ready to do it, he jokingly responds, "Not so."

"Then let's get rid of it," Woody immediately says.

Surprised, he answers, "No wait, I'm really happy to do it."

Just his sham ambivalence is enough for Woody to decide to drop the shot. "The second he said to me, 'Oh, I don't want to do it,' in a half-joking way, I said, 'Great, don't do it.' Then I was able to play the big shot for a moment, a gesture of great grandiosity." But of course he never decides to drop a scene as a gesture of great grandiosity; he does it because he thinks it has lost its purpose in the film. "It was scheduled, and I figured, 'Well, I could shoot it and if I hate it later I can always throw it away.' If he had said, 'It is my favorite scene and I have been dying to do it,' then I would have shot it." *Shane* was made in 1953, and it is unlikely that the students would know it—or, unfortunately, many of the audience. (It could be said that Abe romanticized himself as Shane, avenger of those who harm the harmless.)

Instead, most of the morning is given over to scene 124, one of the most emotionally pyrotechnic of the film. Abe has so far gotten away with murder, and only Jill has figured him for the crime. Then in scene 123, Jill's father reads her a story in the local paper:

> Police are certain they have the person who poisoned Judge Thomas Spangler, the family court judge who was murdered in Lippitt Park. The alleged killer, Albert Podesta, a medical laboratory worker, had access to the same kind of cyanide that was used in the murder. Podesta, who denies he had anything to do with it, had testified before Judge Spangler two years ago and had been enraged with the judge for his ruling in a case against his brother. If convicted, Podesta faces life imprisonment.

124 INT. CLASSROOM—DAY

(Abe has just finished a class. As the last of the students exit, he straightens papers on a windowsill at the back of the room. Jill bursts in, furious.)

JILL

What do you plan to do about this?

ABE

I don't know. I didn't expect it.

JILL

What do you mean you don't know? You're surely not going to just sit back and let this man take the rap for you?

ABE

I've been up and back over it since I heard the news.

JILL

Up and back? What does that mean?

ABE

It means I tried to bring off a perfect crime and apparently I succeeded all too well.

JILL

Yes, but all your big talk about the moral high ground.

ABE

I have to think this out.

JILL

There's nothing to think. An innocent man is about to have his life ruined.

ABE

Okay, I'll give myself up. Isn't that what you want?

JILL

Isn't that what YOU want? All the talk, talk, talk about making the world a better place.

ABE

Okay. Okay—if they don't see they're making a mistake and let him go in a few days, I'll turn myself in.

JILL

Oh god, Abe—you have to. I've had a hard enough time living with this as is but there's no way I'd let an innocent man be prosecuted for it.

ABE

I know—I agree—let me just see if my luck holds out and they come to realize he didn't do it.

JILL

How scared he must be. By Monday—then I want you to do it—or—

ABE

Or?

JILL

Or I have to do it.

ABE

You won't have to do it—give me till Monday.

JILL

First thing in the morning.

(She slams the classroom door as she exits. The next scene is a voice-over with Abe sitting in a coffee shop.)

ABE (V.O.)

But I had no intention of giving myself up. A few months ago my life meant nothing to me. I got no enjoyment out of it, no pleasure—I'd have been fine if that little game of Russian roulette ended it. But since I planned and executed the elimination of Judge Spangler, my life had taken a new turn. I understood why people loved life and saw it as something joyous to experience. I did get pleasure out of living. I didn't want to commit suicide or spend my remaining days behind bars. I wanted to live—to teach, to write, to travel, to make love.

The last shot in the classroom is scene 127, a wide of Abe and his students as he patrols the aisles between the desks while they take an exam a day after his confrontation with Jill. There is no dialogue, just a chilling forty-five-second voice-over.

ABE (V.O.)

The police had their suspect. Rita Richards, who was never really serious about suspecting me, would see it was another man and that her crackpot theory was crackpot. Europe with Rita was beginning to have an exciting ring to it. Her passion for love and lust was contagious. Only one thing stood in the way. I had a few days before Jill would insist I clear the wrongfully accused man—was there a way to keep her from talking? I guess she was right when she said that one murder opens the door to more.

8

"I'm hoping that I'll have a fighting chance for that second draft in the editing room."

The film is meant to wrap at the end of the week, but that won't happen. The task now is to keep the extra days to a minimum. On Tuesday, Helen Robin, Loquasto, the locations crew, and Woody gather on the sofa and chairs in a lounge in a nineteenth-century stone mansion that is now used for classrooms, its intricate woodwork and high ceilings a reminder of old Newport's grandeur. The forecast for tomorrow is rain. Everyone looks at their weather app to see how bad it will be: very bad, a hundred percent chance and up to two inches. Also, there remains the problem of whether to rewrite and reshoot scene 137, in which Jill and Roy walk off together to end the movie, or leave it alone.

"In *Midnight in Paris* and *Blue Jasmine,* the endings are dictated, but not here," Woody says. The final scene of *Midnight* is Owen Wilson's character serendipitously re-encountering Léa Seydoux's, and *Jasmine* ends with Cate Blanchett's descent into madness. "In those you knew he was going to go off with her, and that she would end up in the street talking to herself. Not here. This picture really ends with the scene before." He mentions to Robin that he may not know what to do until he edits: "You never know what you'll do when you're desperate in New York," and he adds that he's not certain about reshooting anything now.

"I'm sure I could scramble and get back here and do something and end up with the first anyway."

Robin looks at him askance, surely stifling the urge to start her reply with "Are you nuts?" Instead, she simply says, "It's much cheaper to do something here, even if it takes an extra day. You have to start from scratch with bringing a crew back if you're in New York." He decides to write a new scene so that he will have a choice when he edits.

After a long discussion, several scenes are reordered to accommodate the weather, and a couple that need locations are settled, including two outdoors that can be done near each other this afternoon. One is a re-do of 99, the hopeless horse scene. The notion of shooting it in a yoga studio with the actresses doing headstands has given way to Woody's other idea: Jill narrates as she runs into Ellie coming out of a store, who then tells her about Rita's theory of Abe's involvement in the murder. The other is 84: Jill calls Abe to tell him of the judge's death, apparently of a heart attack, which is in the paper, and he replies:

> Yeah, I read it. It's just the most amazing thing. I know. No. Why should we feel guilty? Listen, if anybody had it coming it was this guy. Hey look, we should go to dinner tonight. You got any plans because I think we should have a wicked celebration. 7:30? Perfect.

. . .

The rain the next morning is diluvian, swamping several parts of Providence and drenching the crew, who waits under a leaky tarp outside the restaurant for the reshoot of scene 86, the romantic dinner between Jill and Abe to celebrate Spangler's death. This is the scene in which, after seeing dailies, Woody felt that Jill's dress and hair were too sophisticated and Abe needed to be looser and more upbeat. Woody arrives, his shirtsleeves soaked. He puts his right thumb and forefinger together in front of his forehead and says, "I had a paper Mai Tai umbrella." The rain is at times so heavy that its pelting the roof interferes with recording the dialogue.

Both Abe and Jill are more relaxed than when they first shot the scene, so much so that they break into laughter several times while the camera rolls. With only five days of shooting left, "it's like the end of school," Woody says later. "There's a tendency to get silly. You saw Emma this morning, she couldn't stop laughing in the scene."

As the crew prepares to move on, Khondji says he understands why Woody wanted the restaurant scene reshot. Even though he liked the first version, today's is much better.

"Yeah," Woody says later. "I felt it was better too, not a lot better, but better because you're doing it a second time so you have the advantage of hindsight. And also the actors have been playing and they get more confident, they loosen up a little bit, so it was definitely better. Whether it was worth all the money to do it again—I'll know it in the cutting room. But I do think it will be better. [It is what he will use.] I think she looked better in this one, and he was more casual. Everything looks better the second time. I wish I could reshoot all my pictures. Chaplin always shot them and looked at them and shot them again. In those days you could do that."

Khondji earlier cited *Klute* (1971) as an example of a film that looks good in Panavision. The eeriness of that film is what he wants to capture in Abe.

"Yes," Woody says when told this. "It's great, but I'll be happy if we have a lens that just stays in focus."

• • •

A full day is devoted to the setup and carrying out of the murder: Abe stalking the judge to learn his routine, summarized in the production schedule: "Scene 60: Judge jogs and then reads the paper on a park bench; 71: Abe spying on judge jogging; 75: Spangler jogging; 76: Abe watching Spangler; 77: Spangler buying orange juice and newspaper; 78: Abe follows Spangler to his usual park bench." And then 79, the all-important scene in which he leaves the judge with the cup of poisoned juice in Lippitt Park, a square block of grass, trees, a playground, benches, and a couple of paths through the green.

Nearly six hours of the day are spent on Abe coming to the bench under a tree where Spangler reads his newspaper and quickly switching his identical cup of juice—its contents laden with cyanide—with the judge's. To be sure every possible angle is covered, there are eleven setups: a full shot that starts on Spangler then includes Abe as he enters and exits from the left; one of the orange juice cups—Abe sits into the shot from left, places his cup down, takes Spangler's cup, and exits from left; Abe sits on the bench pushing his cup over in one shot and not pushing it in the next, both times exiting left; Abe in profile with Spangler in soft focus; a close-up of Abe exiting left; a medium close-up of Spangler; a close-up of Spangler; a full-medium-full (the actor from the knees or chest up) of Abe and Spangler shot first with the focus starting on Spangler and then Abe, then first on Abe and then on Spangler; a full-medium-full of Abe and Spangler; a Steadicam medium close-up of Abe; and from behind the bench, a dolly wide full (the camera moves on the dolly frame showing the whole body) that starts on Spangler, then Abe enters and exits from right as the dolly slowly pushes in. Woody thinks that the shot from the back will be "the money shot." Thirty-five takes are made, twenty-nine printed, a total of twenty-six minutes of film for a scene that will play out in a minute and a half.

The scene is more difficult to shoot than it appears. A man comes and sits on a bench next to another man, who is engrossed in reading his newspaper, a cup of juice at his side. The first man surreptitiously swaps an identical cup and leaves. "The problem," Woody says between setups, "is how do you poison a perfect stranger without, you know, mailing a cake to his house and poisoning all his relatives? It's not an easy thing to do. So this was one way I figured out, that he was able to see the judge's habits—he jogs and then has juice or something. [He decided against coffee because there is no way to know how the judge drinks his, though it is possible to know what he orders.] So the question is, how do you get the poison in his drink? Well, you can't because his drink is covered, you can't just go and slip poison in it. You have to have a duplicate cup that has poison in it and make the switch.

"I'm doing a lot of angles on it with two things in mind. The most pressing is that it doesn't look silly or comical, like in an Abbott and Costello movie, when they are switching drinks. And the other thing is, if it does work, then I can get a modicum of tension by stretching the time that it takes place."

Although he and Khondji had thought the most dramatic shot of the switch could be from the rear, Woody, already mentally cutting the scene, has second thoughts as they do more takes from the front

The scene in which Abe poisons Judge Spangler (Tom Kemp) required much of a day to shoot.

and sides. "It seems like we may get away with it more easily. Now I'm sensing that if we show Joaquin's face and then the judge's face and then the drinks and then his hand goes around the drink and then you cut back for a second, and you do it in montage where you're never really seeing the whole action, that I can get away with it, that it doesn't look comic and the audience doesn't realize how difficult it would really be. If I'm sitting on a bench reading and not concentrating and have no idea that anybody's got murder on his mind, I'm not going to pay attention if a guy sits down next to me and switches the drink—it's certainly feasible. I just have to make the audience believe that. There are so many ways it could go wrong. You know," he adds, starting to laugh, "a little kid could see him do it and yell, 'Mommy, Mommy, that man stole the other man's drink!' "

After yesterday's torrent, the sky is blue and the air clear—a pleasant summer's day. While the crew readies one of the shots, Woody wants to see how well he can catch a ball gauging its flight with only one good eye. He takes a tennis ball from the prop master, and we toss it back and forth for half an hour, the first time he has done this

Woody at leisure, tossing a ball for the first time in years, between takes in the park where the judge is poisoned.

in ages. His throws are fluid and easy, the perfect infielder's motion across the body. On the way to lunch, Greg Miller, his driver, says that the Teamsters told him, "Hey, your guy can play ball."

With four days of filming left, the question of what should be in the opening montage is finally answered. Instead of Abe driving across the bridge, there will be a series of shots of him driving along the narrow beach roads that lead to and from Newport while we hear his voice-over:

> Kant said that human reason is troubled by questions that it cannot dismiss but also cannot answer. Of course science progresses while philosophy doesn't because the most profound questions asked by philosophy can't be answered. Okay, so what are we talking about here? Morality? Choice? The randomness of life, aesthetics, murder? Luck? Everything—it's all those things.

Then over shots of campus life, the students going to and fro, the classes:

JILL (V.O.)

I think Abe was crazy from the beginning. Was it from stress? Was it biology? Was he disgusted by what he saw as life's never-ending suffering? Or was he simply bored by the meaninglessness of day-to-day existence? He was so damn interesting and different and a good talker and he could always cloud the issue with words.

ABE (V.O.)

(still driving)

Where to begin . . . you know the Existentialists feel nothing happens until you hit absolute rock

> bottom. Well, let's say that when I went to teach at Braylin College, emotionally I was at Zabriskie Point. I took the job at Braylin because it was a pretty little college in Rhode Island where I could teach and maybe pull myself together. Of course my reputation—or should I say, a reputation—preceded me.

Woody had assumed this would be a chance to look over the college campus, but having used the most photogenic spots, he thinks it would be "arresting if right after the final opening credit you have a close-up through the windshield of Joaquin driving and you hear this narration about Kant. Then looking out the car window at Ocean Drive would be nice and then you could hear Emma's voice come in over it." He didn't push earlier for this solution "because it's expensive and a pain in the ass to do, and because I hate car shots. You're up on the trailer that's pulling the car and looking down at the monitor."

The shot will give the audience their first view of Abe. Woody not only wants to give his leading ladies a good entrance, depending on the story he often does this for his leading man—Javier Bardem in *Vicky Cristina Barcelona,* for example, is shown leaning against a pillar, a glass of red wine in hand, wearing a red satin shirt and a louche look; it is instantly clear he is both sexy and trouble. In this instance, however, Woody feels, "I don't want to see Joaquin until the car pulls up to the college—he's just a mysterious voice—and he gets out with his sunglasses on. So he'll still get a good entrance this way but not the way I wanted to do it because there's not enough campus to go around."

Much of Friday morning, starting early so as to have the prettiest light, is spent making eleven shots of Abe behind the wheel as trees, hedges, and ocean roll by. Abe's old Volvo is on the bed of a trailer pulled by a truck with the camera mounted in the rear. There is, however, a major problem with what is filmed that no one will notice until the penultimate day of shooting.

At six the next morning, again to get the best light, Woody shoots the just-written alternative final scene (138): Jill walks alone along the wet sand in a deserted cove, the open ocean filling half the screen. It will cover her forty-five-second voice-over:

> As I think back on Abe Lucas I have to admit it was quite an experience. For me a learning experience. It led me to thoughts about life, love, psychology, philosophy, and who am I really?—I even experienced, for one terrifying moment, the closeness of death. I also learned to beware of anyone who becomes convinced he has the high moral ground. And although it was painful, it was not without its special moments. As Abe would say—it was a lesson in life you couldn't get from any textbook.

When Woody sees the dailies on Tuesday he says, "I wish we could see a little more face in screen. It's not fatal. We can work around it, but it's a little disappointing."

There remains an unsolved problem. The music for an Allen film is almost always jazz mixed with tunes from the 1930s and 1940s, with a heavy reliance on such personal favorites as George Gershwin, Cole Porter, Irving Berlin, and Rodgers and Hart. Often he has an idea of what sort of music he is going to want even if the title is yet to be chosen. This time, with only a couple of days to go, he still has no clue of what he will do, and for the first time in weeks he is giving it serious thought.

"This is an ominous movie, a melodrama. When I did *Match Point*, I used all opera because opera suggested itself: the story was operatic and the family loved opera and invited him [the tennis pro who turns killer] to the opera, so it worked out very well, and I was able to use all those old Caruso records; it sounded great to my ear. [He used vintage recordings, mostly of Enrico Caruso arias, and one operatic tune by Andrew Lloyd Webber.] Here, nothing suggests itself. She's a piano player, but I don't think classical piano would be very exciting.

So I'm trying to think now of counterprogramming. I wouldn't do this but it could be something in which all the tunes have the word 'crazy' in them—'You're Driving Me Crazy,' 'Crazy Because I Love You.' I can't use 'It's a Wonderful World' because it was used ironically in *It's a Wonderful World* [1939, with Claudette Colbert and James Stewart, directed by W. S. Van Dyke]. If you get the right piece of music you can do that. Maybe there's a Rodgers and Hart or Cole Porter tune out there that would say something about it. When I did *Husbands and Wives,* we found that wonderful old recording of Bubber Miley on cornet, Eddie Duchin on piano, and Lew Conrad singing 'What Is This Thing Called Love?' That said it very nicely. In *The Notorious Landlady* [1962, with Jack Lemmon, Kim Novak, and Fred Astaire, directed by Richard Quine], they used 'A Foggy Day in London Town' because the picture took place in London and anytime there was any music—or at least very often in the picture—they played it. So if there was some song, some Johnny Mercer blues nightclub song—ironically, it could be 'I've Got the World on a String.' I used 'Murder, He Says' sung by Betty Hutton in *Crimes and Misdemeanors.*

"If I could find something lively, it would be great because when people are walking across campus and driving their car, a piece of music that's fun to listen to takes up the slack tremendously. In *Psycho* [1960], when Janet Leigh is driving to the motel, it's ominous, foreboding music and it's great, she's still on the run. But you have to find a piece or have somebody write one for you. Quincy Jones's music for *In Cold Blood* [1967] is not my favorite of his, but it certainly evokes tension. But again, nothing in this picture suggests anything, and that's why I'm sort of kicking myself for not going with my first instinct [which he mentioned some weeks earlier]. I had them buy a disc player for Abe as part of his unloading into the apartment, and I thought when he came back from the cocktail party he'd put a disc on and what he liked was ironically only Jelly Roll Morton or something—that kind of intellectual could justify that highly specialized taste in low-class boogie-woogie and it would ring reasonably true. But I didn't follow up on it, why I don't know. Then this morning in the romantic scene, I almost—almost—was going to run up to

Joaquin and have Emma say to him, 'The music here is pretty.' I was going to put in source music, cocktail music—and he would say something like, 'The only music I really like is boogie-woogie,' and I could use that thematically and not have to justify it, but it didn't seem quite right. No music is another way to go. Now naturally when they go to the teachers' cocktail party you've got to put something in, and for the fancy restaurant you've got to put something in to cover the rain. But there's nothing that suggests itself."

People forget that *Annie Hall* had no scoring, that it was all source music, and although Woody has mentioned once or twice during filming that no music was a possibility, now he says, "I was braver then, and for this picture I'm not as confident—that was a comedy and romantic. You could try it here, but it's not shot to be without music. No music is good with a lot of cuts, but when you have master shots you want some music. And for me, the fun is putting the music in. I hate to deny myself that day when I sit with Alisa [Lepselter, his film editor for the past nineteen pictures] and we start to put in the music and suddenly scenes that were just boring as hell suddenly liven up because you're listening to a Louis Armstrong or a Cole Porter song."

Armstrong is a particular favorite of Woody's. A few days earlier he said that he would love to find a place in a film sometime for his versions of "Shadrach, Meshach, Abednego" and "The Night Before Christmas." But not here. "I could never use anything like that, none of that applies, but I love to hear him sing—he's talking 'The Night Before Christmas'—I love anything he does. But it still doesn't help me in this movie. I used a lot of blues in *Blue Jasmine*—King Oliver, Sidney Bechet, and Louis Armstrong—and I don't want to do the same thing here."

August 19 is the next to last day of shooting. These two days will be in a shuttered cement high-rise that was once a bank and office building. (It is known as the Superman building because it resembles that of the *Daily Planet* in the Superman TV series.) Woody's feelings about the film, which have yo-yoed through the past six weeks, have settled into their usual end-of-shooting ambivalence. "It would not surprise me either way at this point if when I put it together I say, 'Hey this is good, the story works.' And it would not surprise me if the audience didn't care for it at all or if they don't believe the story. They may feel I've mixed a kind of dramatic story with a kind of Hitchcockian thing and it's too much intellectual patina for this sort of a story—or that it works just fine. I'm hoping that I'll have a fighting chance for that second draft in the editing room."

He is anxious to finish and get back to New York and sleep in his own bed. "Ahhh! I can't tell you," he says with a smile and brimming pleasure in his voice. "There's no way to convey how I feel when I come down those steps in the morning from my bedroom, go to the front door to fetch *The New York Times,* and outside there in all seasons is my beautiful street. It's New York, it's Manhattan, it's right out my door. I *live* there: I actually own a piece of Manhattan. I can't tell you what a thrill it is. I could stand there for five minutes and just look—the trees, the people passing, it's Manhattan and I'm just on the other side of the door." He laughs at the intensity of his delight but does not shy away from it. "It's amazing pleasure for me. It was always and still is considered one of the most beautiful, if not *the* most beautiful, blocks on the Upper East Side. It's tree lined on both sides with small private houses. Before we moved there I had always loved to walk on the street, always remarked on how beautiful it is. It's where I had Alvy [Singer in *Annie Hall*] live."

His reverie is ruined when Helen Robin brings the dailies of the process shots of Abe in his car. The seat of the Volvo was not tied down tightly enough and Abe looks like a kid excitedly bouncing on his way to get ice cream. No one mentioned while shooting how pronounced and steady the bobbing is, but it is all too clear now. Several of the crew did notice but, thinking Woody wanted it this way, made no comment. Sometimes a crew can be too deferential to a revered director.

He fast-forwards through all the takes and quickly concludes there is not enough usable footage to cover all that is needed. His mood sinks. Half an hour earlier he was excited about going home tomorrow, but now he has no choice but to reshoot, which will mean at least another day. There is plenty of deflation to go around. No one in the crew wants yet another day tacked on, least of all Robin and the others in the production department, who are fighting to keep the film close to budget. She calls the police to see if they can get Ocean Drive blocked off again but is told nothing can be done before the weekend.

The day is literally saved when Virginia McCarthy, who has quietly gone to a corner of the deco lobby with the dailies and her stopwatch, says she has found enough snippets of fourteen seconds or twenty-three seconds in which Abe does not look like he is on a pogo stick to make the montage work.

Woody did not have to think twice about continuing the film an extra day or two, the approximately $175,000 a day coming from his pocket, even though the production was already three days over schedule. Staying to get everything you might need is a tough lesson he learned long ago. "A number of times I've been in the cutting room and didn't have what I needed because I rushed or I overcompromised. I was so relieved that Virginia could find good pieces for me."

With other films, he was not so lucky. After he watched the rough cut of *Crimes and Misdemeanors,* in early 1989, he said that the dramatic portion of the film with Martin Landau looked better than he thought it would, but that his comic section with Mia Farrow and Alan Alda did not work at all. Over the next few weeks he threw out fully one-third of the story and revamped the storyline and plot; in the end he reshot 80 of the film's 139 scenes either during principal photography or in the second go-round, and he bore the entire cost for the extra work.

But such heroics are not needed here. The present crisis resolved, the company settles in to get the six scenes for the day. Four are of Jill going to or taking a piano lesson interspersed through the second half of the story. The exterior for where she studies is a seven-story brown brick business building. The interiors for her lessons and the elevator that will be the scene of the film's denouement are in this much taller building with the right-looking elevator apparatus for playing out Abe's plan to prevent Jill from turning him in. The hallway from the piano teacher's studio to the elevator, all dingy white and scuffed before, has been transformed by two shades of green paint on either side of the chair railing Loquasto installed three feet up the walls "to give tension," he says. The railing pulls the eye along the corridor to the door at the end of the seventy-five-foot-long hall, where Jill's teacher has her studio. The dirty wall-to-wall green carpet that has been on the floor for years somehow looks new. By the elevator there is a directory of offices on the floor. Although the names cannot be made out in the shots, they include Kordish and Kordish in number 613 (Scott Kordish is Helen Robin's assistant); T Me Do, a chiropractor; and M. Wildmann, piano. A shiny copper fire extinguisher on the wall by the elevator adds a pleasant touch. A window insert has been constructed to make it look like a wall is just past the elevator rather than the spacious corridor that is actually there.

Loquasto calls his design of the room for Jill's lessons "a classic analyst's greenroom, with a piano." Two 15-kilowatt lights held up by condors on the street shine through the opaque curtained window. Green and red linoleum tiles have been put on the floor, and a poster of the great early music, baroque, classical, romantic, and modern composers from Guillaume Dufay to Igor Stravinsky hangs on a wall. A bust of Beethoven rests on the bookcase filled with tomes on classical music—and for Woody's amusement, out of context with everything else in the room, *The Way to Tin Pan Alley* (a compendium of musical scores and songs between the Civil War and World War I), with such titles as "I'm Going to Do What I Please" and "$15 in My Pocket." "A nod to the audience," Loquasto says to Woody as he looks over the room: "Don't worry folks, the next one will be funny."

Scene 91: Abe watching Jill's lesson in the bloom of their romance.

JILL (V.O.)

I remember how much fun it was the day Abe watched my piano lesson. He was so inspirational. I told Roy that I needed some space. God, what a

> clichéd way to put it—but space is what I needed. Distance from our relationship so I could explore my feelings for Abe, whom I adored.

The shot is of Jill, the teacher, and Abe, seated by the curve of the baby grand. The camera is positioned in front of the piano so as not to show Jill's fingers on the keys, since Stone can't play. "Bring in Deanna Durbin," Loquasto calls out while the shot is set up. It needs to cover the eighteen seconds of voice-over. Woody says to put ten seconds on Jill and then pan toward Abe. Between each take the hair and makeup artists rush in to touch up Stone. Woody is impatient. "You'd think this is a product shot," he says loudly, referring to a commercial for a beauty aid; "let's go."

The reason for scenes of Jill at her piano lesson and saying goodbye to her teacher is not so much for plot as it is to provide momentum in this sequence. Some narrative pieces are needed while Abe is in the basement fidgeting with the elevator: "Cut to her and she's going in to her teacher while he's walking up the stairs; she's with her teacher playing chords and scales; he's hanging out in the hall; and she's leaving her teacher. I need little stuff to make the sequence go."

Scene 130 begins the climax to the film. Various cuts show Abe following Jill as she walks to her lesson.

ABE (V.O.)

> Did I love Jill? I thought she was a fabulous young woman but I valued my own life too greatly to allow her to destroy it.

Jill enters the building and Abe follows presently. He walks downstairs to the basement elevator room. The controls are in the foreground, the shaft and elevator in the rear. In scene 25, Abe and Jill walk and talk for the first time, and in telling her about his past he says, "I drove a cab, I was a handyman in a building, I ran an elevator." Now he plays off that setup.

ABE (V.O.)

Her death would have to look like an accident and I ran through all the ones she might have and it hit me—my brief time running an elevator during my college days might now pay off. Funny how often your best ideas come under the pressure of a deadline.

Scene 132: Abe in the elevator room. He pulls on rubber gloves and fusses with the control box. The elevator moves a bit and then stops with a thump.

ABE (V.O.)

It was perfect. Saturday was her piano lesson. Most of the offices were closed. There was very little action in the building. I couldn't make it look like the elevator had been tampered with but I knew enough how to make it seem broken—

A camera with a 50-millimeter lens is set up in the doorway. This gives a closer look at Abe but does not show all the room and the elevator shaft, the most important things here. Woody says to pull the camera behind the doorway and put on a 40-millimeter so the audience will see the shaft and the elevator being stalled in it: "We just need a sense of Abe doing his stuff. To me, the shot is about the room. There's no need to see Joaquin doing that mischief in close-up, no need to see the expression on his face or what he's doing with his fingers. What's appealing to me is the room. The shot is really about the elevator shaft."

The one shot outside the building is at the courthouse across the street. It is made last to take advantage of early evening light. Scene 58 is one of the several of Abe tracking the judge to learn his daily routine in the hope of finding a time and place to kill him unobserved. Spangler comes down the courthouse steps, walks toward the camera, and exits from the right. Abe, watching in the far background, enters from the left and exits near right. Woody wants to get Abe in the shot without him "skulking" or having to cut to him. We have seen Abe track the judge in many ways—from a park bench, in his car, and on foot. There are a dozen beige-clad extras who walk through the scene. Woody tells the camera operator to "hang more on the judge. We haven't seen him before. He can't look like he's an extra who happens to be in front of the camera. It has to be, 'Ladies and gentlemen, here's the judge!' "

A take is made but there are too many people in the frame to make out Spangler immediately. "Lose the extra in front of him so he comes out alone and there is no question of who he is," he says, "and Abe needs to be farther in back."

But still too many people come up the steps behind the judge. Arthur Penn offered good advice: about 80 percent of the people in the first take are out for the third. "Abe should be walking all the time, not lurking," Woody calls out. Take 4 is better, take 5 nails it. "It really helps to flush out all the extras," Woody says, "then you know what you're looking at." Seconds later he is in his car and on the way to Newport.

August 20 is the thirty-second and last day of shooting—four days longer than scheduled, three less than originally planned. Only scene 136 remains, the most dramatic of the film. There are three setups: Jill comes out from her lesson and walks down the hall; cut to Abe waiting by the elevator; she turns the corner to the elevator, sees him, they do their dialogue, and when the door opens, he grabs her and tries to shove her into what we see is an empty shaft. The plan is to be finished by lunchtime and for Woody and his family to be on Edward Walson's plane back to New York at five o'clock. He is thrilled to be going home even though, "after I am away for a while I can't remember whether the movies are in the two hundred or five hundred channels [of his television system], the code to the alarm, or where I keep my vitamins."

The crew are crammed into the small space in the hallway and around the elevator. Woody leans against the wall by the camera. "I'm reflexively and inexplicably sad," he says. "Inexplicably because I'm dying to get out of here and glad it's over. I can't wait to edit it. But what happens is, you do a project and you work so intensely with the same people every day—you see them at seven in the morning and you're with them all day and their problems are your problems and vice versa for months at a time. And then"—he claps his hands once—"it's all over. There is no real connection. I have no real connection to Emma, no real connection to Joaquin or Darius, I don't even know the names of most of the people in the crew. I guess humans get comfortable in a situation."

This scene is one he has given thought to for months as he planned and changed details, and after all that he is still unsure how well it will work. "I hope that when I see the film that I don't feel, 'You just don't buy it that he would kill her, he's been too romantic with her.' It worries me. I don't know if I'm going to earn it, if people will feel, 'Oh, god, it was so romantic. She was falling in love throughout the picture with this old burned-out guy, but I didn't think he would try to kill *her.*' [The film is similar to *Match Point* in that the audience does not anticipate an attempt on the life of the lover.] You'd buy it if he gave himself up or he felt riddled with remorse. Yes, he's crazy, and I'm counting on the title *Crazy Abe,* but I don't want it to be that his behavior is just dramatically irrational and is not consistent. Not just, 'He's crazy,' but that he could do anything—he could take tap dancing lessons."

The first two parts of the scene are made easily. Now comes the all-important action. Jill walks down the hall from her lesson and when she turns to the elevator, she sees Abe.

JILL

Abe—omigod, you scared me. What are you doing here?

ABE

I just wanted to talk to you before I go to the police.

JILL

If it's about anything but giving yourself up—

ABE

No. I see no other way. I just wanted to apologize for all the trouble I've caused you.

(He pushes the elevator button.)

JILL

It's a nightmare but the only way out is to tell them the whole story.

ABE

What? That I murdered a judge?

JILL

I'll certainly say whatever I can as a friend—I'll stand behind you.

ABE

It won't matter—it's premeditated murder—they'll put me away for life.

JILL

Maybe not. Maybe with a good lawyer—

ABE

Who are we kidding?

JILL

I just don't know what to say—the whole thing is so tragic.

(The elevator door opens to a dark shaft with no cab.)

Actually the top of the elevator cab is three feet below the door. A mattress is atop it to soften Abe's fall, but it is far enough down that his feet will disappear completely. Phoenix wants to do the fall himself, but first a stuntman rehearses it several times to be sure there is no extra danger, and for Khondji to decide how best to film it; he records the falls on his iPhone and shows them to Woody. Stone will do some of the wrestling, but a stunt double (hired through a specialist stunt coordinator) will handle the most vigorous portion. Two cameras will film the shot to capture the action with different lenses and at different angles and speeds to make the scene cut together in a more exciting way, the first time in the picture more than one is used. A little bit of light is put on the six cables to emphasize there is no cab, but otherwise the shaft is black.

Between rehearsals Woody once again plays chess on his phone. "I have never won," he says.

There is no further need for the day's script pages. He abandons the game to rip his sides into the customary eight pieces and dangles them near McCarthy's mouth. She takes them with her thumb and index finger.

"Don't let these fall into the hands of the jihadists," he says.

"I know my job is to eat them," she answers with mock solemnity.

"Yes, I can see you have put on some weight eating the script."

"It's a heavy story."

Two hours pass and the first shot is yet to be made. Woody slips into kick-ass mode: "Can we shoot finally? Or we're never going to get out of here."

There is some excitement about the shot, both because it is the last of the film and because it is so dramatic, even if it is all make-believe—at least until the action starts. Suddenly it all seems completely real: A man is trying to shove a woman into an open elevator shaft. The woman is fighting for her life. The man has the upper hand, but the elevator door closes and he has to adjust to press the down button again. The woman is writhing and resisting with all her might. In the tussle her bag falls to the carpet and its contents—among them sheet music and the flashlight she chose at the amusement park—spill out. Their feet momentarily slip on the sheets of paper, but the man now has her in a better grasp and is almost at the point where he can turn her into the shaft. Just then, he steps on the flashlight; it rolls forward, and he falls back toward the open door. He lets go of the woman to catch himself on the frame but grasps only air and screams as he drops to his death. She picks up the flashlight, its beam shining at the camera, looks at it, then down the dark elevator shaft.

A few of the well-seasoned crew audibly gasp when Abe falls. All applaud as Phoenix pops up from the void. Still, the emotion of the scene is evident on the actors' faces and, for that matter, on the faces of many of those watching. This is the key moment of the movie, and Khondji and Woody carefully watched their monitors to be sure everything they want is in the shot. No one wants to have the star—or a stuntman—fall into an elevator shaft again unless absolutely necessary.

The shot is good and they move on. To give a variety of visual angles from which to piece together the struggle, shots are made of Jill and Abe: Abe with the stunt double for Jill; their legs as they fight; the purse and flashlight on the ground; another of just the flashlight; and one of Abe's feet, the right one slipping on the flashlight, done at thirty frames a second rather than the usual twenty-four to imperceptibly slow the action. A little over nine minutes of film is printed to construct a scuffle that lasts twenty-five seconds on the screen.

It is after one p.m. when "Cut" and "Check the gate" are ordered for the last time, followed by more applause. The cast and crew immediately go to a large room on the floor for the customary group photo, and Stone and Phoenix pose for shots with members of the various departments. Phoenix then walks over to Woody and bows from the waist.

"Maestro," he says as they shake hands.

There is a wrap party that night but Woody is home in New York before it begins.

CHAPTER 6

The Edit

The glamour of the movie business, almost always absent in a film's shooting, is never present in its editing, which in this case will take 200,000 feet of multiple takes from various angles and shape around 9,000 of them into a story. Woody's three-room combination office/editing/screening suite plus a bathroom and projection booth is in the rear of a Park Avenue apartment building; it is windowless save for a tiny pane that looks out onto a dreary inner courtyard. He rented the space, a former bridge club, in the 1970s as a place to watch films and found he could consolidate his work here. The eight-by-sixteen-foot office has a wooden desk and a couple of chairs and bookcases. A poster of *Mighty Aphrodite* hangs by the entrance to the tiny hallway that leads to the water cooler, bathroom, and projection booth. The twenty-by-forty-foot screening room has half a dozen plush chairs upholstered with forest green velour fabric that matches the color on the walls. A golden beige loveseat on a raised platform under the projection window is for him. Along one wall is a specially built case that holds the hundreds of LP albums of jazz, show, and classical music that he draws on to score his pictures. When it is unopened it is simply a nice wooden countertop. Beneath it the records are in bins that mimic those in a record store, at least when such things were common, and to which Woody was a constant visitor. The only thing that has changed over the years (the upholstery included) is the method of editing in the narrow seventeen-by-thirty-foot cutting room.

The cumbersome Moviola that had been a staple of constructing a finished film out of thousands of snippets of celluloid since its invention in 1924, and which Woody used for his first dozen films, was replaced in 1981 by two Steenbeck editing tables that each held a reel of film (1,000 feet) and two of sound track. Woody, who hates to waste time, bought two (they cost about $30,000 apiece) so that if he was cutting a scene on one he could instantly compare it with another version on the second without dismantling the reel in progress. Both these devices required careful monitoring of the many clips of film being considered to assemble a scene. They hung like streamers on a half-open paper clip through a sprocket hole and fell into a canvas bin rather like a large laundry bag. It was tedious and time-consuming work. For example, if the director and editor wanted to see whether an additional three-quarters of a second—eighteen frames—made a shot better, the frames had to be cut and spliced by hand and then removed by hand if they didn't help.

In the early 1990s, Avid Technology, Inc., introduced software that allows for digital editing on an Apple computer with a custom keyboard and stores as many versions of a scene and film as desired. What used to take hours to edit can now be done in minutes and even seconds. A push of a few buttons adds those eighteen frames and, if necessary, subtracts them just as quickly. Woody started using the machine in 1998 on *Sweet and Lowdown*. It was the first film with Alisa Lepselter as his editor. A soft-voiced, steady whiz at the Avid, she could pass as a red-haired cousin of Julia Roberts. Before joining Woody, she was an assistant editor on two of Nora Ephron's films and Martin Scorsese's *The Age of Innocence* (1993), on which she worked with his longtime editor Thelma Schoonmaker, whom she credits with offering invaluable lessons. After Lepselter edited Nicole Holofcener's *Walking and Talking* (1996), she was recommended to Woody when word went out that he was looking for a new editor. They met for a ten-minute interview—a long one by his standards—and he offered the job a few weeks later. She is his third editor in nearly forty-five years.

Her predecessor was Susan E. Morse, who edited twenty-one Allen films beginning with *Manhattan*, in 1979, and continuing through

Celebrity (1998); she also was editor for the TV version of *Don't Drink the Water* (1994). Prior to that, she was an assistant editor on Walter Hill's classic *The Warriors* (1979) and to Ralph Rosenblum, who did the final edit of *Take the Money and Run* and then *Bananas, Sleeper, Love and Death, Annie Hall,* and *Interiors,* and whose forty credits include *The Pawnbroker* (1964), *A Thousand Clowns* (1965), *Long Day's Journey into Night* (1962), and the 1967 Mel Brooks–directed version of *The Producers.* There are many instances of a longstanding collaboration between a director and editor. Martin Scorsese has worked with Schoonmaker since 1967; Clint Eastwood with Joel Cox since 1977; and Steven Spielberg with Michael Kahn since 1977.

Rosenblum came to *Take the Money and Run,* which is largely a series of comic bits told in documentary fashion, after its original edit simply did not work. Woody says perhaps 80 percent was in good shape but that Rosenblum truly salvaged the picture. He showed Woody how more sprightly music would make scenes come alive; encouraged him to use pieces of a long interview with the parents of inept crook Virgil Starkwell (Woody), most of which had been cut, as a funny bridge between segments that did not naturally flow into each other; moved sketches from one reel to another to give the picture better pace; got him away from a dark and realistically bloody ending in which Virgil is killed in a hail of machine gunfire purposely akin to the fusillade at the end of *Bonnie and Clyde* (1967), but completely out of sync with what is otherwise a just-for-laughs comedy ("I didn't earn the ending," Woody says); and added more of Virgil's voice-over along with narrator Jackson Beck's interviews with Virgil to link the mélange together.

Narration remains a favorite tool of Woody's because it allows the audience to hear what is going on in a character's mind. It is the thread that binds the stories of *Zelig, Radio Days, Broadway Danny Rose, Another Woman, Husbands and Wives, Mighty Aphrodite, Vicky Cristina Barcelona,* and this one, among others. A ploy of some directors of comedies is to leave a little space between a funny line and the next bit of dialogue to allow the audience to laugh and not miss what is said next. Herbert Ross and his editor, Marion Rothman, did that in *Play It Again, Sam,* and the Marx Brothers did it in their films, but for Woody, pace is too important for that.

Comedies and dramas have their own considerations and demands. With comedy, a snappy pace is paramount. *Scoop* (2006), for instance, had a first cut of two hours and fourteen minutes and was released at an hour and thirty-six.

"The most prevalent problem was keeping it moving along," he explained, shortly after he finished. "It's a comedy, and a *light* comedy, and you don't have a lot going for you except a light story that has to bounce along amusingly. Once you bog down, it's death. I learned this—I never learned it, I observed it and failed to learn it—on my first play, *Don't Drink the Water* (1966), where I wrote a ton of extra material. You tend to write too much to make things clear and developed. I wrote about five pages between Tony Roberts, who was playing the ambassador's son, and the daughter of Lou Jacobi and Kay Medford, and the second the family walks in with the young daughter and she looks at him and he looks at her [*snaps fingers*], you didn't need any of it. It was superfluous. This kind of thing holds true in the movies. I've learned it [*laughs*] a thousand times and I always screw it up, and that's what I did with this movie. You think the audience is not going to get it so you explain it, clarify it, but the truth of the matter is, they're *always* far ahead of you."

It is common practice in both film and TV for an editor to make an assembly of the dailies during shooting so that the director can come in and immediately see what he or she has and then proceed from there. Not with Woody. He wants to make his own. No editor cuts a frame without his guidance, although he will leave Lepselter to put together changes they have discussed or to try an idea she has. During shooting, she and her assistants put the dailies in order, gather sounds and bits of incidental music that can be placeholders during editing, and generally ready everything to make editing go as quickly as possible. Then Woody comes in and starts with scene 1. He has, Lepselter says, "a photographic memory of scenes, takes, and dialogue, in part because he wrote the picture and lived every shot." He is always thinking ahead and changing the film in his mind. He often wants to move a scene even before they come to it because he already sees it in another place. Within a week or two at most of the completion of filming, he is in the editing room. It takes about ten days to assemble the first cut, with much more work over the next month. Even when he finishes that first iteration, he is not sure of what he has until he looks at the whole thing straight through.

"As I'm cutting it," he said one day with a sigh, "you don't get an inkling of what the whole effect will be. It's all very self-congratulatory and confident and buoyant and optimistic. And then you see what you wrought [*he laughs ironically*] and your heart sinks. It's always too long, it's always too slow. Invariably stuff you thought was funny is not very funny and stuff you thought was so wonderful is not wonderful and relationships you thought would go a certain way don't. Everything that can go wrong goes wrong and nothing is as good as you hoped it would be."

David Picker, among Woody's champions at United Artists, once told a first-time director, "Don't worry. No movie is as good as its dailies or as bad as its first cut."

In mid-September 2014, following a trip to France to attend the premiere of *Magic in the Moonlight* and give interviews to promote the film, Woody and Lepselter settle in to begin editing *The Boston Story*. Woody is still inclined to call it *Crazy Abe* but has told no one connected to the film other than his sister and Helen Robin.

He and Lepselter sit beside each other at the Avid, in the right rear corner of the cutting room. To his right is a forty-six-inch monitor, to give him an enlarged view of what they are working on, and a wooden end table that he sometimes uses to put up his feet. Behind them on the upper part of the wall are dozens of one-and-one-half-by-ten-inch cards held in by rails and stacked in columns. Every scene has a color-coded card to follow the thread of the story, and it is placed to show its spot in the movie as it is currently ordered. A scene written for one part can easily end up in another. Other columns contain the lifts, scenes that have been dropped. Along a wall behind them is a clothing rack with twenty-seven dresses from *Magic* that still have to be sold, donated, or warehoused. Two assistant editors work on computers at the front of the room. A three-cushion sofa rests behind Woody and Lepselter's chairs. To her left is a music stand to hold the script and continuity with the details of every shot in a loose-leaf binder; she tells him how many takes there are of each before they look at them.

Woody's focus while editing is the same as his focus while writing, which is to say complete. There is no food, no background music, nothing for amusement during a break—there are no real breaks anyway. He arrives every weekday morning between nine and nine thirty, works through until about noon, walks home for lunch, returns around one, and edits steadily until five or a bit later. There is no chitchat or personal talk, only attention to the task at hand. He is the same in the editing room as he is on the set: calm, polite, and uninterested in what is happening in the lives of his crew. He is there to work, not socialize. If there is a hiatus while Lepselter makes agreed changes to a scene on the Avid, he will either sit quietly beside her or meet with his assistant to return calls or emails and take care of whatever other business is at hand.

"Editing Woody's films is different than it would be for most other directors," Lepselter says. "He doesn't shoot enormous amounts of coverage. The hope is to choose the take with the performance that best serves the story. Selecting takes, moving scenes around, lengthening or shortening certain sections of the picture—it is always about what best serves the story, if the story is being told authentically. The narrative should have a natural flow; it should be efficient while having room to breathe. The rhythm and pacing of a scene should be organic to how the scene was shot. I believe that the film tells you what to do if you pay attention." Among the things to watch for in editing are the rhythm of the voices, the intonation of the words, and a harsh or soft delivery. There also is the emotional ebb and flow of scenes to consider how they are best combined to advance the story. Woody will always choose the take with the best acting over the prettiest, even when there is a small problem with the focus. One reason he is comfortable with technical flaws is that he never wants his pictures to look "slick and commercial" in the way that studio films prize technical perfection. Plus, as he points out, audiences seldom see the glitches caught by professionals. So whatever seems most real to him is what makes it to the screen. Even though he does not get an inkling of the whole effect of the film as he edits, a sense of its pace does become clear, and that is when he knows what to cut. "You just *feel* at the editing machine that you want to move on to the next thing, and I look at Alisa and she looks at me and we both know the same thing: Who wants to stop for that now?"

They start the edit of each scene by first looking at the dailies, but everything that was filmed is digitally in the Avid, so there is access to all the material. Lepselter notes which take each of them preferred or if they agreed on one; sometimes one may like the delivery of a particular line. As with most every film, usually the order of cutting begins with an establishing shot followed by medium shots and then close-ups. It usually is pretty clear to them how the scene is going to fall into place for the first pass.

The annotated script next to Lepselter has a line through all the dialogue for when a certain character is on camera, for instance, Jill in A92. If Woody asks what coverage they have on her, Lepselter can immediately see exactly how many angles there are. On the facing page are helpful notes for many takes: best for sound; best for camera; a reminder that a boom is visible; that the take is incomplete; if there are airplanes overhead. But to a remarkable degree, Woody already knows this information, to the point, Lepselter says, that she is "amazed sometimes by the grasp he has of what takes he has in his head. He remembers from when he was on set. If there were twenty takes of something he'll say go to the last two, because he'll remember he was going for something. And so we'll look at the last two first and then we'll go back and look at earlier ones; it will jog his memory from what happened on the set that day." He listens to her suggestions and accepts those that offer a better solution than his, but unlike other directors who will say, "Here's an idea, you work it out and I'll come back," he is hands-on for every frame.

Lepselter has developed shortcuts over the years and has programmed the keyboard in a way that makes her remarkably fast. Even so, reconfiguring a scene can take a while. "Sometimes," she says with amusement, "I know there is something that can be done differently that he'd like better, but it's going to take me some time to make it work. I'll say, 'This will take me a few minutes, go out and come back,' but he'd rather just sit there and wait for me to figure it out because he doesn't want to get up and go."

Woody finds it "unthinkable" for him not to be in on every inch of the movie, because to him the screenplay, casting, locations, directing, editing, and music are each a part of the larger creation. The script is just a guide. "You're writing with film when you edit it and put in music. This is all part of the writing process for me."

As with the drafts of the script, the edit is the time to sharpen or smooth out scenes, reorder some to make the story flow better, and to cut whatever seems extraneous. Unlike with writing, it is no simple matter to do something new; you are stuck with the footage you shot. The one thing easy to change is a voice-over, and Woody will rewrite several of Jill's. Until about twenty years ago, he budgeted his films to allow him time and money to go back and redo scenes. "Basically, I shoot the script," he said while making *Another Woman*. "I like to get a first draft on film and then see where I am. I discover radical things I never would know otherwise. A script is only a guide for the work to come." But less so now, in part because after so many films he has a pretty good idea of what he needs, in part because of the reality of budgets and locations. Now if he wants another chance at a scene, he generally redoes it right away. The days of being able to completely reshoot a film, as he did with *September,* have passed. Plus, when he was making his films solely in New York, often with many cast members with whom he was friendly and who lived there and could make time for the extra work, he could ask them to come back. Actors' contracts usually had a clause that kept them available for up to a couple of months after production ended. He no longer has the luxury of reassembling a set and bringing actors back to, say, the South of France. So, as he puts it, "I've had to adapt." There are no more instances of having thirty-five hours of film to wade through after 101 days of shooting, as was the case with *Sleeper.*

Sometimes when Woody knows how he wants the score to sound, they edit with the music as they go along, not moving to the next scene until the one they are working on is scored. "But," he says, "when you don't do that, you often have to make a lot of trims subsequently. Because when you are editing a chase scene or a walking scene or a driving scene without scoring it, you make it to a length that's appropriate when it's silent. And then suddenly you put a piece of Django Reinhardt or Benny Goodman behind it and you think, 'Oh, it should be triple this length. It's very disappointing that it runs out here.' Or vice versa."

Woody and Lepselter put together the first eighty-six of the film's 138 scenes in four days. Over the course of the month that follows they will delete twenty-one, four of them in the first dozen, all vignettes with or about Abe that slowed the progress of the movie without adding more to understanding him, instances of Woody falling prey to explaining too much in the script. Another dozen short takes of Abe, two of them voice-overs, the rest without dialogue, also go: him distraught after the faculty party; eating alone in his kitchen; rushing to class—altogether perhaps two minutes. Three scenes with Jill will be cut to keep the story moving ahead—in total, 15 percent of all scenes. Another five are moved to other parts of the film to strengthen the story.

Among them is Scene A84, Abe's voice-over as he stands overlooking the ocean at sunset:

> I'm Abe Lucas and I've murdered. I've had many experiences and now a unique one. I've taken a human life—not in battle or self-defense but I made a choice I believed in and saw through. I feel like an authentic human being.

It has been moved ahead several scenes so that it now follows 92, Jill telling Abe and Rita the news that the police say the judge was murdered. Abe's ability to feign surprise so well and play along with Jill's earnestness gives his interior confession and justification of his actions more resonance than when it followed 82, Abe seeing the report of the judge's death in the next day's paper.

The bar scene (101) with Jill and Rita that was shot the first day has more than twenty minutes of footage and easily cuts back and forth between the two women. A few of the takes are in soft focus, but that does not bother Woody. The question is, on whom should it end? He decides on Jill because it is more about what she makes of Rita's "crackpot" theory of Abe being the killer. The one rough spot is the end of the scene—from when Rita finishes speaking to when Jill leaves. There needs to be a nuanced reaction from Jill.

"We don't have a face from her?" he asks. "Look for a bit in any take for a reaction shot where she's not impervious to the implications but not crushed by them either."

"A moment where she takes it seriously but seems to take it lightly," Lepselter suggests.

"The normal charming Emma Stone reaction."

But Jill comes across as having taken that part of the conversation more seriously in all the ensuing footage, so they decide to use a shot of her sipping her wine and saying, "I'll weigh it out" to end the scene.

Some fixes are small. In 103, Jill and Abe are at the lake. She stands against a tree, he on the dilapidated dock while we hear her voice-over:

> There was no question I was rattled by Rita's outrageous theory. I knew Abe had had a very angry reaction to the judge's unfair treatment of that poor woman. And what was he doing out at 6:30 on a Saturday morning? My thoughts were very mixed up and troubled and more devastating revelations were to come, but for the moment I lapsed into complete denial and told myself this was too absurd to even contemplate. I must not get carried away with my overactive imagination and yet a dark cloud had crossed the moon, resist it as I did.

But there is not enough head—lead-in to seeing Abe—on the shot and he comes into it before she finishes properly. They try several alternatives without success, so Woody says to put in what he likes as her best reading and adds, "Maybe we don't need, 'Resist it as I did.'" Dropping the line makes for an easy fit.

Other fixes are complex. In scenes 105–108, Jill's rising suspicions of Abe lead her to break into his house to see if she can find anything incriminating. As written, there are two voice-overs, the first one leading to her entering his house through a porch window. She goes upstairs to his bedroom and office and looks through drawers and on tables for anything that might tie him to the judge's death. She finds it in his handwritten list of names of murderers, himself included, in a paperback copy of *Crime and Punishment.* As she does, we hear her saying:

> Once inside Abe's house I felt I was betraying him
> and I felt guilty and stupid. I couldn't imagine what
> I expected to find and yet on his desk was a copy
> of *Crime and Punishment* with margin notes that
> had Judge Spangler's name and a quote of Hannah
> Arendt's [about the banality of evil].

Moments later she hears Abe come into the house and to cover her intrusion quickly undresses and jumps into bed as if there for romance.

Woody wrote the scene to give the story some suspense and action. It seemed it would work fine as it was shot but now he is not so sure. "Do you think the whole sequence is too broad for the picture? The book is not the smoking gun—the smoking gun is April saying she saw Abe in the lab. Everything before has kept the picture basically believable." He puzzles over this, his head down.

Lepselter gives him time to think, then says, "The entry in the book is so on the nose to me—the list of murderers, and Abe Lucas at the end—it seems heavy-handed."

"The only reason to have it is that otherwise every scene is with everybody talking to everybody else," he replies. "There's no physical stuff, no action. This gives action. We could do just the book and no Abe coming in."

After watching a revised version he asks, "Is it a little farcical?"

"We could have her looking around but not get caught."

Woody shakes his head. "There's no punctuation point we learn. We just go straight to the parents' house for dinner. Is there anything we've left out?"

"Without his coming home it's nothing. Are you thinking of cutting the whole scene?"

"Going to the house adds suspense. If nobody's coming there's no tension. Let's try and cut it properly once we see if we can make it work."

The sequence they try is: Jill opening a window and entering the house; Abe getting ready to leave class (the first part of the scene, him lecturing, is cut) and putting papers in his briefcase; the students walking out; then a shot of Jill in Abe's house.

"Do we need to see her coming upstairs?" Lepselter asks.

"Yeah, let's use the second half of the take, then she goes in the bedroom. Or do you want to bring her around the corner?" She does.

Woody is still thinking about Jill sneaking into Abe's house. The segment is in two parts, Jill rummaging and then quickly undressing and jumping into bed when she hears Abe come home. They watch Jill enter through a window.

"I buy that cut," Woody says. "It doesn't seem ludicrous if it went someplace."

"If she finds nothing that would not be ludicrous," Lepselter offers. "The stuff that feels silly to me is the pseudo-tension of him coming home."

"But if she doesn't find something, it's shoe leather. I agree with you that it is artificial tension, so let's have her go in the window and read the book and say, 'There it is: twelve o'clock Spangler' or something. Or do an insert, which is the hardest but as we're going to get Emma back, that's OK. Do we do a V.O. with her in the study?"

"I feel cheated if we don't see the book."

Woody wonders whether the insert with the list of murderers written on it will be clear enough for the audience to make the connection with Abe. It looks okay on the monitor—if you know that Raskolnikov, Stavrogin, Kirillov, and Verkhovensky are Dostoyevsky characters. All he cares about, though, is that the audience be able to read the names; if they don't know who these killers are, so be it. "I don't want people looking at a list of names and wondering. We could have her read some of it in a voice-over then cut away, right? This sequence is now over." After talking through a couple of alternatives he pauses to think and shakes his head. "We'll revisit this."

They revisit it several times. A few days later, after yet another look, it seems better if the manufactured tension of Abe coming home while Jill snoops is cut, leaving only Jill entering through the window and eventually finding the book with the handwritten list of murderers on the page. This advances the story and gives information to Jill without having to resort to a plot gimmick that is not germane.

Later, as Woody gets up to go to lunch, he says, "I made a lot of

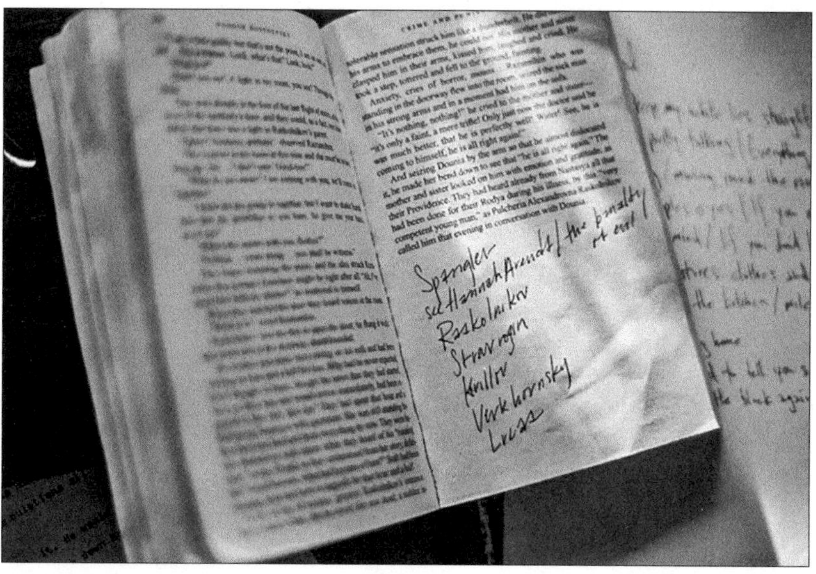

The list of Dostoyevsky's murderers written by Abe—his own name added—in his copy of Crime and Punishment.

blunders in writing and shooting. That into-the-house sequence was meant to be some action. Now I have a lot of dialogue and no space between it. I'm going to have to tap-dance."

Lepselter is smiling after he goes. "It's always like this," she says. "There are no insurmountable problems in the film. It's like he wants it to come full-blown out of his head. He's impatient. This is just editing, but for him, it's torture."

After he returns, they set to work on scene 117, one of the most dramatic of the film. Jill has just figured out that Abe is the murderer and confronts him on the patio of her parents' home. Her disillusionment is also a predicament because she has gone from admiring Abe to loving him but now realizes he is not the man she thought. She is in emotional shock, trying to sort out what to do. The long exchange lasts more than five minutes, and there is a lot of choreography to keep the characters moving—Jill comes down the stairs, the pair sit on a couch, and each stands at different times. There is an establishing shot, two over the shoulder, and two close-ups of Jill, four and a pickup (a minor shot to augment footage already filmed) of Abe plus three of his close-ups; thirteen in total, which is not unusual, but they are not all consistent because it was hard to match the blocking in each.

Woody wants to be sure he has the best shot of Jill for a sequence to play over one of Abe. Halfway through the scene Jill asks: "And you're ready to go to prison for the rest of your life?" Her line overlaps Abe's: "The police are not thinking of me." At first it is annoying to Woody, but after some thought he feels that the overlapping lines are appropriate for the turbulence of the scene. "This opens the doors for us," he says.

His hopefulness is short-lived. After a few minutes of working on another shot he exclaims, "Oh, god, this is so annoying."

"I'm going to give it one extra frame on Jill and that might help," Lepselter says. It does; one twenty-fourth of a second makes a difference. Woody perks up.

He says to try two shots over Jill's shoulder, then go to a wide master for Abe to say, "Is the world a better place without this rotten judge?" Both agree that it is too wide. He says to cut to a single on Jill asking: "How could you do it?"

Then, after a moment, "Is there any value to making a few cuts and make it manic and apoplectic—or would that be too much shrieking?"

"I want more, I feel they're holding back," Lepselter says.

She runs this combination. Woody is intrigued. "The intensity of the performance is really lively," he says. They keep this, at least for the moment, but look at another of Jill saying the line as taken from over Abe's shoulder.

"That's a good reading," Woody says, but he is sitting back in his chair, his arms folded.

Lepselter notices and asks, "You're not enjoying this?"

"Yes, I am. That was okay, that was a heartfelt reading." But he is speaking in the detached voice he has when he is not yet satisfied.

"We started her off melodramatically, so it's hard to pull back now," he says.

They have spent three hours on this go-round of the scene.

"I'm trying to squeeze every last drop out of this," he says.

Abe and Jill get up from the couch, followed by a long piece of dialogue:

JILL

Just leave here, Abe. I don't want to see you again.
I won't say anything. I believe you actually thought
you were doing something morally worthwhile
even though it's reprehensible no matter what
kind of bullshit romantic spin you use to distort all
that postwar French coffeehouse rationalizing—
it's murder and murder opens the door to more
murder. I don't have the intellect to refute your
arguments but you taught me to go with my instinct,
and without having to think, I feel it's no good.

ABE

Okay—I'll finish off my last weeks here and go. You
won't see me again.

The scene ends with three short exchanges of dialogue by each. "Just play this two-shot out?" Woody asks. "Or go out on 'I feel it's no good'? It's all one piece after they get up. I like that, it's no cutting. I'm sick of cutting." He asks her to put together the scene as they have discussed, then adds, "I feel for these actors—so many takes."

Lepselter tells him that David Fincher (*Gone Girl* [2014], *The Social Network* [2010]) regularly does thirty or more.

"Really?" he responds in genuine surprise. "Well, his movies are terrific." Then he walks home for lunch.

Lepselter says, "He's willing to accept technical flaws if he likes the take—but this is hard for all the professionals who are doing their best to get everything close to perfect."

After he returns he proves her point. She says that she hopes Khondji can fix the light shift in the scene during the color correction as it goes from dark to light in a couple of places, and there is a sun blotch on the sofa.

"I never worry about that," he answers blithely. But he is happy with how she assembled the scene.

"I like the roughness," he says. "You made it more exciting than it was. You picked out the best spots. We can come back this afternoon for it."

By the end of the day, they have edited a couple more scenes and return to finish 117. They drop the opening lines:

ABE

Why are you acting so strangely and what's on your mind that's so important that we have to go over it right now? Are you pregnant?

The scene cut together better without them and now begins with Jill's response, a statement in the form of a question: "You killed Spangler, didn't you?" Woody liked but does not really mind losing the pregnant line. The one he does regret losing was from Abe: "You're talking rules but there are no god-given rules." This attitude reinforced his existential thinking, but it, too, did not fall within the optimal cut.

Despite his regret, his response is merely a rueful shrug: "They are casualties that drop out over the course of the movie." (One line he had no compunction cutting was in a voice-over by Jill, about not believing anyone who feels he has the moral high ground, "because we wanted to shorten her dialogue and I thought it was speechifying.") This version is intensely acted, the emotions on the surface for the audience to see. When Jill says, "I'm so crushed. I'm lost. What do I do?" they have used the one take in which she suddenly starts to cry, her face contorted. The back of her hand comes across her face, as if to at once wipe her nose and wipe away her grief. Abe speaks with the sincere emotion of someone explaining he is certain in what he did, making his delivery all the more chilling. Woody is pleased with the performances as well as the editing.

"I knew they would both be good," he says. "Joaquin had less drama because he doesn't need it; she's the one that's stunned by what he's done. I choreographed the scene when we were in the yard. There wasn't much you could do because it was so confrontational. It's just two people in conflict with each other, not in an argument exactly but in a moment of crisis. I didn't want them sitting in two chairs, so I tried to move it around. Because all they could do was talk, I had them come in and stand up and then sit down and then he got up and walked to the other chair and then came back—there was no place to go. I did the best I could to keep that going, knowing that most of it would be up and back arguing, dependent on performance. We cut it toward what we felt was the most realistic and the best-performed material. There were takes where she was lower key and others where she was more hysterical and you're not sure which is the right way to go until you get into editing it. The right way to go *seems* one way to you as the author and often it is, but many times it's not. You find that the quiet way that the actors instinctively did it was more correct—you imagined fireworks between them but the quiet tension that they instinctively bring to it is better. That confrontation required what we have in it."

The fiasco with Jill and Ellie and their horses looks at first like it can still be used to establish them riding together. A bit of narration meant to go over the shot runs between eight and ten seconds, exactly the amount of usable footage before the horses stop. For a moment it looks like it can be connected to a second shot of them talking in the barn (scene 119), in which Jill tells Ellie that Abe has decided to leave the college and that she is not as "cutting edge" as she thought. But then Lepselter notices they are wearing slightly different costumes. So the short horseback ride is put following scene 98: Jill has given no thought about who might have murdered the judge until she runs into Ellie coming out of a store, and Ellie says that she heard Rita expounding her theory at a party. The last line of the two on the street is Jill saying they should go riding again soon. The scene in the barn is poignant. An idealistic young woman who was comfortable with her broad education and high ability, and who thought she would be able to soar with a brilliant if tortured professor, instead sees that the safe and reliable boyfriend and largely sheltered life she has had are just fine.

A shot of the Rhode Island coastal highway through a car windshield, meant to be used in scene 1, segues into a voice-over by Abe as he drives, saying that what he did was justified. These short scenes are the turn to the end of the picture.

The five scenes that lead to the climax at the elevator fall together fairly easily: in a voice-over, Abe says he will not turn himself in; Abe and Rita meet in a bar and talk about going to Europe together; Abe paces the aisles in the classroom as his students take a test and in a voice-over considers murdering Jill to keep her from going to the police; Jill and Roy get back together in a coffee shop; and Rita breaks up with her husband in anticipation of a new life with Abe.

Woody asks what time it is: 5:13 p.m., enough for one day. "Let's nail this and tomorrow we'll finish the picture. And tell me how much time because it's really bothering me."

Lepselter checks the Avid. "Eighty-five and a half minutes." In the beginning, Woody had hoped it would come in closer to 120 but now is relieved that it will hit 90.

"A film like this should be larger," he says softly.

"Nobody objects to a ninety-minute film."

"Check *Match Point,* I'm sure that was more substantial."

She goes to IMDb and says with some surprise, "Over two hours—one hundred and twenty-four minutes."

"Wow!" Woody says.

By early afternoon the next day they are ready to construct the final sequence of the picture, short takes of scenes 130 to 137, which apart from voice-overs by Abe in 130 and 132, has no dialogue until 136. It begins with Jill walking along the street to her piano lesson. Abe follows unnoticed at a distance as she goes into the building. After he enters, Jill walks down the hall to her teacher's studio; cut to the elevator control room in the basement where Abe carries out his sabotage; Jill at her lesson; then Abe walking up the stairs. "Maybe use some of a couple of takes to imply he is going up a lot of stairs," he says. Even that does not convey enough, so there is a second cut of him in the stairwell as Jill finishes her lesson. Woody asks, "Can we keep that sound of footsteps going so it sounds like he's going up another flight?"

Jill leaves her instructor's studio and walks up the hall toward the elevator, where Abe stands in front of it, hidden by the corner until she turns it and sees him. The question is where to cut from Jill to Abe. Woody's first thought is that it should come the moment she says, "Hi." But he decides to drop her greeting before the cut because he turns toward her later and her line ("Abe—omigod, you scared me. What are you doing here?") will cover it. They play the master through the struggle. When Abe slips on the flashlight and drops into the empty shaft, it is so realistic that Lepselter gasps and puts her hand over her mouth, as some had when it was shot. It does not matter that she knew this was coming and had seen it in dailies many times.

"He did it so *well,*" Woody says of Phoenix. "It looks like he falls in."

Now comes the task of piecing together a mix of close-up and medium shots from different angles to add more tension and drama to the scene. These shots are a mixture of Stone and her stunt double, Becca G. T., the latter doing the most violent takes. Woody starts with

Stone, then goes to a close-up of her after they've cut back to the double. He wants to hold a wide shot of Stone for as long as possible, then go to the double, then more of Stone—it's her close-ups that reinforce the notion that she is in all the action. During the fight when her bag drops, spilling sheet music, keys, and the flashlight, he says that if there is not enough footage for this, to cut to the flashlight, then the double wrestling with Abe, then to his foot on the flashlight, "but not so long that it ruins the fall, because it looks so natural." He uses two cuts of the bag and its spilled contents, then Abe plunging into the darkness, which works, though Woody is not yet sure just how well.

"I guess that's a reasonable cut of this," he says but then asks, "Does it have the same impact—does it look as good with the cut to his foot on the light rather than the flow of the master without interruption?

"One thing," he adds. "Tell me how much time it is up to here. We have only one scene left and it is about a minute. Let's get the bad news over with." He is still worried about being under 90 minutes, but he's not. This already is 91½ minutes with another scene to go. They run the fight with these cuts and it is clearly better with the flashlight. Woody had worried that if they "didn't show it in the master and showed him stepping on the flashlight we'd break up the thing that creates that feeling in you just being witness to a simple scene. But it's more effective actually seeing him step on the flashlight." He pushes back his chair.

"Okay," he says, to Lepselter. "Nail on one of the endings [Jill and Roy walking on campus; he has not yet decided whether to use the alternative he shot] and let's start on the music. I don't see it having classical; that takes the movie in too serious a direction. Not pop. Not eclectic like boogie-woogie." He pauses to think. "Different parts of the movie require different music: we need classical for the piano and cello scenes [Jill's recital and the performance she and Abe attend] to make them romantic and tense. But the picture can't have a musical theme because it has too many disparate parts."

Lepselter, who has a fondness for scored films, asks, "Will a real movie score with appropriate music for appropriate themes work?"

Woody, who dislikes scores, both because he enjoys selecting the music himself and does not like working with a composer, immediately says, "No. In *Hannah and Her Sisters* we used whatever was appropriate for the scene, it was completely eclectic, and no one noticed but us." The twenty-four titles in that film include Bach's Concerto for Two Violins in D Minor, *Madama Butterfly,* and *Manon Lescaut,* Cole Porter's "I'm in Love Again," four Rodgers and Hart tunes, and Benny Carter's "The Trot" played by Count Basie and his orchestra.

Woody usually thinks about scoring in general terms while cutting and often while shooting—but the only way to say he is closer to an answer is that he has decided on a couple of genres that *won't* work. "There's no suggestion of anything in this picture," he says, repeating how he felt close to the end of filming. "I'm not going to score one ever again. I don't want old-timey jazz. Charlie Parker's not going to work, John Coltrane's not going to work; maybe [Thelonious] Monk because he's halfway between old and new in a way. Classical would be boring and pretentious and I wouldn't do that to the movie." Jazz was once an option really only because jazz is usually an option. Boogie-woogie still is not tempting enough. "I once thought of using silly songs like "Mairzy Doats" but that won't work. I thought of doing this movie without music, which would have been fatal. And I don't want that kind of heavy this-is-serious-stuff Philip-Glass thing [which he used to good effect in *Cassandra's Dream*]. This has always been an unresolved problem and I've long kicked it down the road but today I have to face it."

He leaves Lepselter to add on a take of the final scene, then pushes back his chair and stands up. "I'll take a quick look at our record albums," he says, heading toward the screening room.

CHAPTER 7

The Music

Working on the score is a rich dessert for Woody. Pairing music and his movie is something he long anticipates and thoroughly enjoys. "You've cut the picture together," he says, "and every addition you make is a plus. There's no downside. You can't do anything but enhance it." Music, particularly jazz but also classical and the American songbook, is more than a passion for him, it is integral to his life. To understand just how much is to understand why he so enjoys selecting the music for his films. He has used a composer on only five: Marvin Hamlisch for *Take the Money and Run* and *Bananas*, Mundell Lowe for *Everything You Always Wanted to Know About Sex*, Dick Hyman for *Zelig*, and Philip Glass for *Cassandra's Dream*. Hyman also arranged music for *The Purple Rose of Cairo*, *Bullets over Broadway*, *Mighty Aphrodite*, and *Everyone Says I Love You*; altogether he has contributed to eleven Allen films. Woody has jazz as well as classical and standards piped into his shower, his phone is loaded with New Orleans jazz albums that he listens to whenever possible, he practices his clarinet daily without fail, and he plays along to recordings by favorite jazz players such as Albert Burbank or the Bunk Johnson Band. The large callus in the middle of his lower lip from gripping the reed is testament to decades of steady playing. He often will whistle an old jazz tune while waiting on the set or in another idle moment, and sometimes when he has trouble falling asleep, he makes up playlists for imaginary concerts (other times he mentally writes a newspaper account of a professional basketball game he's seen). Each of his band's performances, whether on Monday nights at the Carlyle or in the many concerts they give in Europe and the United States, is different. On the road he tells the band the first two numbers before they go on. After playing them, he stands to make a few comments to the audience, then tells the musicians the next song as he takes his seat. The remainder of the program is chosen spontaneously.

Authenticity is a serious matter to Woody, who makes every effort to achieve it, even if he is the only one who notices. For the score of *Magic in the Moonlight,* since the story takes place in the 1920s, he wanted music from the period.

"You are faced with three choices," he said during the edit of that film. "You can do authentic music from the twenties; you can do music from the twenties that's re-created, so you can have Dick Hyman or my band playing something like 'Ain't She Sweet' or 'Five Foot Two'; or you can do as they did in *Splendor in the Grass,* which took place in the twenties but is scored just like a regular movie. When a band plays at a party, they're playing the Charleston, but when, for instance, you see people driving cars, it's scored from the 1950s with saxophones. In a back-and-forth conversation with Alisa, I made the decision that I wanted authentic twenties music, which put us in a very difficult position because there's *very* little, almost no romantic music. No strings. When you hear any of those songs of the twenties, it's all jazz. We cheated a little bit by taking some music on the borderline, hoping no one made a fuss over that. If we had to cheat into the thirties, we stuck to the early part. Once you get later into the thirties you get that swing thing: Benny Goodman emerged in the late thirties."

After he has settled on the type of music he wants comes the pleasure of finding the right tunes. He has in memory a vast number of the songs written between 1900 and 1950 (he has used more than 450 of them), which, as far as he is concerned, is the end of musical history. With a few exceptions he knows nothing about what came after because "listening to it is a punishment. I only like classical and jazz. I like cosmopolitan instrumentation—a singer in a piano bar, someone playing trumpet quietly. I want what I grew up on, and younger people are saying, I want what *I* grew up on. But I've been able to put the music I want in my movies, the music that's meaningful to me."

So he checks the playlists on the backs of his many albums or when he is stuck looks through the ASCAP title book, which lists all songs registered with the American Society of Composers, Authors and Publishers. If he is unable to find a suitable recording on the albums, there is a backup collection of CDs in canvas books to consult, but he prefers vinyls. Before the great Manhattan record store Colony Music went out of business in 2012, when no amount of thinking and searching yielded the right number, Woody would have a member of the editing team call the store and say they needed a tune along the line of, say, "Sing Sing Sing," something in a minor key, and ask for suggestions. He called the people at the shop "the fishmongers" because he always relied on them for something fresh.

While a composer might perhaps bring a polished and unified score to the picture, for Woody it means handing over an important portion of it. Moreover, if he doesn't like a choice he's made himself, he is happy to throw it out and try another, but that is much harder to do with another person in the equation. A composer works for weeks or longer on a score and, no doubt pleased with the work, plays it for Woody. But one person's pleasure is not always another's, and he often has had to say the music is not exactly right for him. "And the composer is brokenhearted and it takes him a lot of time to write a new piece and you might not like it. And this goes on. He plays the songs and you know it's taken him forever and still they don't work. I don't see any percentage in it at all.

"I couldn't take any of that, it was too nerve-wracking. I thought to myself, 'Why?' I've got all of Cole Porter and all of Louis Armstrong and all of John Coltrane—I have a choice of the world's greatest music. If I don't like something, I run through a hundred things, where a composer would be heartbroken and work for six months on something new. It's a much simpler way for me to work."

However, he says that he was very lucky to have worked with Philip Glass on *Cassandra's Dream.* Apart from his moody, edgy score, Glass had the added value of being the exception to the rule. "He was so quick. If you didn't like something he couldn't care less and the next morning there would be something else. He was just relentlessly creative." Plus, his style was suited to the film. "The movie is kind of tragic in feeling, and he seemed like someone whose work was full of, you know [*smiles*], suffering and angst. It seemed like it wouldn't be a routine score, it would be one full of feeling that was appropriate to the story."

A score in an Allen film needs to do only two things: heighten the mood to the greatest degree and please him. If no one else has ever heard of the songs or has no taste for them, that's their loss. Just as he makes the movie *he* most wants to make at the time, not what it is presumed his audience might like, his choice of music is his final personal stamp on an entirely personal picture.

"Music," he says, emphasizing something he deeply feels, "enhances the film and sometimes is a lifesaver to a scene—without the music, the scene doesn't work, and with the music, it does. [The point will be proved when he finds the right accompaniment for the opening of this film.] If you have a good picture and you put in good music, it's like pushing a winning hand in poker. If you have a mediocre picture or a bad picture and you put in good music, you can help yourself a little bit, but you can't save a bad film with just music."

Woody's scoring is a study in low tech and high memory. There is no music editor. There is no catalogue of choices or even notes about them. There is only his sensibility of what works and what doesn't; as he puts it, "It's very homespun." When a music publisher recently proposed doing a book on the music in his films he warned them, "What you have to understand is there's a cupboard of records in the other room. We just take 'em and put 'em on and we do the musical editing right there to make them fit."

In addition to using Woody's collection of records, Lepselter and the other editors spend a lot of time searching for music online. "If he mentions an artist we can do a quick search and come up with many songs to sample before he needs to go to the LPs. Sometimes he wants to search in his collection, but often it is quicker and more productive to audition things right at the computer."

Unlike directors Mike Figgis, Clint Eastwood, John Carpenter, David Lynch, Satyajit Ray, and Charlie Chaplin, who composed original scores, Woody composes by weaving jazz, classical, and standards into a film. Where to use music and what song to use is instinctual to him. If a scene feels like it needs music, he either reprises something or finds something else he likes. He does not set out to find themes for characters. He feels his way through to the end and then inevitably finds he erred in an instance or two where "it's annoying to hear music there," or he finds a scene that should have it. But for him "there are not too many mistakes because it's not such a hard thing to do."

Because music transforms a picture, Woody wants a good first cut of a film before concentrating on the accompaniment. He prefers to wait as long as he can, "like when I get a pizza and not drink my beer until I'm way into it and I can't stand it anymore and then the beer tastes so great. It's the same thing with music. I try to hold out if I can. When you put it in it is such a treat. Because after all, what am I putting in? I'm putting in, always, wonderful music."

There are occasions when he knows from the start of the film what music he wants, the best example being *Manhattan*, which, with the exception of Mozart's Symphony no. 40 at a concert, is all George Gershwin. But the notion of what music he wants is often in the back of his mind. When he was shooting *Blue Jasmine,* he frequently thought, "I have to get a good blues piece for this scene, and I want a King Oliver piece for that scene, and this scene would be great if I could find the right Louis Armstrong piece. I was thinking very frequently of blues songs."

This is a good example of his choosing what few others than he will fully appreciate. "Woody thought using blues music for *Blue Jasmine* was a bold stroke," Lepselter said one day. But his idea of a bold stroke fell on unknowing ears. Because audiences lack his knowledge of the many plain and subtle differences in jazz and blues styles, "most people just thought, 'Oh, Woody Allen music.'"

• • •

After Woody leaves Lepselter to make the changes he suggested in the elevator scene, he walks around the corner into the screening room to sift through his three bins of albums. Two have jazz and American songbook albums, the third classical. He opens all three but immediately puts back the cover on the classical and starts to go through what is in the middle. He flips through the albums, occasionally pulling out one to examine its content, making a soft "Hmmm" as he reads and decides whether to listen to it or put it back. After ten minutes he has a stack of twelve records: The Modern Jazz Quartet's *Pyramid; The Chico Hamilton Quintet; The Greatest Hits of Ramsey Lewis; "Basie 'E=MC2' "; The Art of Dave Brubeck: The Fantasy Years;* Gerry Mulligan and Chet Baker's *Timeline; Jelly Roll Morton Plays Jelly Roll Morton;* Thelonious Monk's *The Riverside Trios;* Thelonious Monk's *It's Monk's Time;* Thelonious Monk's *Straight, No Chaser;* The Modern Jazz Quartet's *Vendome;* and *Giants of Boogie Woogie.*

He gathers them and heads back to the cutting room. Assistant editor Morgan Neville brings a black plastic bin to hold them. A floor lamp is brought beside him and turned on. Lepselter puts the opening sequence of the film up on the screen, frozen on the first frame, Abe at the wheel.

"I want to start to test music to see the effects of some of these things," he says. Looking at the track listings on the back album cover he asks assistant editor Sharon Perlman to put on the fourth band of the Chico Hamilton album, Fred Katz's "The Sage," which begins with a rather morose cello. He stares for about a minute at the freeze-frame of the picture, then asks her to put on Basie's "The Kid from Red Bank," featuring a snappy piano before the band pops in. Neither does anything for him. He asks for the third track on the Basie album, "Splanky," offering muted trumpets and a piano at a nice pace. "I like it," Lepselter quickly says, and Woody, nodding, says, "I can see that." But not for the start of the film.

He picks up the cover for *Vendome* and asks for the title tune, a jazzy glockenspiel and piano. An immediate no. He moves on to *Giants of Boogie Woogie.* The first track is "St. Louis Blues." No good.

The third is "Bass Goin' Crazy." The same. Side 2, track 2, "Blues 'de lux.'" Ditto. He picks up the Mulligan and Baker album, studies the list, then puts it aside. He looks over Monk's *Straight, No Chaser.* It is lively enough, but suddenly there is narration in the tune. No way. From *It's Monk's Time* he asks for the first track, "Lulu's Back in Town," jazzy piano in Monk's signature style but way too up in sound and tempo. His routine is the same for each song. He imagines it in the film by looking at the frozen frame and decides whether or not it has a chance.

The next dip into the bin brings up the Ramsey Lewis album. He asks for side 1, track 1, Billy Page's "The 'In' Crowd," which starts with a driving beat. Woody sits still, staring at the screen. The four others in the room are clearly taken by the track.

"Try it," Woody says, and Lepselter starts the first scene as the music plays over it. The performance was recorded live, so there is applause at the start. For most directors this would be ruinous, but Woody doesn't mind. The tune is perfect accompaniment as it plays over the opening scenes, turned down for Abe's initial voice-over, then back up until he pulls into the campus. What had been a static shot of someone driving is now completely energetic and interesting.

Woody learned how the right piece of music can enliven a scene when Ralph Rosenblum played Eubie Blake over Virgil comically getting ready for a date in *Take the Money and Run.* Marvin Hamlisch had written a doleful Chaplinesque piece that made the scene play flat. Rosenblum suggested trying a Blake ragtime piano piece behind the scene that brought it to life in the editing room. Hamlisch then composed something similarly upbeat for the film. That one incident opened Woody's eyes to scoring.

"As Marshall Brickman says," Woody remarks after viewing the scene with the Lewis tune, "music in a movie is borrowed grandeur.

"What are we seeing here?" he continues. "Do we want a piece of music binding all of that together? And if we do, it can't be too loud." He pauses. "We could drop it out and bring it back."

"Continue it from the credits?" Lepselter asks.

"Or no music on the credits."

"No music feels like a mistake," she says quickly.

Woody shrugs. "We've done that before. It depends on the music."

In *Annie Hall,* there is no music over the credits and virtually no scoring at all in the entire picture. The one exception is Eric Coates's "By the Sleepy Lagoon," performed by Tommy Dorsey and his orchestra. It starts when we first see Alvy's house under the roller coaster and plays through to his kissing a girl at school, and again when Alvy, Annie [Diane Keaton], and Rob [Tony Roberts] visit his home in a flashback. Whatever other music there is comes from a car radio or at a party, and, on two occasions, at a club, Annie singing, "It Had to Be You" and "Seems Like Old Times." When Woody made the film he was very much under the sway of Bergman, who once said music in movies was "barbarous," and it did not matter to Woody whether the audience shared his view. "I felt he must know something. I figured, 'He's so good, if he doesn't think music is right, I probably have a blind spot.' I used source music [background music from a radio, for instance]. And I didn't use music in *Interiors.*"

But as Woody made more pictures, he realized that although his are influenced by Bergman, they aren't *by* Bergman. "As I started to get a little more confident I thought, 'Well, that's really not the way *I* feel movies. I feel them with music.' To me, music has a special meaning. It is vitally connected to the material." Now, he says, his films "overflow" with music, not just because the music is connected to the story and visuals and emotions of the film but also because it is equally connected to his own emotions.

Lepselter suggests they need to hear the music under Jill's narration as well. Woody agrees. "One possibility, for instance, is we come in on Abe and no narration and then cut to her [Jill walking across the grass with books in her arms] and start the narration. Take Abe driving and we cut for POV from the front window or something." A shot through the windshield comes up. "Let's play recklessly here. Go to the side shot—does he take a drive in the side shot? I think we looked for one and couldn't find it." He pauses. "Once we get into the story everything is indicated rigorously but here it is free." He listens to Abe's voice-over:

> Kant said human reason is troubled by questions
> it cannot dismiss but also cannot answer. So, what
> are we talking about here? Morality? Choice? The
> randomness of life? Aesthetics, murder? Luck? All
> of that—it's all those things.

"So if we just use the line about Kant and then go to 'what are we talking about here?,' I'm operating under the theory that this might be of interest to the audience aesthetically and is not aimless palaver. Also, if we're going to pad the picture, this is the place to do it while we still have some good will from the audience, before they turn on us." Then he adds, looking at a shot of Abe drinking from a flask while driving: "Let's see if we can have a picture that he narrates, too, before we get to the third reel. Let's try it with Lewis, 'The "In" Crowd.' After Jill's narration ends we go to Abe's 'Where to begin . . .' so we can justify this shot."

This is followed by two short shots of teachers and students reacting to Abe's arrival, saying things like "That should put some Viagra in the philosophy department" and "He's this totally interesting guy but he looks totally wasted."

These shots of Abe in the car are what Virginia McCarthy salvaged from the many minutes of him bouncing. They put in one on the open road that ends at a picturesque inlet with a grand house overlooking the water. It has the added benefit of showing Abe from the side, so he is not seen just straight on.

"Now, take it from the start of the actual movie [after the opening credits] and play the Ramsey Lewis. It may be the wrong length. If it starts with applauding you can put that over the 'Written and Directed by' so the picture can start with it. [It does.] We don't need to use all of it or maybe just begin with the bass intro, that little vamp." After they look at it this way he tells her to "drop the music down and bring Jill's voice really up."

Woody explained later, "I thought the picture would have so much more dramatic impact if the titles had no music and the first cut was '"In" Crowd' on Abe. *Bonnie and Clyde* begins with no sound, and the stark silence over Bergman's credits causes an emotional effect. It's that my pictures have a reputation of having sound, so I didn't want the audience to think, 'Oh, is something technically wrong?' I also thought that *if* it turned out that utter silence was no good under the titles, I could do something like have a clock ticking so that the audience would know that the sound was on in the theater and it would imply his time bomb personality and time passing, a lot of pretentious—I meant to say portentous—symbolism."

The music plays through Jill walking across the lawn, Abe's saying, "Where to begin" and then drinking from a flask in his car, snippets of two teachers' dialogue, and then three female students talking. Woody says to let it play on until Abe meets the college president. This long piece of music over the action covers the first eight scenes of the picture. In this time we meet the two central characters, hear what others have to say about Abe, and know there is trouble ahead, all without taxing the audience. It is essentially free time as far as their attention goes, several minutes that they do not need to deal with the complexities of the story but can simply sit back and listen while the music and narration carry them along.

Woody has done this at the start of many of his films, beginning with *Take the Money and Run,* in which the first eight minutes play as an introduction to the early life of Virgil Starkwell before the titles appear. A few others: *Manhattan* begins with nearly four minutes of narration as "Rhapsody in Blue" plays over romantic black-and-white shots of the borough; *Vicky Cristina Barcelona* has nearly eight minutes of a combination of "Barcelona," narration over introductions of the characters, and beautiful shots of Catalonia; and *Midnight in Paris* has more than three minutes of Sidney Bechet's soaring rendition of 'Si tu vois ma mère' while shot after gorgeous shot of the City of Light illuminate the screen.

Woody likes the applause and cheering on the track, even though the accepted wisdom is to have music alone. He wants this to be "less slick," in the same sense that he wanted the Caruso arias he used in *Match Point* to have in them the tics and scratchiness of the ancient recordings they were taken from. He thinks the applause and cheering sound better and are consistent with Abe's spirit, along with the audience seeing and hearing other people besides him. "It just sounds, it feels better to me," he says. Other occasions when "The 'In' Crowd" is used over the action—for instance when we see the judge jogging—some in the audience on the record are yelling with the band. "It gives it a nice lift," he says.

He knows that the Lewis piece is not the only song that could bring the scene to life; it is just that it is a *right* piece for it, and that is what is important. As he says later, "*So* much music is right. If I didn't have any Ramsey Lewis here we would have found somebody else—boogie woogie or Erroll Garner—and it would have come to life. Ramsey Lewis has a kind of sinister drive, a real bluesy-nasty quality that works well for the movie. That kind of pulsating, throbbing music lends itself to anxiety and action. It's not 'Clair de Lune.'"

Fitting music to a scene often reveals problems that were missed in the general edit. Woody decides against music over Abe and Rita walking beside a tall hedge toward her home but realizes that the scene is too long. Lepselter suggests they think of the dialogue they want and cut the walking, as in much of the shot their mouths are not seen. The sequence, their first since meeting at Abe's welcome party, is meant to show Abe and Rita developing a relationship, as well as her wanting an affair with him even though he is distant. About one-third of the lines are cut.

The party where Abe demonstrates Russian roulette requires contemporary music. "We have some music for this but you're not going to like it," Lepselter warns him. It is modern pop by Mike Ballou, and although it is something he would never know about on his own, it works. For scenes that require contemporary tunes, Woody leaves it to Morgan Neville to find something appropriate. When a modern, seductive song was needed for a scene in *Melinda and Melinda* (2004), Barry White was immediately suggested. Woody had no idea who he was, but "Come On" was perfect for the action. His greater concern than the music here is that the start of the Russian roulette sequence is not right. During several takes the night the scene was shot, he exhorted the students at the party to be more demonstrative; the problem remains. Lepselter puts in some stock voices for the track while they edit, and other voices will be recorded and added during the mix to achieve the desired effect.

He wants music under Abe waking up in his bedroom excited over the prospect of killing the judge (scene A50) because "otherwise it's empty," and says to try "'In' Crowd," which ends up being used four times over long blocks of scenes: the first eight of the film, the last nine, and two chunks of six in the middle—about 20 percent of the picture. In this instance, it begins as he wakes; plays on as we see him, his appetite renewed by his decision, enjoying a huge breakfast; and on to meeting Rita on campus, who remarks on his newfound enthusiasm. Three scenes later, Abe begins to surreptitiously follow Judge Spangler to learn his daily routine—leaving the courthouse, jogging, buying orange juice at the same stand, going to a park bench to read his newspaper after every run—and it is time to introduce something new. Lepselter asks if he wants "stalking music."

"No, I want something like Ramsey Lewis but we've been using it too much."

A Basie number is suggested, but it is not quite right. Lepselter asks if he wants to put Basie's version of Neal Hefti's "Splanky" over it. He does but then it does not sound right to either of them.

"Too 'Pink Panther,'" she says.

"Too Jerry Lewis," he says and asks for more Ramsey Lewis tracks. "They did a great version of 'Hard Day's Night.' [A rare instance of him ever thinking of using a sixties pop tune, although this score will end up being all 1960s jazz.] It will probably cost a fortune but it will be great for us." Playing it makes the point, but then he says, "I don't know if we can afford it."

"No, Beatles songs are too expensive for us," she tells him. His music budget used to be about $750,000 but now is half that or less. So they put in Lewis's upbeat "Wade in the Water," which begins with a trumpet before going to the piano and accompaniment. (The next day it is moved to a three-scene sequence in the middle of the movie and is replaced by Lewis's "Look-A-Here," which stays.)

"Let's find something for when he steals the poison," Woody says when they come to the three-scene sequence of Abe researching poisons at the Athenaeum library, then stealing Rita's key to the chemistry lab supply room from her purse after a tryst and walking across campus to the chemistry building. Abe says in a voice-over, "The killing would be an act of creativity."

"Want to try 'Wade in the Water' since we have it out?" Woody asks. They do and both say, "Sounds fun." "Do you think we'll have the trouble of it sounding like '"In" Crowd'?" he continues. Lepselter doesn't. "Okay, put it in. Now, run the picture right from the cue to '"In" Crowd' so we can hear both cues together." They work well.

She reminds him that he used "'In' Crowd" in *Mighty Aphrodite*. "Yeah," he says, "but just once," when Woody's character, Lenny, knocks on the door of Mira Sorvino's character, Linda, and while she shows him her apartment.

"'In' Crowd" starts over the end of Abe's voice-over and carries through his crossing the campus and into the lab to steal the cyanide. As he finishes pouring the poison into the container he's brought, it's suggested that the music end when Jill's friend April surprises him. Woody says instead to try playing it softer beneath their dialogue, which ends with her asking him a question for a philosophy paper as they walk out together.

"Yeah," he says, "we have to leave it there and blend it in with the next scene because it has such a relentless beat; it's like Ravel's *Boléro*. I wish we could use it all the way through and make it the theme of the picture." A few days later, he decides to use Lewis's "Wade in the Water" over the sequence to allow a break before using "'In' Crowd" five scenes later under a six-scene sequence.

It starts to play as Abe's alarm awakens him the morning he kills the judge. Woody asks to try it without the alarm to see what it's like to have him wake up naturally.

"You still want the music when he opens his eyes?" Lepselter asks.

"No, on the cut." They watch it that way and he says, "No, I think it's going to be better the way you had it." They look at it again. Woody is not satisfied. "Let's try two beeps on the alarm and have the music go on then." Lepselter adds some head—a few additional frames—to the shot to give the extra time. They watch this version and Woody says, laughing, "And now you better bring it up to four beeps and play it long—whatever we can do to lengthen the picture." The alarm is a be-be-be-beep sound. "Are the beeps too close together?" he asks.

"Sounds like my alarm clock," she says.

"Can you bring that music in when he sits up and we'll work backward from there?"

The beeping ends when the music begins and continues through Abe standing in his kitchen putting poison in the juice; the judge jogging then buying his juice and paper and going to the park bench; Abe walking to the bench, the judge vaguely seeing him and turning his body away for more privacy; then Abe switching cups and walking away, his face demonic, his eyes rimmed in red. They watch it again. Woody asks to put in the judge jogging up to the counter at the juice shop, then adds, "If you want to start in the middle of getting the order that is okay, then cut to Joaquin." They like this.

Lepselter wants to see him brooding. Woody is not so sure. He says to put in the take where, after switching the cups and waiting a few beats, Abe pushes the poisoned cup to about where the judge originally put his. But this doesn't work for Woody, who echoes his concern when he shot it: it seems "too amusing, too Abbott and Costello."

A wide shot of the judge taking a sip of his juice before Abe comes is added. This improves the scene. Then Abe sits near him, makes the switch, and walks away toward the camera.

Woody wants a piece of music over Abe and Jill's dinner to celebrate the woman being freed of her bad judge and likes a Les Paul guitar rendition of Hoagy Carmichael's "Stardust." Later he changes it to Jimmy Van Heusen's languid guitar and sax melody "Darn That Dream," played by the Jimmy Bruno Trio.

Jill's dream of love with Abe will soon become a nightmare, and although this particular song was not the first choice for the scene, the tying of a song's title to the action is something Woody often employs. A small sample: *Magic in the Moonlight* has Cole Porter's "You Do Something to Me" over the opening credits (it also plays when a couple go on a first date in *Mighty Aphrodite*); Lew Brown, Buddy G. DeSylva, and Ray Henderson's "It All Depends on You" in the penultimate sequence in which Aunt Vanessa leads the romantically dense magician Stanley along until he sees he loves Sophie; and Fred Ahlert and Roy Turk's "I'll Get By (As Long as I Have You)" as they unite at the end (it also is used at the end of *Zelig*); *Husbands and Wives* has Porter's "What Is This Thing Called Love?" over the titles. In *Hannah and Her Sisters,* James V. Monaco and Joe McCarthy's "You Made Me Love You" plays after Mickey tells Holly how much he liked a script she has written; *Mighty Aphrodite* has Jack Palmer and Spencer Williams's "I've Found a New Baby" playing when Lenny hopes to find the name of his adopted child's mother by covertly rummaging in the files at an adoption agency; *Everyone Says I Love You* has the eponymous Harry Ruby and Bert Kalmar tune. *Oedipus Wrecks* has Harry von Tilzer and William Dillon's "I Want a Girl (Just Like the Girl That Married Dear Old Dad)" over the opening and closing credits and also within the film at appropriate spots. Those in the audience familiar with the songs get an added treat; for others, the music simply complements the action.

He finds that music helps a comedy, whereas a drama can be effective without it, "but it's better to use music," he quickly adds. "It's part of the pleasure of a certain kind of movie that you deliver to the audience. As Noël Coward said [in *Private Lives*], 'Strange how potent cheap music is.' "

Following a short scene originally earlier in the story but moved to here, Abe and Jill attend a twilight cello concert illuminated by torches, which puts the film back in sync with Woody's first cut. The music is the prelude to Bach's Cello Suite no. 1 in G Major, which sounds good as it matches the bowing of the cellist.

"There's no cello music that keeps pace with jazz music," he muses.

The story is in the home stretch. In scene 103 Jill and Abe revisit the lake where earlier they had made love. This is the first time she presses him for information as she tries to square Rita's "crackpot" theory with Abe's actions. For instance, why was he, a notoriously late sleeper, seen leaving campus at six thirty a.m. on a Saturday morning? He says he had to go to Providence for an MRI. This scene is the last in which Jill can contain her denial.

In the next she is obsessed with Abe's story. Woody again turns to "Look-A-Here" over this and the following two scenes of Jill looking through Abe's house and then finding the copy of *Crime and Punishment* with the list of murderers written in his hand.

Woody is still not happy with how he's edited the scene, which begins with Jill walking down Abe's street. There is not as much footage from which to choose as he would like.

"This is unexciting," he says and changes the start to Jill opening the window and climbing in. He laughs and says, "You know, we're very economical when we shoot."

He pauses in thought, then looks over to Morgan Neville and asks her to make a *Crazy Abe* title card for the credits. This is the first time he's said anything about it to the editors, even though he first mentioned the idea on the set three weeks ago and it has been floating in his mind for months.

"The title's *Crazy Abe?*" Lepselter asks.

"Uh-huh."

The title has stuck with him and he has not thought in any detail of alternatives. He did wonder for a while if *Crazy Abe* was the right choice, but as nothing else suggested itself, he kept it. "I didn't want to have one of those serious titles like *Crimes and Misdemeanors,* and I wanted the picture to have a lightness to it," he said later. "I guarantee that if people accept the picture, ninety percent of them will take it as a black comedy, because they take everything I do as a comedy. And here, what do you have? A story of a guy who feels impotent in every way and then the moment he decides that he's going to murder somebody, everything turns great for him—he's just fine and he can sleep with the girls and he likes his breakfast and his life is good. It has a comic quality to it." When he had Helen Robin clear it he said, "It's a bouncy title, it's not serious, and it tells the story."

The remainder of the music quickly falls into place, Ramsey Lewis all the way. Several scenes have been cut so that the action goes directly from Jill finding the book in Abe's apartment to April telling her that she encountered Abe in the chemistry lab and then to Jill confronting Abe that she knows he killed the judge. These play with no music. "Look-A-Here" is brought back for the two following scenes, Jill distracted in class and then telling Ellie that Abe is leaving the college. "Wade in the Water" plays while Abe is driving, feeling justified in what he has done.

No music is needed as Jill reunites with Roy in 128, and Rita breaks up with her husband in 129 because the dialogue carries the story of each couple. But then "'In' Crowd" comes on for the final nine scenes, which begin with Abe following Jill to her piano lesson and finishes as Jill walks on a beach at the end offering her summary of events.

Woody's use of a sort of coda as a final scene is not new and in fact appears in many of his films going back to *Take the Money and Run.* In *Crimes and Misdemeanors* Cliff (Woody) and the unrepentant accomplice in a murder Judah (Martin Landau) sit on a piano bench at the wedding reception of the daughter of Ben, the blind rabbi played by Sam Waterston. The scene provides a chance for Cliff to sum up his (and Woody's) feelings about the randomness of life. He felt in that instance it worked with him doing the lengthy solo speech because of his training as a monologist, and because he feels that "my films are such a personal statement that I'm shameless about moralizing in the end. It's like the old Caesar show joke among the writers. Sid would sum up a sketch and say, 'If there's one thing I've learned . . .' Maybe all the writers were nice Jewish boys brought up to have a little idealistic lesson at the end."

He is content with the use of two narrators to advance the story, even though one—as in *Sunset Boulevard* (1950)—is dead. But he has not used Abe here in the way that Billy Wilder used William Holden. Wilder, he says, "always wanted to do a dead man. It meant something to him. But it didn't mean anything to me who told this story. Abe represents one of those instances where I don't care what the logic is. The film is supposed to be a fable, a tale, because it's not realistic." He is a fan of Wilder's work, although, he says, "*Sunset Boulevard* is very entertaining and fun but I think it's campy fun. However, *Double Indemnity* [1944] is one of the best American pictures, and I loved *Ace in the Hole* [1951]."

The music for this picture came together much faster than usual. In fact, the three hours that Woody spent unsuccessfully trying to fit "Bye Bye Blackbird" into *Magic in the Moonlight* was longer than it took him to lay out the basic sound track here, though of course there were many more hours of fiddling before it was as he wanted.

"The music fell in as soon as the Ramsey Lewis came along, but that's sheer luck," he says later. "I could be still breaking my neck with Alisa, trying to find music for this movie. With Ramsey Lewis, the music is kind of down and dirty and sexy and you get the feeling that something's going to happen. It's got everything going for it. So now I'm just waiting on the information" [*he laughs*] "that I can't get it because it's too expensive.

"The music is transforming. As soon as you hear it the movie goes from dead as a doornail to pleasurable and alive."

CHAPTER 8

The Color Correction, the Mix

1

"All that matters is the effect you're having on the audience."

While doing the last of the editing and music, Woody screened the film a few times for several friends to gather their impressions. He does not expect the critical reaction that a stranger would offer. "You can't get your kicks from critical response—from bravos. Friends are rooting for me, so they say, 'This was great' or 'That was great.' But if you show the same film to six people who are not in my corner, they could really dislike it. It's very subjective and that's why only the actual making of the film has to be the pleasure."

He knows as well that no matter how many times he and Alisa Lepselter have seen a film in progress, the moment a fresh viewer comes in, regardless of who it is, everything changes. "When you watch it by yourself, it's one thing. But when you watch it with someone else—the guy who comes to deliver the coffee—and he starts looking at the screen, your whole psychological perception of what is going on suddenly changes. There's now somebody watching your picture and it's no longer that which you're indulging yourself on and doing what you want. Suddenly you're a little embarrassed if it's slow and you want to say, 'Hey, coffee delivery guy, we're going to take that out and it's going to move much faster.' It changes your perception. It really helps to watch it with people. You don't have to get into long conversations—I ask about specific things such as, 'Do you understand that he did this?' or 'Were you shocked when this happened?' But you can feel, you can actually feel, what is needed. It's like that sense I had when I was doing my routine as a stand-up comic. You know right away, 'Cut this joke and go right to that joke.' You feel something that's in the air; it's the only place that joke can be. It's not tangible and yet it's as real as if it was a footstool or a lamp. And you're almost always right."

After these few screenings, and having fiddled more with the picture, including making the start faster, he is ready for the last two steps of production.

Once a film is edited and the music is properly in place, its hues and sounds are balanced, scrubbed, polished, and highlighted, first by the color correction and then by the sound mix. The color correction, also known as timing, uses a computer to brighten, dim, or deepen colors to make what is on the screen look as vivid as possible. There are two types of correction. The primary alters the midtone colors—red, green, blue, and gamma, the relationship of each to the other—the highlights, or whites, and the shadows, or blacks, of the entire image on the screen. The secondary concentrates on hue, saturation, and brightness without altering the rest of the color spectrum. The work is slow and is entirely subjective, but those who do it well bring a beauty and richness to a movie far beyond what is on the developed film or in the digital image. Among the best at doing this is Pascal Dangin. He and his colleagues at his firm, Box Studios, retouch photos for fashion shots, magazine covers, and advertisements, and he is widely sought after to put the finishing touches on a film to make it jump to life on the screen. For a week at the end of November, he and Darius Khondji worked on every frame of this one.

It is the second Allen film Dangin has color corrected, and he well understands the director's taste and needs. Woody in turn trusts him and makes his comments as he watches; he writes no notes, here or at any screening of the film. Although he is satisfied with most of the adjustments, inevitably he requests small changes. He wants the opening shot to be brighter when the camera is on Abe's full face, and the color a bit brighter on Jill in the second scene, as she walks across the grass, so there is less contrast after seeing Abe. Dangin removed a bit of blue from the shadow on Abe with Jill on their first walk across campus and erased a piece of production equipment that accidently was in one shot in Abe's kitchen with Rita. "I put some beige in there," he says, matching the color to the wall. He made the sky brighter in the scene where Abe and Jill walk out of the movie theater and added a touch of blue to the shadow. He also added a bit of brightness to the scene in the diner where they hear the mother's tale of woe.

"It looks nice," Woody tells him.

The first sex scene with Abe and Rita is a point darker, and it looks moodier. Woody is happy with that but asks to check Rita's face when she and Abe are in the kitchen prior to the bedroom.

"That we didn't touch," Khondji says.

"I want to be sure she doesn't look too pasty," Woody says. Khondji, who speaks excellent English but whose first languages are Persian and French, is not sure what "pasty" means.

"Embalmed," Woody tells him.

The first shot of the judge and another of him playing cards with his cronies are slightly brightened. "The other was a struggle," Woody says, referring to its not being rich enough. Khondji agrees: "We made it cleaner."

Many minutes are spent on Roy sitting on the porch before Jill comes out and breaks their date to go to a concert. The scene begins with him alone and, Woody says, "It looks melancholy. When she comes out it looks fine." This shot follows Abe stealing poison in the chemistry lab, which is dark, and Woody wants the contrast. "After the lab it would be good if we had a nice afternoon shot to pick up the energy on the porch." Dangin tries to put in late afternoon sun but, he says, "There is not a hard shadow anywhere."

"I don't need to know if it's morning, noon, or night," Woody says. "Just a pleasing change from the last cut."

"You go too much brighter you start losing the skin," Khondji says. They try for a honey gold color but it looks garish.

The shot as it is looks nice enough and so any change would have been minor. Woody is not troubled to leave it as Dangin has it. "Okay, moving on from here. These things are all so subjective, and if you are happy, okay."

Dangin has made a scene in which Abe walks away from Jill cleaner, "not so drab."

"I prefer it a little more warm," Woody says.

"Less grey," Dangin says.

"Warmer, which is positive," Woody replies. This is a standard correction for him. His preference for "a warm picture" has not changed over the decades.

The outdoor concert that Abe and Jill attend in the flush of their new romance has been made moodier. There is more gold on them and the sky over the water at the back of the shot is bluer, an easy fix. But they fiddle with the scene in which Jill and Roy break up. Like an ophthalmologist checking one lens against another, Khondji takes the color down a half point, then up a half, and asks after each adjustment, "Do you like this . . . or this?" Not surprisingly, Woody prefers the slightly lighter to the slightly darker. The scene under the vine-covered pergola, in which Abe gives Jill poems he has written, has been enhanced. Khondji added gold and removed green. It looked beautiful the morning it was shot but this is more so. "I love the 'good dark,'" Woody says later, "the Gordon Willis dark that can be real dark, but the 'bad dark' is just dreary."

Things that pass unseen during editing on the Avid are suddenly evident on a bigger screen. In the scene with Jill and Rita in the bar, a microphone that was reflected in Jill's wineglass has been erased; when Rita breaks up with her husband Paul in their car, the yellow has been taken out. "That was always a problem because we shot it so early," Woody says. The time is meant to be late in the day, but

Rita (Parker Posey) breaks up with her husband, Paul (Robert Petkoff), sitting in their car in the rain outside their home.

even with the rain and flags to block out what sunshine there was, too much brightness still came through the windshield. The shot is similar to one in *Magic,* in which Stanley's car breaks down and he and Sophie are engulfed in a thunderstorm that sends them fleeing into a nearby observatory for cover. That shot, however, was made in sunshine, the dark sky and rain inserted digitally. In this case, there was a rain machine dumping water on the car. One question here is whether the rain is strong enough or if more should be added digitally. Khondji says to Woody, "I thought we were going to add rain like we did in *Magic.* We don't need to do it if you don't want to. A big tree shelters the ground from the car to the porch but not the rain you see in the unprotected area of car." A little more is added.

There are other fine-tunes. For a better transition from the preceding scene, they feather in color as Jill walks on campus. Roy breaking up with Jill is too blue in comparison to the preceding shot. Abe in the elevator room is too dark, as are Rita and Abe walking by the hedge at her house. The cocktail party welcoming Abe is made a little brighter to help bring the audience into the story. Abe and Jill driving to the lighthouse is lightened: "Too drab," Khondji says. Woody, always looking for warmth, happily goes along and adds, "I'm not sure that even in Emma's house you can't come up half a point."

"These are subtle things," Khondji says. "If you feel emotionally you want to do it, we should. We won't add any contrast, just brighten."

"I don't want the audience to resign themselves to a gloomy story," Woody says. Khondji tells him that it is fine brighter.

They come to the final scene, Jill walking on the beach as her narration plays over the picture. Woody tinkered with the color on this quite a bit during editing.

"Is this last shot too cold?" he asks, still uncertain. "Does it need yellow?" Khondji says that he likes the gilt on the sand and also on the seaweed strewn about.

"Is it warm enough for you?" Woody continues.

"You can change it, but you don't want to affect the look of the blue of the ocean; that is beautiful. Do you want to see it with a touch more gold?" The blue of the water as it is has a lovely Scandinavian hue.

"If you want to look at it that way," Woody says. But the gold doesn't work. "It's not the kind of gold you can really add. It looks fine."

Although Woody does everything he can to give his films the best look possible, he feels all this polishing can only get you so far, and that despite the technical wizardry, in the end none of it really matters. The day after this session he says, "I've preached to Darius for years, and I've preached it to the editors, that only the effect is relevant. It doesn't matter if you see the flag in the background or the mics overhead or the edit doesn't match or the color is not realistic or it's too red—none of that matters. To be accurate and perfect doesn't mean anything. It's nice, but all that matters is the effect you're having on the audience."

2

"It's not a picture until it's mixed."

The technological feats of the color correction are matched by what can be done in the mix, which binds together all the elements of a film. If even a single letter of dialogue sounds mushy or trails off, it can be replaced with one from another word in another take or even another voice. If there are extraneous sounds—cars, a plane, the hum of a generator—they can be erased or counterbalanced by computer magic and the keen ear of the mixer. As Lee Dichter, who has overseen the mix of Woody's films for the three decades since *Hannah and Her Sisters,* says, "I can lower a sound, raise it, change its pitch, make it longer, make it shorter, or reverse it." He even can make a room seem larger or smaller by using different reverb programs. Yet, he adds, "it's hard to talk about sound because it's in a subjective place." But all art is subjective, and he is an artist.

Woody calls Dichter "the best mixer there is. I always wait for him if he's not free—you have to book Lee a year in advance, and I don't know *how* it doesn't make him crazy. He comes into that dark studio and sits there all day. It's such meticulous work."

Along with Dichter, who has mixed nearly three hundred films, are Sylvia Menno, the dialogue editor on Woody's films for years, and Harry Higgins, the mix technical assistant. Robert Hein, the supervising sound editor, will insert approximately five thousand sounds of footsteps, glasses being put down, doors opening, and so on, drawn from additional thousands of choices that he has assembled and in many cases created.

The team works in a small screening room behind a console of seven twelve-inch screens with eight rows of tracks and eight equalizer knobs and a sliding fader at the bottom of each track that automatically returns to its last setting; the knobs look like the keys of a player piano as they go up and down. Dichter's board has the separate sounds recorded by the actors' individual mics and the boom. Menno has every line of dialogue in her computer, also separated, so lines recorded by the boom microphone are separate from the individual actors' mics. She edits them with Pro Tools to take out extraneous sounds and has alternatives ready if the recording she thinks is the first choice has a blemish. Dichter equalizes the sound, something that almost requires the hearing range of a dog to do well. Sometimes the dialogue is too brittle or bass-y or muffled, and he has to dig crisp lines out of the aural mire. For instance, the confrontation in the classroom between Abe and Jill had an underlying hum from the generator that powered the high-wattage lights outside, so he found the frequency and equalized it. First the words are made as clear as possible, then the music is added, after that the sound effects are inserted.

What is recorded on the set can be foggy or it can have not enough chest tone if the actor's lavalier microphone is tucked in wrong. Sibilants are easily lost. Sometimes a body microphone picks up the actor's heartbeat, and so Dichter must use only what the boom gathered. Two voices not recorded together will be unbalanced, so he needs to align them to keep the tone even. Actors unknowingly help each other with their readings. For example, in the confrontation between Jill and Abe in the classroom, one of her lines includes the words "up and back." Her "k" comes out as hard ("*kuh*"), making it clear. But when Rita breaks up with her husband in the car, her "k" in "talk" in the last line is hardly audible, so Dichter copies Jill's and slips it into Rita's. In another instance, he wants a little more "juh" in someone saying "just"; the mic was buried in the actor's blouse and so the sound is not as clear as it could be. Menno searches through readings and finds another word with a sharper "j" and drops it in.

The correction and the mix are exceptions to all the other parts of the film, in that Woody is not there for every moment, making every decision. For perhaps his first fifteen pictures, he went to the mix "the second it started, and never left for a moment of every frame." Then he realized that he didn't need to do that. His tastes were so clear and consistent that he felt "everyone knew what I wanted. I could have the editor do the laborious work of sitting at the mix and then at the end of the day or perhaps two, I could check it and just say, 'Yeah, this is perfect,' or 'No, this is not loud enough,' or 'Gee, that was great, but can you just turn down those cricket noises?' I've worked with Alisa now for a long time and I've worked with Lee for a very long time. They know what I want."

So much with sound depends on how the words are said by a character in the preceding scene. When Abe says in a voice-over, "I wanted to live—to teach, to write, to travel, to make love," the monologue sounds fine on its own but compared to how he speaks in the next scene, it is a completely different tone. Most directors would simply have the actor back for additional dialogue recording (ADR), but because Woody does not like to do that, Dichter has the computer make a digital shot of every word—actually the analog waveform of the word—and then plays with that. It is the same with Rita's breakup with her husband in the car. Rain on an auto's metal body is a problem; turn up the dialogue and you turn up the rain as well. Another director would have the actor come to a sound studio to match lip movement for the scene as the dialogue is rerecorded. The equalizer helps, but not as much as Dichter would like. Still, after the high level of improvement they have achieved, it may be only he and a handful of others who can notice the difference.

Woody's longstanding problem with the level and intensity of the voices of the partygoers' reactions to Abe playing Russian roulette is at last resolved. When preparing his effects, Hein recorded several actors in an ADR studio. He had no more than two speak at a time so that he could build on the voices, and the layered result gives the emotional response Woody has wanted all along. For the thump of the elevator stopping before Abe sabotages it, he dropped large hunks of metal on a recording stage. The hum of the elevator is from piano wires processed so they sound nothing like piano wires but rather give a sense of a moving cable. Most sounds are subtle and suggestive, heard but not remarkable.

The violent elevator scene is enhanced by small changes in sound. The first two screams from Jill as Abe grabs her were recorded in filming but then filtered and augmented by Dichter. The loud high-pitched scream she makes when his hand is over her mouth is discarded. Lepselter wonders if there should be a sound when Abe hits the elevator cables as he falls down the shaft. Or maybe it should be quiet until there is the sound of him hitting the bottom? They try that but it seems too isolated, they need to put some scuffling around it but with less sound. Dichter comes up with one that cuts through.

"He's definitely dead now," Hein says.

Dichter, still unhappy with the confrontation between Jill and Abe in the classroom, wants to work on it a bit more. Part of the problem is that the dramatic argument is high-pitched. He adds some bass to take away the harshness but not reduce the emotion.

No detail is too tiny to matter. When Roy and Jill make up, the sound of a car in the background is heard before the vehicle—more a blur—is seen in the background, and the two are matched. As the credits conclude, the music fades out after the card for Sony Pictures Classics, the film's North American distributor. Dichter asks, "Should it go one foot longer? It seems a little short." One foot is sixteen frames—three-fifths of a second. Later, after they watch the whole reel through, Dichter suggests extending the music one more phrase, one and a half seconds—thirty-six frames. On a shot of a door that closes at the end of a scene, he removes a short squeak that he missed earlier. He recently did the mix for Wes Anderson's *The Grand Budapest Hotel* and says, "The more he listened to his movie, the fewer the sound effects he left."

The effects for the elevator coming to a stop at the bottom of the shaft with a bang encroach on Abe's voice-over, so they are moved two frames—one-twelfth of a second—ahead to put it in sync with the music, and Hein adds a "zzzt" sound to accompany the spark that shows Abe has disabled the mechanism. Dichter notices a slight dip in the music as Jill walks in the hallway toward the elevator and sees Abe before the audience does. He wants no change so there is more of a surprise. "I almost want her voice to cut the music off," he says. The adjustments ratchet up the tension.

Hein has added slaps to the fight between Abe and Jill to match her hitting him, but it is still not right. They try different screams and add one to a close shot. In addition, the sounds from two different mics are not quite synced. The boom mic is a little distant, so adding reverb makes it sound strange, and the body mic is muffled. Dichter eventually succeeds in combining them. Finally, just before Abe falls into the shaft, a faint breathy sound from Jill offscreen is removed.

Lepselter finds Jill's first line of narration in the final scene ("With the passage of time the awful vividness of what I had experienced . . .") "a little low" and asks to "fade the music in just a wee bit earlier. I felt the music was fighting her." They also reduce the sound of the small waves lapping the beach so her voice-over is not as crowded. Waves, seagull cries, music, and narration are all in this scene and need to be balanced so that one does not override the others.

The next day, Woody comes in to look at what they have done to reels 4 and 5, the last forty minutes of the film. (For theatrical presentation, reels hold two thousand feet, twice the amount on those used for shooting.) He has already seen the mix for the first three and made tiny changes. He saves his visits other than to see a reel or two "for a special sequence in the mix that requires creativity that affects the story." He is invariably satisfied with the technical corrections and so virtually every change he makes is "a creative tweak." The opening titles serve as a good example. Woody likes to have music come in strong, and he wanted no music over the titles. Dichter persuaded him to have the audience hear a moving car come in over the title card, which appears a few seconds after the film starts to roll, just to let the audience know that the sound is on. The car is still heard when "Written and Directed by Woody Allen" comes up, and it lasts for three seconds before fading out. Then the applause that greets the start of "The 'In' Crowd" is heard for a split second before the screen goes black and then Abe appears behind the wheel. But Woody wants it to come in differently: "On the record, the applause hits too hard and vitiates the music hit," he explained later. "I asked them to take the applause down so the music is the dramatic hit. That's a decision that I would make. The rest of the reel was perfect."

In reel 5, when Abe walks around the classroom supervising an exam while his narration plays, Woody says, "Make sure the music cue doesn't peter out enervatingly." He asks to lower music under Abe's narration ("But I had no intention of giving myself up . . .") in a coffee shop. Dichter softens the cue from Jill slamming the door in the classroom to Abe's voice-over in the coffee shop, but Woody says, "It doesn't give you quite that thrust into the next scene." He prefers it as it was. "It needs a little goose there. I'm too insecure to have it softer."

His greatest concern is Abe's fall: "Is the sound of the body hitting the bottom okay? It seemed almost comical." It has a sound almost like "boom." They look at it again. "It sounds like a vaudeville crash where the guy falls off the stage into the orchestra pit," he tells them. Hein makes the sound less resonant and a bit softer. Woody continues, "The second one had a hitting-the-snare-drums-and-cymbals quality." The boom sound is removed, but the sound of the body hitting the elevator cables is slightly raised. They watch it again. "It definitely helps to have the cable sound. It's not as comic," Woody says, then adds, "better, not as amusing."

"I see what you mean," Hein says. "It sounded like someone fell on a tympani."

Woody is finished within an hour. After he leaves, Dichter says, "Most of Woody's films are so narrative, the film almost tells me how it has to be mixed. This one is so dialogue-driven that maintaining the dramatic flow is key. There are many multiple takes that are edited together to make a scene happen. We work hours and hours and on one scene to make it flow as though it happened in real time. Any distractions I hear must be addressed, then minimized or removed. My top priority is to keep the dialogue in focus, however it was recorded, and then make it play within the entire sound mix. In the editing process Woody and Alisa create a guide mix as a reference for what he wants, but he is open to ideas at the mix. Still, you don't want to hit him with surprises but rather help him bring his vision to fruition. The point is to get as much as possible out of the actor's performance and keep the emotional content at the highest level."

As Woody puts it, "It's not a picture until it's mixed."

CHAPTER 9

The End

In December 2014, Woody showed Sony Pictures Classics executives the edited movie without the sound mix. They liked everything about it except the title, something they did not tell him directly but rather took up with his sister. "They walk on eggshells all the time when they want to do something," he said afterward. "They told Letty, 'We love the picture but don't you think that *Crazy Abe* suggests comedy, since it's Woody's picture?' " This is a recurring problem with all his dramas, but the executives at SPC were not the first to have concerns about this title. Juliet Taylor, his friend and former assistant Jane Martin, and his publicist Leslee Dart all had a similar reaction. Sony's concerns finally convinced him that he needed to make a change, much as he still liked *Crazy Abe.*

A couple of weeks later, he had "a plagiarism inspiration, to call it *Irrational Man.*" William Barrett's book that explicated existentialism "was famous—well, famous with my little crowd. I thought that it would be a great title for this. It's not *Crazy Abe,* but it's a serious way of saying it. It's human generic." Helen Robin was checking to see if there were any legal problems in using a book title. If there were none, she would then try to clear it with the Title Registration Bureau. As backup he also had her check on titles from Nietzsche (*Beyond Good and Evil*) and Kierkegaard (*Fear and Trembling*). There was no problem with the latter, but it turned out there is a picture in preparation called *Beyond Good and Evil.* After some thought, he decided to go with *Irrational Man,* but he had one concern.

"I would hate for the heirs of William Barrett to sue me, only because I like the book and I like William Barrett. There is no connection between this and his book, but I don't want to be in the papers with a lawsuit from his children. I thought, 'It is the best title, so let's use it and hope it doesn't mean anything to them.' Now I'm waiting to hear," he laughs, "for the other shoe to drop. For this movie it's perfect." And, it turned out, legal.

With the work on the film nearly finished—at this point he still had the color correction and sound mix ahead—he had perspective to consider the result. "I feel okay about it," he said. "I feel it is an honest picture. I don't feel there's anything in it where I have to close my eyes and hope I can get by this scene. It's close to what I wanted. I don't feel, 'Oh, god, I blew this and even if people love it I'm heartbroken.' I feel that I did a good job executing it. Joaquin was terrific and Emma was beyond terrific. The cast did a great job.

"I hope people aren't put off by the philosophy in the story, that they think it's an intellectual picture," he continued. "I want them to be entertained and get interested in the story. I think there's a good chance they will, but I don't know." He shrugged. As always with his projects, which have an interest span of about a year to him, the present was quickly becoming the past. "When it comes out I'll be well into another."

By the end of 2014 he had already turned his attention to his next two projects, the script for his 2015 film and what idea to write for the series he had at last agreed to make for Amazon Studios. The company had made him an offer a year earlier, giving him complete freedom to produce anything he wanted. Each segment could last approximately thirty or sixty minutes; he could be in them or not.

"This all stems from my agent, John Burnham, telling them, 'He's not interested,' when they approached him," Woody said one day during his yearlong debate about whether or not to accept the offer. "That's immediately the best thing you can say: 'He does movies, he doesn't watch television, it's not an interest.' And that was true. But as soon as you say that, they say, 'Well, can we meet with him?' And then, 'What would you want to do?' When they want you, they'll give you anything you want. And when they don't want you, you can't get them on the phone. It's the Jerry Lewis thing. There was a time they said about him, 'If he wants to burn down the studio, give him the matches.' And then by the time I got around to wanting him to direct *Take the Money and Run,* they said, 'No, we don't want him.' He had burned too many bridges."

Woody's greatest dilemma was in coming to terms with the fast ascent of streaming video. "I'm having trouble accepting that those things are becoming in a sense more important than movies," he said some days later. "The voice of reality says, 'Let me tell you, movies are slowly fading away and what people talk about at the water cooler and what they look forward to are no longer the weekly Jean-Luc Godard movie or the Martin Scorsese movie. What they're really looking forward to are the *Homelands* and *The Sopranos* because those things have reached a level of artistic importance comparable to movies.' But they're all seen on laptops and phones, so you wonder, 'Do I really need Darius Khondji to be lighting these things? If you see it on a big screen, it's magical. But if you're seeing it on a television set, or worse than a television set, on your iPhone—it hasn't captured my imagination, but it has captured the public's. Apparently the shows are good and meaningful and adult and well written, whereas movies, with a few exceptions, are corporate enterprises conceived in venality. They're trying to make an audience-friendly, likable comedy or thriller, and they'll do anything to get that. The pictures have no individuality, there's a corporate look to the photography and the whole film."

The allure of the Amazon project was enhanced by an uncharacteristic lack of enthusiasm for any of his ideas for his next film. He was taking some time off to write a couple of stories to submit to the *New Yorker.* "I'm at a dead end with my films," he said in mid-November. "I don't have anything that inspires me at the moment and coming down the pike is this thing for Amazon. They keep meeting with Steve [Tenenbaum] and they keep giving him everything he asks for. They want it to happen so much that they are amenable on every point. So he calls me and says, 'Look, I don't know what to tell them. Do you not want to do this? Because everything I say to them they go along with.' There are no restrictions on me and it's lucrative and it seems a shame not to. I'll never get a television offer like this again."

He had plenty of thoughts for series ideas but even more ambivalence about making one of them. "Now I really know that feeling that they talk about but I've never had, where you do everything to keep yourself from starting to write," he said with both frustration and amusement. "I just don't feel like doing it but I have to. Six or eight episodes, my choice. I'd like to get away with six. I could make more money with eight because I get a piece of each one, but if after I write two or three and Helen budgets them it looks like I would be able to make the money I want to make from six, I'll make those. If I need two more to have made a lucrative investment, I'll do them. But I really don't know what I'm doing; I'm in over my head. I've never, ever, seen a miniseries. I've never seen a single *Sopranos* or *Mad Men* or *Breaking Bad.* I don't watch those things, only because I'm never around. I go out for dinner or if I have dinner at home, I go upstairs and turn on the basketball game immediately and by the fourth quarter I can't keep my eyes open. If I do get through it and I am up I watch the news for a while. The latest I ever go to sleep is eleven thirty."

His being at a rare dead end with his films lasted three weeks before he had an idea he liked for his 2015 movie project. At the end of January he finished the script for what would become *Café Society* and quickly moved on to the series. Finally, "out of frustration," he reworked a screenplay called *A Rainy Day in New York,* which he wrote about fifteen years ago and then decided against and put in his drawer. From time to time since, he has taken a bit of it here, a piece of it there, for one or another of his films. For the series, he broke up the script, changed the things he'd used already so as not to repeat himself, and made it into six episodes, none of which he would be in. Problem solved.

But then he had another idea, set in the 1960s, in which he could act. A year or so earlier he had spoken of it as a film idea that had been rattling around for some time. "I said to myself, 'Write it.' I agonized over it. I've earned my money," he said at the end of April. "Today I finished four of the six chapters. It will take me another two weeks at least because it's a drone-on way of writing. It's not one thing, where you build and build and build to a single climax, and that's caused two problems. The first is that I have to end an episode; then do the next and end it; and do that again and again. That's been killing me. The other is, I'm trying to tell a story in a financially reasonable way to keep the budget down."

The story, of an aging couple in a wealthy New York suburb beset by the arrival of a friend's radical daughter sought by the police, is a clash of generations and political persuasion in which Bob Hope could have played. One of its appeals is "it would work as a one-set stage play very well with everything going on in that house. That helps in the economics because it's not enormous scope where it's costing me a fortune. Now, I may finish it and type it up and feel it is just abysmal and go back to the other one."

It will be another month before he finally chooses. His ambivalence has been at flood stage for months. "I'll be very happy when the Amazon experience is *over.* I can only think back to Martha Graham. When I was growing up there was a moronic but very popular radio show called *Truth or Consequences.* Once a year they had the Miss Hush contest. The first week they gave you a clue that was so obscure nobody would get it. Each week they would add another and the whole country was asking, Who is Miss Hush? Martha Graham was not well known in the United States then. [This was in 1947.] I figured her out, you know, the twentieth week when half of America did. I had to go to the library to do it. The clue that got me to it," he starts to laugh, "involved something around Graham crackers. I saw, 'Oh, there is a dancer called Martha Graham.' [He later came to know her.] She hated that she did it. This Amazon thing is the Miss Hush contest to me." Despite this, he has found that the Amazon executives are "the nicest people, and artistically they could not be more free and nonencroaching. I'm trying to work on it in the cracks so as not to disrupt my normal filming schedule."

He might have felt differently if he had known that a year later,

Amazon Studios would pay a reported $15 million plus at least an additional $5 million for prints and advertising for the North American distribution rights for *Café Society* and then offer even more for financing *Wonder Wheel,* released in the fall of 2017. The company wants to establish itself as a theatrical power and paid him millions more than he had been receiving from conventional distributors—Sony Pictures Classics for the last seven.

Eventually he will settle on the young woman who comes to the house, with the title *Crisis in Six Scenes.* His wife will be played by Elaine May, who, like Woody, came to prominence with her partner, Mike Nichols, under the management of the late Jack Rollins. Miley Cyrus, who he thinks is "terrific," plays the felonious girl. But he will have to finish writing it before he can make that choice.

The next morning he lay fully clothed on his bed, his face pressed close to the page, writing a script in longhand.

ACKNOWLEDGMENTS

Since 1971, in what has become the oldest established permanent floating interview in New York and elsewhere, Woody Allen has answered my questions with candor and good humor, and has allowed me complete access while he works. Over the course of forty-six of his movies, I have seen him by happenstance rather than intent. Something new was always going on and there was time to talk, and so I have had the rare opportunity to watch and write about an artist through virtually all of his career in film to date. My gratitude to him is matched only by the pleasure I have gained.

Juliet Taylor, Letty Aronson, Helen Robin, and Santo Loquasto have been enjoyable and helpful company during preproduction and on sets for decades. My thanks for their many kindnesses come with my admiration for their singular abilities.

Darius Khondji was always generous with his explanations of the fine points of cinematography, in which point and shoot is not an option. I am grateful to Parker Posey for our conversations and for her emails that so thoroughly detail some of her experience during the making of *Irrational Man;* my thanks as well to Emma Stone and to Jamie Blakely for their thoughts and insights. Virginia McCarthy, who once literally saved the day, was a great companion every day. Suzy Benziger could costume the darkness and make it look good. Thanks to Edward Walson for many lunches, and to the crew, especially Danielle Rigby, Christie Mullen, Billy Weberg, Brad Robinson, Mike McGuirk, Carl Sprague, Faith Brewer, Julie Snyder, Jen Gerbino, Lindsay Boffoli, Greg Miller, Frans Wetterings, Scott Kordish, Amy Trachtman, and David Schwartz. Sabrina Lantos took the excellent stills that accompany the text and the jacket photo as well.

Alicia Lepselter has been a generous guide in the editing room for almost a score of films; my thanks for the view over her shoulder and for her helpful answers to countless questions. Thanks also to Morgan Neville, Kate Rose Itzkowitz, Sharon Perelman, Lee Dichter, Patricia DiCerto, Lauren Cheung, and John Doumanian. Ginevra Tamberi, Woody's nonpareil assistant for many years, was a constant help to me. She has my affectionate thanks for that, as well as for her continuing friendship.

I am indebted to Wayne Kabak and James Gregorio for their valuable guidance and contractual skills, and to Don. C. Skemer, Curator of Manuscripts, and his colleagues at the Princeton University Library Rare Books and Special Collections Department.

The incomparable Susan Stroman kindly let me hang around for the rehearsals and staging of *Bullets over Broadway*. I had hoped a section on the show, which came to life during the year *Irrational Man* was made, would fit into this book. Alas, my account of her genius as a director and choreographer is for another time.

Moses Farrow and Soon-Yi Previn spoke with me at length about difficult matters and offered new context to an old story, and Linda Fairstein graciously provided invaluable perception and opinion on it. I am deeply obliged to them.

At Knopf, Chip Kidd came up with yet another jacket that instantly distills a book. I am happy to have one of mine judged by his cover anytime. Iris Weinstein created her usual wonderful design. My appreciation to Amy Ryan for again bringing her clear-eyed copyediting to bear on these pages, finding errors both large and small that would have made me cringe had they made it to print. The brilliant Victoria Pearson once more shepherded a manuscript through production with care, humor, and suggestions that were always on the mark. It is enormous fun to work with them both. Much of our communication is through notes in the margins, but they are written in a manner that makes it seem we're sitting side-by-side discussing a comma, fact, or dangler. Production manager Roméo Enriquez turned the work of all into a gorgeous book. Grateful thanks to Meghan Hauser and Julia Ringo, Jonathan Segal's dazzling assistants, who handled hundreds of phone calls and emails from me with grace and alacrity; Anke Steinecke for her acute legal advice; Nicholas Latimer and Michael Lionstar, who found my inner author; and my lifeguard Kathryn Zuckerman, who once again put him on display.

Endless gratitude to good friends who provided thoughts and help: Robert B. Weide for his Allen expertise; Andrew Wolk for casting a director's eye over these pages; Linda "Sherlock" Amster for her always stellar sleuthing; and E. C. McCarthy, Robert Wallace, David James Fisher, Dexter Cirillo, and my son John Lax for their helpful readings of the manuscript. My appreciation in general to Walter Hill.

My love, as ever, to Constance Lax Midgley, Joy Lax Lloyd, and Margaret Lax Winter. The same with thanks to Cathy Sulzberger and Joe Perpich for years of shelter.

Jonathan Segal is unsurpassed in his ability to get to the heart of what a sentence, paragraph, or chapter should be, and no one in publishing endeavors more to make a book sparkle. Every manuscript Jon edits is vastly improved by his intellect, passion, and care. His pencil hovers over each word, but its marks are invisible to the reader. I am fortunate that we have worked together and been pals for thirty-five years now; somehow he has not aged a day.

William Tyrer and David Wolf have read and reread works in progress for decades, always offering candid criticism along with unwavering support, encouragement, and friendship. Their help shows in every book I write; this one is dedicated to them.

My love for my wife, Karen Sulzberger, and our sons, Simon and John, is unbounded, and theirs means everything to me.

INDEX

Page numbers in *italics* refer to illustrations.

PHOTOGRAPHIC CREDITS

All photographs are by Sabrina Lantos, copyright © 2015 by Gravier Productions, Inc., with the exception of the following, which were taken by the author.

11 The first page of the first draft of *The Boston Story,* with the idea of calling it *Crazy Abe* in the upper-left corner

12 After Woody revises his handwritten script, Helen Robin types it into proper script form. As action is delineated only by the initial of the character, she often has to discern a scene's end.

119 Sheets of a reflective material called Ultrabounce keep the light the same from shot to shot. Natural light would change as the sun moves or is darkened by passing clouds.

158 Helium-filled balloons over the verandah of the house for Abe's welcome party

250 Lights for Abe's classroom, second story, left. Air-conditioning tubes are connected to keep the interior, where there are more lights, cool.

A NOTE ABOUT THE AUTHOR

Eric Lax is the author of, among other books, *Life and Death on 10 West* (a *New York Times* Notable Book of the Year); *Conversations with Woody Allen; The Mold in Dr. Florey's Coat; Faith, Interrupted;* and *Bogart* (with A. M. Sperber). His biography *Woody Allen* was a *New York Times* best seller and Notable Book of the Year. Lax's books have been translated into eighteen languages, and his writing has appeared in *The Atlantic, The New York Times, Vanity Fair, Esquire, The Washington Post,* and the *Los Angeles Times.* He lives with his wife in Los Angeles.

A NOTE ON THE TYPE

This book was set in Caledonia, a typeface designed by W. A. Dwiggins (1880–1956). It belongs to the family of printing types called "modern face" by printers—a term used to mark the change in style of the type letters that occurred around 1800. Caledonia borders on the general design of Scotch Roman but it is more freely drawn than that letter. This version of Caledonia was adapted by David Berlow in 1979.

Composed by North Market Street Graphics, Lancaster, Pennsylvania

Printed and bound by Berryville Graphics, Berryville, Virginia

Designed by Iris Weinstein